Persuasive Pro-Life

Trent Horn

Persuasive Pro-Life

How to Talk About
Our Culture's Toughest Issue

Catholic
Answers
Press

Published by Catholic Answers, Inc.
2020 Gillespie Way
El Cajon, California 92020
888-291-8000 orders
619-387-0042 fax
www.catholic.com

Printed in the United States of America

ISBN 978-1-941663-04-2
ISBN 978-1-941663-05-9 Kindle
ISBN 978-1-941663-06-6 ePub

For John, Melanie, and Steve, my pro-life mentors

Contents

Appendices

Foreword

Human life can never be a casualty on its own. Reason will always be a casualty right along with it. That's why I am so grateful for this book. As you will soon discover, it is a resounding affirmation of both life and reason, which are so intimately related.

Since my high school days in the mid-1970s, I have been presenting, arguing, and defending the pro-life position. In my role as a national and international pro-life leader, as well as in my work with the media, I have always placed a high priority on helping people to *speak intelligently* about abortion. Although as a Catholic priest and as the leader of several clearly *religious* pro-life organizations, I would be expected by most to put a priority on the religious arguments against abortion, I have always pointed out that the most religious defenders of life need to be able to argue the pro-life position *on the basis of human reason*, and that in doing so they are being completely consistent with their faith. Why? Because the God of faith is the God of reason, too. He created it, he redeems it, and he expects us to use it. And this book does that brilliantly.

When I give talks on abortion to predominantly pro-choice or skeptical audiences, I will often start by holding up a pencil and asking the audience what I have in my hand. Of course, they will say, "A pencil." And then I guarantee them, "By the end of our time together, some of you will be denying that this is a pencil." What I mean is that the mental gymnastics necessary to deny that a baby in the womb is a baby are quite sufficient to deny that a pencil is a pencil.

Ultimately, when you examine the core meaning of the term "pro-choice" and try to determine what meaning it may have beyond the superficial level of a slogan, it means what the Supreme Court asserted in its 1992 *Planned Parenthood v. Casey* decision: "*At the heart of liberty is the right to define one's own concept of existence, of meaning, of the universe, and of the mystery of human life."* In other words, *I create my own truth and therefore my own moral code. Any value in things is there because I put it there.* Ultimately, it is the original temptation, "You will be like gods." Pro-choice, then, means self-validating choice. In other words, *what I choose is right, not because the thing I choose is good but simply because I choose it.*

While this appeals to many as the ultimate freedom, it really enslaves us, because it cuts us off from one another. If everyone's truth is his or her own self-isolated creation, then reasoning and dialogue are no longer possible, because there is no common truth that we have to acknowledge outside ourselves and which then serves as a bridge between people. Conversation and authentic debate become impossible, because common truth cannot be grasped, and ultimately human solidarity disintegrates.

At the risk of generalizing, I often say that it only *appears* that we have been having a debate over abortion in our country for the last several decades. In reality, if human reason cannot find truth, and if people discussing abortion cannot begin by knowing that when they say the word *abortion* they are talking about the same thing, then we are simply talking past each other.

But far from concluding that we should therefore not debate or discuss abortion, all this means that we as a movement need a profound reaffirmation of the value of reason and the necessity of engaging the abortion debate. We as pro-life people who believe in life also believe in reason. We also know that the last thing abortion supporters want to talk about is abortion. It is in fact indefensible and has been so from the beginning. But all the promises of its supporters to create positive results for women, families, and society by legal abortion have turned up empty. Abortion supporters have run out of arguments, and their only remaining response to ours is "Shut up!"

Many of our fellow citizens, however, can and are being persuaded by reasoned arguments, which this book helps us to utilize. Building the culture of life requires much more than logic, and this book acknowledges that. But this is no time to lose faith in reason, to grow tired of making the case for life or to conclude, "People don't want to hear about abortion, and reasoning won't persuade them anyway." In fact, it will persuade many, if it is done within the intellectual and emotional framework that this debate calls for.

A key to that framework is to take a positive and compassionate stance, in our own minds and hearts, to those we are seeking to persuade. Even the most ardent supporters of abortion are our brothers and sisters. *They are not our enemies; rather, they are captive to the enemy,* who specializes in destroying both truth and life. We are not better than those who disagree with us, for we are all subject to a truth that none of us created. And we all fall short in living it.

We realize, too, the *pain* that characterizes this debate. Pain keeps many from seeing the obvious truth of the pro-life position—pain over involvement in abortion, or pain over the fact that if they face up to abortion, they will not be able to live with themselves unless they do something to stop it, but that if they do something about it they will suffer persecution or loss of some kind.

When we acknowledge that pain, when we accompany our skills of reason with a heart of compassion and a hand of fraternity, and when we are willing to absorb—and help others absorb—the suffering necessary to bear witness to the truth, we will know the joy of using reason to advance the culture of life.

— Fr. Frank Pavone
National Director, Priests for Life
President, National Pro-life Religious Council
www.priestsforlife.org

Acknowledgments

Most of the techniques and arguments I present here are not original, and I have tried to give credit where it is due. In particular, I am grateful for the work of Greg Koukl, Scott Klusendorf, Francis Beckwith, Patrick Lee, William May, Stephanie Gray, Christopher Kaczor, Robert George, Christopher Tollefsen, Peter Kreeft, Stephen Wagner, David Lee, Josh Brahm, and the many other knowledgeable pro-life advocates who have trained or influenced me. I am also grateful for Tim Ryland's editing of this manuscript. Finally, I am indebted to Arizona Right to Life and to Justice for All for allowing me to use in this book material I created during my time with them.

Introduction

Many people who oppose abortion are hesitant to do so publicly.

The media has reframed the issue of abortion and made it one facet of a so-called "war on women." Since no one wants to go to war against half of the electorate, politicians might choose to say nothing about abortion. They're also worried that if they speak about the issue they will make a gaffe that will haunt them every time their name is searched on the Internet.

Students are worried their friends or college professors will think they are some kind of fanatic who wants to impose their opposition to abortion on everyone else by making it illegal. And regular people are scared that if they mention the "A-word" in mixed company it will ignite a shouting match with coworkers, friends, and even their family members.

Talking about abortion can be scary, but so is anything with which you're unfamiliar. The goal of this book is to teach pro-life advocates how to talk about abortion in ways that inspire confidence in the truth of the pro-life position. We must talk about abortion *because* we are afraid.

I am afraid for a country that thinks it's acceptable to kill innocent human beings simply because they are unwanted. I am afraid for men and women who don't realize that abortion is a permanent and tragic answer to a temporary life problem. And I am afraid for pro-life advocates who think we are "winning" because some polls say a majority of Americans call themselves pro-life.[1]

The fact is that we are holding our ground, at best. One survey shows that 35 percent of self-described pro-lifers think abortion should not be made illegal, and whenever general abortion bans are put on the ballot (the only polls that count), they always lose.[2]

I've engaged in the rational defense of the pro-life world-view for longer than a decade. I've developed a set of principles based on the work of pro-life scholars and activists whom I consider the best. I've field-tested them in tough environments like public university campuses and augmented them to help the average person answer arguments for abortion he's never heard before.

The goal of this book is to teach you how to use those principles to change people's hearts and minds on the issue of abortion; specifically, to persuade them to believe that human beings matter not because of what they look like or how they benefit us but because they are members of the human community, and all members—regardless of age or level of development—deserve to be treated with respect and given basic rights. And the most important of these rights is the right to life.

My story

The first time I was confronted by abortion, I was twelve and asked my mom what it was. She told me not only what abortion was but told me tearfully that I would have had an older brother had he not been aborted. All I knew at the time was that abortion was a bad thing. I mean, how could it be a good thing if it made my mother cry so bitterly?

Fast-forward five years.

I stopped by the home of my friend John, whose daughter I had escorted to prom a few weeks earlier, and he was watching a video in his study. He was quiet, illuminated only by the television's blue light. John told me he was reviewing a graphic pro-life video for use in schools and churches and invited me to watch it. His brief description and warning couldn't fully prepare me for the video's gruesome imagery.

Dismembered body parts. Bloated late-term fetuses. Blood. An abortion in progress. As my heart pounded in my chest, I couldn't take my eyes off it. I knew abortion was bad, but I didn't know it was evil. Fortunately, my experience with my mother kept me from condemning or hating women who had chosen abortion. I just knew at that moment that there had to be a better way than this "choice."

John helped me navigate the pro-life movement and introduced me to my first pro-life books. After months of intensive study, I knew I was a "pro-lifer," and I could artfully defend my views in front of my secular friends. Of course, I didn't think I was supposed to actually *do* anything about abortion except believe it was wrong.

Fast-forward four more years. I was at Arizona State University on my way to a philosophy class when I saw a crowd outside the student union. From a hundred yards away I saw what looked like giant billboards set up behind steel barriers. As I got closer, I saw why the crowd had gathered: The billboards contained pictures of aborted fetuses.

As I walked through the crowd, I noticed that while the pro-choice students were loud and angry, the pro-life volunteers with the billboards were calm and rational. I was intrigued. Later the pro-life group hosted an open-mic session where anyone could debate abortion. I noticed some of the pro-choice students were monopolizing the microphone and making terrible arguments in defense of legal abortion.

Just then John's daughter, the one I had taken to prom, pulled up next to me on her bicycle. As we watched the spectacle I said, "Someone needs to show these pro-choice people they're wrong."

She didn't miss a beat. "Maybe that someone is you," she said.

I was nervous, but I also couldn't resist the challenge. I walked up to the microphone and said the protester's appeals to choice, law, and privacy in order to defend legal abortion were the same kind of appeals used by those who defended slavery 150 years earlier. I turned to the pro-choice advocates and asked them, "If you believe in choice and not imposing morality on others, then can you tell me it's wrong to own slaves?"

Instead of refuting my argument, the pro-choice woman turned her back to me and proceeded to yell about contraception to the crowd of onlookers. A pro-choice heckler even noticed the pro-choicers' reluctance to debate and said to me, "Wow, they didn't touch your argument with a ten-foot pole!"

After the microphone session ended, many people asked if I was with the pro-life exhibit. "No," I said, "I'm just a student here." When I got to my philosophy class, the professor asked why I was late.

I said, "Sorry, sir. I was at the abortion exhibit practicing philosophical argumentation."

"With one of those anti-abortion nuts?"

"Actually sir," I replied, "I am one of those anti-abortion nuts."

Passion for pro-life

The next day the exhibit was still on campus, and I spent as much time as I could talking with pro-choice students. I later learned the exhibit was presented by Justice for All (JFA), a national organization whose mission is to "train thousands to make abortion unthinkable for millions, one person at a time."[3] I wanted to learn its approach to dialogue so badly that I joined a group of friends who followed the exhibit to its next stop in California. The exhibit staff members called us "JFA groupies."

I traveled with several more exhibits until I finished my undergraduate degree. During that time, my friend Melanie drafted me to help her local pro-life group. Being a national chastity speaker, Melanie trained my speaking partner, Brooke, and me to speak persuasively on the issue of abortion. We not only learned pro-life arguments, we learned how to convey them as public speakers. During my training as a speaker, I thought that pro-life advocacy would be a hobby while I worked as a high school teacher. But with Melanie's help I eventually landed a full-time job right after graduation with our state's right-to-life organization.

After a year and a half there, I felt called to take my mission of teaching pro-life apologetics to the national level. I contacted Justice for All, and for the next two years I traveled the country speaking and training students at more than twenty public university campuses. In fact, many of the stories I describe in this book are from that invaluable time when I was in the company of good friends who always taught me something new about defending the pro-life worldview.

My approach

This book is not a systematic philosophical defense of the pro-life position, though I have drawn heavily from those kinds of works.[4] It is also not a book of one-line comebacks pro-life people can give to those who disagree. It is instead designed to help people have sustained and meaningful dialogue with the goal of persuading others.

Chapters 1 and 2 outline what is at stake in the abortion debate and how pro-life advocates must model a gracious approach. The subsequent chapters describe how to communicate the pro-life message to different types of people. The types aren't separated by familiar demographics such as age, gender, race, or occupation. Rather they represent the different views pro-choice advocates hold and the reasons they give for wanting abortion to be legal.

It's important to remember that the people we speak with do not belong to just one "type," and they probably have many reasons to think abortion should remain legal. I hope readers

will understand that I am not using these types out of spite
or as name-calling but as a way to help pro-life advocates
understand the complex views that are at play in the debate.

By engaging people's complex views on abortion, while
at the same time respecting the people we disagree with, the
pro-life movement has the chance to reframe the abortion
debate and create a culture that respects human life. There is
no magical, silver-bullet law that will create a pro-life culture.
Such laws will be passed only when pro-life advocates engage
our culture through persuasive dialogue—one person, one
conversation at a time.

PART I

Understanding the Abortion Debate

I

What's at Stake?

There were about thirty of us huddled in a dressing room getting ready for yet another rehearsal. Opening night was two weeks away, but because it was a musical there was still a lot of preparation ahead. As I sat on a wooden bench in the dressing room, I watched one group of actors argue whether the video game Dance Dance Revolution was a game or a sport. At the same time, I overheard another group having a more serious discussion.

One of the cast members said to my friend Cindy, "You're pro-life? But don't you believe in the right to choose?" Cindy gathered some of the other actors into a circle and started to play the role of teacher. She said, "You see, there are really only two positions. Either the unborn are human or they aren't human. If they are human, then abortion is killing a baby. But if they aren't human . . ." As Cindy continued to teach, I noticed that one of the other female cast members became more and more uncomfortable.

"But what about the woman's choice?" one of the actors asked Cindy.

"Right, but the baby never chose to be murdered, did she?" Cindy responded.

One cast member, whom I'll call Mary, was in her late twenties, and she began to mutter under her breath as she heard everyone talking about abortion.

"Guys, let's focus on the show," she said. "I really can't hear all this abortion stuff right now." But the conversation continued, and finally Mary shouted, "Guys, can't you just freaking knock it off?"

"What's your problem, Mary?" Cindy asked.
"I'll tell you my problem! I had an abortion, okay?"
Mary stormed out of the dressing room in tears. Everyone sat stunned. I broke the silence the only way I knew how. "So . . . Dance Dance Revolution. I vote that it's a game. Anyone care to challenge?"

The emotional powder keg

Ever since that day I think of Mary and the range of reactions people have to abortion. What makes this issue different from all others? Why is it that when the word *abortion* is mentioned in public it feels like a chill overtakes everyone present? Abortion is different from any other issue because the stakes involved are mind-bogglingly high.[5]

If pro-choice advocates are correct and abortion is merely harmless surgery, then pro-lifers oppress women and falsely accuse them of homicide. But if pro-life advocates are correct and abortion ends the life of a human being, then pro-choicers are guilty of defending the killing of millions of people. Also, both sides can't merely agree to disagree, because each side wants the law to reflect its view of abortion. Pro-choice advocates want abortion to be considered legal surgery, while pro-life advocates want abortion to be considered illegal homicide.

Before I discuss the arguments for and against abortion, it's important to clarify the terms I will be using. When I talk about pro-life or pro-choice advocates, I don't mean just professional activists. I mean average people who find themselves in conversations where they have the chance to advocate for their view on abortion (though what I say applies to professional activists as well).[6]

Pro-life advocates are those who believe abortion should generally be illegal. They also believe that unborn children have a right to life, and the reason abortion should be illegal is because it is, all other things being equal, wrong to kill an innocent human being. Now, there may be strange cases in war or other emergency situations where it is moral to act in a way that kills innocent human beings (such as bombing an enemy headquarters near a civilian neighborhood). However, these difficult cases do not annul the general principle that it is wrong to directly kill an innocent human being, which is what pro-life advocates maintain happens in an abortion.

Pro-choice advocates are those who believe abortion should generally be legal. Of course, the terms *pro-life* and *pro-choice* can't encompass every nuanced view on abortion. I've met self-described pro-lifers who dislike abortion but think it should be legal because they can't force their personal views on other people. They sometimes say they're pro-life *and* pro-choice. I've also met people who call themselves pro-choice but think the vast majority of abortions should be illegal. That's why I prefer the terms *defenders* of legal abortion and *opponents* or *critics* of legal abortion. But for the sake of simplicity, I usually use the generic terms *pro-life* and *pro-choice*.

Some pro-life advocates have told me that I should identify defenders of legal abortion as being *pro-abortion*, a term that most people who support legal abortion reject. Many of them say they don't promote abortion but merely support the legal choice to have an abortion, which is why they are pro-choice and not pro-abortion. In order to make conversations on abortion more productive, I simply use the label that each side prefers.

I could get into a lengthy argument about labels, and maybe even win the argument, but if the other person is annoyed by my attitude and doesn't want to hear my reasons for why abortion should be made illegal, then my rhetoric would be in vain. I'll call anyone whatever he wants to be called so long as he is willing to change his mind about the killing of the unborn.

My approach to conversations on abortion, including an appreciation for how nuanced people's views can be, came out of hundreds of conversations during outreaches sponsored by the pro-life organization Justice for All (JFA). This organization travels the country training pro-life advocates to graciously defend their view on university campuses. After hosting a training seminar at a local church or university, JFA takes students of all ages out to practice what they learned alongside various outreach tools that help create conversations on campus.

The tool that probably created the most conversation while I was with JFA was an 18-x-40-foot, three-sided photo exhibit that contained pictures of living and aborted fetuses and embryos. Student responses to the exhibit ranged from thumbs-up support to loud demonstrations of disapproval.

Defusing an explosive issue

"Your exhibit is full of lies!" That's what one girl shouted at me when I stood in front of the JFA exhibit at the University of Colorado in Boulder.

"What do you mean?" I asked.

"You people say that abortion is legal through all nine months of pregnancy, but I know you can only get an abortion in the first three months of pregnancy!"

Rather than get into a "You're wrong," "No, *you're* wrong" squabble, I took out my smartphone and accessed the Internet. As I pulled up the browser, I said, "Actually, I have evidence that abortion is legal through all nine months of pregnancy. In this very city there is an abortionist whose Web site advertises first-, second-, and third-trimester abortions. I even have his Web site bookmarked on my phone. Want to see it?"[7]

The young woman looked at my phone, shook her head, and said, "I had no idea it was like that. . . . So tell me, why are you against abortion?"

"I'm against abortion because it's already illegal to kill unborn children," I said. She gave me a confused look, so I continued, "Currently in several states and under federal law it is illegal to kill a fetus that is wanted by his mother. For example, if a drunk driver kills a pregnant woman, he can be charged with two counts of homicide: one for the woman and one for the fetus. But if the fetus was unwanted by his *mother*, she wouldn't be charged with any crime, provided she had someone else kill the child through abortion. I just think the fair thing to do is to give equal protection to both wanted *and* unwanted unborn children and protect all of them from being aborted."[8]

The young woman looked down at the ground awkwardly for a few seconds and then said with a smile, "Thanks, I never thought about it like that before."

Instead of ending in tears and hurt feelings, like the conversation with Mary in the dressing room, conversations about abortion can end with mutual understanding and even friendship. In order to have these kinds of conversations, pro-life advocates need knowledge and a gracious approach. A calm tone helped my conversation in Colorado, but what really helped was knowing the facts that, when presented graciously, transformed a hostile critic into a curious enquirer.

In this chapter I'll focus on the top five factual questions every pro-life advocate needs to be able to answer. The information comes from the pro-choice Alan Guttmacher Institute, which is the former research arm of Planned Parenthood. Pro-life advocates should use pro-choice sources like this or neutral sources like the Centers for Disease Control so that opponents can't accuse them of being biased or inaccurate.

1. How many abortions take place each year? Approximately 1.06 million abortions occur annually in the United States. This translates to about 2,800 abortions every day.[9]
2. Who has abortions? Fifty percent of women who have an abortion have had a previous one.[10] About

30 percent of women by age 45 will have at least
one abortion.[11] The most common age of women
who have abortions is between 20 and 29. Protes-
tants obtain 37 percent of abortions, Catholics 28
percent. Pro-choice researchers point out, "While
the Catholic Church has strong proscriptions against
abortion, the relative abortion rate for Catholic
women was no different from that for all women."[12]
However, these sources do not describe how frequently the women surveyed attend religious services, and so they may identify with these religious
groups but not fully believe what the groups teach
as doctrine.

3. Why do women have abortions? The most common reasons women give for having an abortion are
social and economic. They include "having a baby
would dramatically change my life" (74 percent),
"I can't afford a baby now" (73 percent), "I don't
want to be a single mother or am having relationship
problems" (48 percent), and "I have completed my
childbearing" (38 percent). Twelve percent of women
said their abortion was related to a health problem,
and 1.5 percent said they were a victim of rape or
incest.[13]

The last two questions—What is abortion? When is it legal?—can't be answered in a few sentences, but they are two
of the most important questions that a pro-life advocate needs
to be able to answer.

What is abortion?

For most people who call themselves pro-choice, abortion is
merely surgical contraception that prevents a baby from coming into the world. Abortion may be distasteful, but it isn't an

evil that merits outrage or legal sanction. Abortion providers facilitate this lack of outrage by describing abortion in sterile terms that hide the procedure's true nature. These providers say that abortion is "the ending of a pregnancy" or "the emptying of the contents of the uterus" (which makes it seem as horrific as taking out the trash).

I prefer to use a neutral dictionary definition so that critics cannot accuse me of being hyperbolic. According to the *Oxford English Dictionary*, abortion is "the expulsion or removal from the womb of a developing embryo or fetus in the period before it is capable of independent survival."[14] This distinguishes abortion from childbirth, whereby an unborn child is removed from the womb when it can survive and there is no intention of killing him or her.

Even the term for the being who is aborted can obscure the reality of abortion. Pro-choice advocates use the term *fetus* (which is Latin for "little one") or refer to the unborn child as "the pregnancy" or even a "fertilized egg." The term *fertilized egg* is especially inaccurate, because once fertilization is complete the egg ceases to exist and what remains is a new human organism. The concept of a fertilized egg is as nonsensical as a married bachelor.

When I talk about the being who is aborted, I use the terms *fetus* (or *embryo* if the child is younger than eight weeks), *unborn child*, and *human being* interchangeably because those terms accurately describe what I am talking about.[15] The term I prefer to use, especially when talking to pro-choice advocates, is *the unborn*, because it is a neutral term that even the media use when describing humans before birth.[16]

Before I describe the different types of abortion procedures, I must warn the reader: The descriptions are graphic, because abortion itself is a violent act, and it takes significant effort to hide that fact. When reading these descriptions we must resist the temptation to lash out in anger against women who seek abortions and the abortionists who perform them. Threats and violence are not the answer, and I condemn all abortion-related violence.

We must instead emulate Pope St. John Paul II's compassionate outreach toward post-abortive women. In his encyclical *The Gospel of Life*, the pontiff wrote:

> The Church is aware of the many factors which may have influenced your decision, and she does not doubt that in many cases it was a painful and even shattering decision. . . . The Father of mercies is ready to give you his forgiveness and his peace in the Sacrament of Reconciliation. To the same Father and his mercy you can with sure hope entrust your child.[17]

I have also taken care to use only medical, legal, or pro-choice sources to ensure that the following descriptions of abortion procedures are accurate and beyond the criticism of abortion advocates. There is no single type of abortion procedure, because the procedure used is based on the size of the unborn child to be killed. Let's start with procedures that are used on the youngest unborn humans.

Medical abortion

Medical abortions involve taking drugs that cause a woman's body to miscarry the pregnancy. In the United States, the most common of these drugs is a combination of mifepristone and misoprostol called RU-486.[18] According to the National Abortion Federation (NAF), mifepristone causes "changes in the uterine lining and detachment of the pregnancy," while misoprostol "causes the uterus to contract, and helps the pregnancy tissue to expel."[19] The NAF also says that women may see "pregnancy tissue," or the body parts of the dead unborn child, as they miscarry. Medical abortions account for approximately 23 percent of all abortion procedures.[20]

Pro-life advocates must be careful to distinguish medical abortifacients such as mifepristone from emergency contraception. As far as we know, only abortifacients such as mifepristone have the ability to cause a human embryo that has implanted in the uterus to detach and be expelled from the uterus. Emergency contraceptives such as Plan B (also called the morning-after pill) work by either preventing the union of sperm and egg (which is contraceptive) or preventing the embryo from implanting in the lining of the uterus and killing the embryo as a result.

The emergency contraceptive Ella (also called the week-after pill) allegedly works in the same way, but there is some data from animal trials that suggest it could cause an implanted embryo to be aborted.[21] Even if it only prevented implantation, that act would be as morally wrong as locking the front door of your house during a blizzard to prevent your toddler from seeking shelter inside. In both cases human beings are intentionally shut out from the environment that would allow them to survive.

Some pro-choice advocates will object to the accusation that emergency contraceptives are abortifacients, because they claim that pregnancy begins when the embryo implants in the lining of the uterus. They say that if a drug kills an embryo prior to implantation, then it acted before pregnancy began and so was contraceptive.[22]

Prior to 1965, this definition of pregnancy was not used in the medical community, and the terms *fertilization, conception,* and *the beginning of pregnancy* were synonymous.[23] After 1965, the definition was changed so that *fertilization* became the preferred word to describe the moment sperm and egg unite while *conception* and *beginning of pregnancy* referred to when the embryo implanted in the womb. (In this book I use the pre-1965 definitions of fertilization and conception that consider these terms synonymous.)[24]

In 1964, demographer and Planned Parenthood ally Christopher Tietze wrote:

> At which point a human life or any life begins is a philosophical question, but I submit that throughout history the theologians and the jurists have always taken into account and have listened to the prevailing medical and biological consensus of the times, and I think this is still true. If a medical consensus develops and is maintained that pregnancy, and therefore life, begins at implantation, eventually our brethren from the other faculties will listen.[25]

In response to this clever use of semantics, the pro-life advocate can simply say, "Alright, drugs like Plan B may not be able to cause what you define as an abortion. They just have the potential to kill tiny human beings by keeping them from implanting in the womb. Is that somehow better than abortion?"

To summarize, medical abortions are the result of drugs that cause an embryo to detach from the uterus and be miscarried. They are effective only until the embryo is seven weeks old, or nine weeks after the mother's most recent menstrual period. Doctors who specialize in caring for pregnant women measure pregnancy from a woman's last menstrual period and not from conception, since there is no way to accurately date when a child was conceived. This process adds two weeks to pregnancies; so, for example, in a pregnancy that is in its ninth week, or nine weeks "gestation age," the fetus will actually be seven weeks old.

Emergency contraceptives and even hormonal birth control usually prevent conception, but they could also prevent the embryo from implanting in the womb and thereby cause the death of a human being. At this time there is no scientific consensus on how often either emergency contraceptives or other forms of hormonal birth control prevent implantation or even if they do that at all.[26] A wise policy for pro-life advocates is to warn people about the potential negative effects of hormonal contraceptives (without overstating the dangers) and to suggest ethical alternatives such as natural family planning, which carry no risk of harming an unborn child or the mother.

Suction abortion

According to the NAF, "If the medications fail to end the pregnancy, a suction abortion should be provided."[27] This procedure is also called menstrual extraction, vacuum aspiration, or suction curettage, and it is used in approximately 75 percent of abortions in the United States.[28] The Michigan Department of Community Health describes the procedure in this way:

> The doctor first widens (dilates) the cervix, which is the opening of the uterus. This may be over a period of several hours by inserting a small rod or sponge into the cervix, which swells as the sponge absorbs moisture. The doctor may choose to enlarge the cervix right before the abortion by inserting and withdrawing larger and larger smooth metal rods until the cervix has been opened to the necessary size. Most women experience some pain, so the physician will give you a pain-killer, either locally by shots in the area of the cervix or, on rare occasions, by a general anesthetic.
>
> After dilation, a plastic tube about the diameter of a pencil is then inserted into the uterus through the enlarged cervix. The tube is attached to a pump which then suctions out the fetus, the placenta and other uterine contents. After the suctioning, the physician may find it necessary to use a curette (a sharp, spoon-like instrument) to gently scrape the walls of the uterus to make sure all the fragments of the fetus and placenta have been removed from the uterus.[29]

Dilation and evacuation

Dilation and evacuation (or D&E) is a form of surgical abortion that is performed during the second trimester of pregnancy when the fetus is too big to fit through the suction tube. The fetus is dismembered and removed from the uterus piece by piece. It accounts for approximately 8 percent of all abortions in the United States.[30] In *Gonzales v. Carhart* (2007), the U.S. Supreme Court described the procedure as follows:

> The doctor, often guided by ultrasound, inserts grasping forceps through the woman's cervix and into the uterus to grab the fetus. The doctor grips a fetal part with the forceps and pulls it back through the cervix and vagina, continuing to pull even after meeting resistance from the cervix. The friction causes the fetus to tear apart. For example, a leg might be ripped off the fetus as it is pulled through the cervix and out of the woman. The process of evacuating the fetus piece by piece continues until it has been completely removed.[31]

Late-term abortionist Warren Hern describes a gruesome D&E necessity in his medical textbook *Abortion Practice*: "A long curved Mayo scissors may be necessary to decapitate and dismember the fetus."[32]

Dilation and extraction

Prior to 2007, some abortionists used a procedure that ended the fetus's life after it was partially outside of the woman's body. The American College of Obstetricians and Gynecologists (ACOG) calls this technique dilation and extraction (D&X), though the more common term is partial-birth abortion.[33]

This procedure involves delivering the fetus feet first and then pausing delivery while the child's head is still in the birth canal. According to the ACOG, the procedure ends with the "partial evacuation of the intracranial contents of a living fetus to effect vaginal delivery of a dead but otherwise intact fetus."[34] In other words, the abortionist cuts a hole in the fetus's skull and uses a vacuum to suck the brains out. He then delivers the child's dead body, since without brains the head is small enough to pass through the cervix.

Martin Haskell, the abortion provider who invented this procedure, admits that most D&X procedures were elective and not done to preserve a woman's health. In testimony before Congress, he said, "I'll be quite frank. Most of my abortions are elective in that 20–24 week range. . . . In my particular case, probably 20 percent are for genetic reasons. And the other 80 percent are purely elective."[35]

Even though this particular procedure is banned under the Supreme Court's 2007 *Gonzales v. Carhart* ruling, abortion is still legal in most states through all nine months of pregnancy. The abortion procedures simply have to be done inside the woman's body. The ruling addresses how these late-term procedures can be done: "Sometimes the abortion provider ends the fetus's life without dismembering him, though this method is rare. Some doctors, especially later in the second trimester, may kill the fetus a day or two before performing the surgical evacuation. They inject digoxin or potassium chloride into the fetus, the umbilical cord, or the amniotic fluid. Fetal demise may cause contractions and make greater dilation possible. Once dead, moreover, the fetus's body will soften, and its removal will be easier."

After reading these descriptions of abortion, it's easy to understand why people become emotional, angry, or willing to do anything to bring attention to these horrors. But remember that abortion is shocking in and of itself. We don't have to run through the streets shouting, "Abortion is murder!" in order to make it shocking. A gracious defender of the pro-life view knows that the facts speak loudly so we don't have to.

When is abortion legal?

Throughout most of U.S. history, abortion was illegal except in rare cases, such as when a woman's life was in danger or the pregnancy was the result of rape or incest.[36] This changed when Norma McCorvey sued for the right to have an abortion. Because her case went through a lengthy appeals process, McCorvey gave birth and placed her child for adoption.[37] In 1972, McCorvey's case finally reached the Supreme Court where, under the pseudonym Jane Roe, she sued the state of Texas, which was represented by Dallas County District Attorney Henry Wade.

On January 22, 1973, the Court handed down its *Roe v. Wade* decision, ruling 7-2 in favor of Roe. Justice Harry Blackmun argued in the Court's opinion of the case that:

+ Abortion had usually been considered a misdemeanor in previous law codes, and anti-abortion laws seem to have been enacted to protect women from unsafe abortions (although several legal scholars have made a compelling case that Blackmun erred on this fact).[38] Since abortions were now relatively safe, there was no compelling reason for the state to outlaw them.

+ The case of *Griswold v. Connecticut* (1965) made the sale of contraceptives legal in the United States and helped enshrine a "right to privacy" in the Constitution.[39]

+ Because there is so much disagreement about whether the fetus is a human being, the Court could not rule on the matter and felt it had to be left an open question.[40] However, the majority of *Roe v. Wade* seems to take the position that prior to the time the child can live outside of the womb (or viability), the child has no interests and thus has no rights under the Constitution.

◆ Citing various amendments in the Bill of Rights, the Court ruled that abortion fell under the scope of other private medical decisions that the state could regulate only in order to protect the health of the woman having the abortion.[41] But even many pro-choice advocates see *Roe's* reliance on privacy to be poor judicial reasoning. Edward Lazarus, a former clerk of Justice Blackmun who himself supports legal abortion, considers the case "indefensible." He writes, "What, exactly, is the problem with *Roe?* The problem, I believe, is that it has little connection to the constitutional right it purportedly interpreted. A constitutional right to privacy broad enough to include abortion has no meaningful foundation in constitutional text, history, or precedent—at least, it does not if those sources are fairly described and reasonably faithfully followed."[42]

Roe v. Wade divided pregnancy into three twelve-week "trimesters" and ruled that in the first two trimesters states could not outlaw abortion, but they could regulate the procedure in the second trimester to ensure the safety of the mother. *Roe* allowed but did not require states to ban abortion in the third trimester. If states banned abortion in the third trimester, they had to allow an exception for abortions deemed necessary to protect a woman's health.[43]

The problem with this exception is that *Roe's* companion case, *Doe v. Bolton*, ruled that "health" included any factor that was "physical, emotional, psychological, familial, [or related to] the woman's age."[44] Abortion provider Warren Hern has even argued that a child unwanted by his mother can be considered a "health risk." He writes, "It appears that 'unwantedness' may be regarded as a major complication of pregnancy with surgical intervention in the form of abortion as the indicated treatment."[45] The Court's definition of health thus made it almost impossible to ban any abortions.

While the majority of abortions (89 percent) occur during the first twelve weeks of pregnancy, a significant number of late-term abortions still occur. Defenders of legal abortion claim that late-term abortions (those that typically take place after a fetus is twenty weeks old) account for only about one percent of all abortions. Let's assume that's true. Since 1.06 million abortions occur each year in the U.S., that still means about 10,000 late-term abortions occur annually. To put that into perspective, about 8,900 people were murdered in the U.S. in 2012 through the use of firearms.[46]

Pro-choice advocates sometimes claim that these abortions are performed only when a woman's life is in danger or the child cannot survive being born. However, a 2013 study on women who obtained abortions in the second and third trimesters found that most women obtained late-term abortions for financial or social reasons rather than health concerns. It stated, "[S]eeking a later abortion was unrelated to women's reasons for seeking an abortion. Thus, among women without fetal anomalies, reasons for seeking abortion are not different whether women sought abortion early or late in pregnancy."[47] A *Washington Times* article about the study concluded, "[R]esearchers found that women in general delayed getting abortions if they are unsure they are pregnant, aren't sure they want an abortion, and are disagreeing with the baby's father. . . . [A]bortion costs were also a major hurdle."[48]

Staring into the abyss

Since 1975, the number of people who believe abortion should be legal under any circumstance has risen by 7 percent, while the number of people who believe abortion should be illegal under any circumstance has fallen by 4 percent. Even though the numbers fluctuate, it's clear that public opinion on abortion has barely changed since *Roe v. Wade* was decided more than forty years ago. It's true that more people identify as being pro-life, but one study found that 35 percent of these self-proclaimed pro-lifers did not want *Roe v. Wade* overturned.[49] These people may dislike abortion, but they do not want to make it illegal.

Rather than give up in the face of this challenge, pro-life advocates must refocus their efforts to make an attractive and powerful defense of unborn children. Even communicating simple statements of fact could change our culture. For example, a 2013 NBC News-*Wall Street Journal* poll found that while 70 percent of Americans did not want *Roe v. Wade* overturned, 41 percent of people in the same poll did not know enough about the decision to say if they disapproved of it.[50] A 2012 Pew Research poll found that 57 percent of adults under the age of thirty did not even know what *Roe v. Wade* was about.[51] For these people, the idea of *anything* being overturned was enough to spark their opposition.

Defenders of legal abortion succeed when abortion is obscured, the facts are hidden, and the discussion is centered on anything but the actual abortion procedure. Social movements such as the civil rights movement succeeded because the victims decided they would not be victims anymore. Martin Luther King, Jr. wrote in his *Letter from Birmingham Jail*, "[F]reedom is never voluntarily given by the oppressor; it must be demanded by the oppressed."

The problem with abortion is that the victims can't become angry and demand change. They can't do *anything* to help themselves. Instead, advocates have to demand justice on their behalf, but to be successful they must do so in a persuasive and gracious way.

2

A Gracious Approach

One of my first experiences with the Justice for All exhibit was at the University of California in Santa Barbara.[52] By the afternoon, thirty protesters were marching around the exhibit chanting slogans like "Pro-lifers lie, women die!" "My body is not your property!" and "Get the U.S. out of my uterus!" Fortunately, the volunteers with Justice for All are trained to take anger from protesters and channel it into productive and civil dialogue.

I remember watching one young man in a tight red T-shirt look at our exhibit. He was wearing sunglasses, but they couldn't conceal the anger on his face. He walked over to where I was standing, and I braced myself for a verbal barrage. The young man abruptly turned and began yelling at the pro-choice protesters instead. It turns out he was a pro-life student on campus whom we had not trained at our seminar the previous weekend. Indeed, his lack of dialogue training became evident as his conversation with the protesters began to deteriorate.

"What's the matter with you people?" he shouted. "This is the murder of babies! How can you be for this?"

"They're not babies, they're fetuses, and it's our choice."

"You don't have a right to take away our choice!" the protesters shot back.

"You had a choice when you had sex!"

"You're a man! You have no rights over my body! We can have sex and not be punished by pigs like you!"

The young man's face flushed with anger. "We wouldn't have abortion if women like you could learn to keep your legs shut!"

"Enough!" I said, stepping forward. "You should apologize to these women and listen to what they have to say. You might not agree with them, but that doesn't give you the right to insult them."

"Forget you, man!" he replied and hurried away.

One of the female protesters turned to me and said, "Thank you so much. I can't stand anti-abortion people." I smiled and told her who I was. One of the women's jaw dropped, and she said, "But . . . you're so reasonable!"

That young man at UCSB was angry that children were being aborted and no one seemed to care. I understand his anger, and I wish more people would be as upset about abortion as he was. But I don't condone his response to that anger or his treatment of those protesters. Instead of hearing a compassionate plea for the lives of the unborn, all these women heard from this man's outburst was "I hate you!"

At Justice for All we taught people how to be ambassadors for the pro-life position, and we often quoted 2 Corinthians 5:20: "So we are ambassadors for Christ, God making his appeal through us. We urge you on behalf of Christ, be reconciled to God."[53] Pro-life ambassadors are effective when they combine knowledge with a persuasive approach. For a while I didn't understand the need to be a pro-life ambassador until one time I failed at it. Massively.

Learning by failing

The scene was the University of Arizona, and I was talking to a belligerent student whose yelling had attracted more than a dozen onlookers.

"If you're pro-life, then you must be against IVF," he said to me.

IVF, or in vitro fertilization, is a process in which human embryos are created outside of a woman's womb and then later implanted there. Often embryos that have genetic abnormalities are destroyed or aborted later in the woman's pregnancy. This prompted me to respond by saying, "Well, if IVF kills embryos, and those embryos are human beings, then, yes, I oppose IVF."

"Ha! I knew it!" he shouted. "I was an IVF baby. Without IVF I wouldn't be here!"

As the crowd formed a ring around us, this young man and I began a rapid-fire debate. For every argument he advanced, I fired the perfect rebuttal right back at him.

"Don't you think creating life is a good thing?" he asked, to which I immediately responded, "Ah, *abusus non tollit usum*, or 'abuse does not annul the proper use' of an act. IVF abuses the natural order involved in procreation, so that makes it gravely immoral."

We argued with increasing franticness. As a result, the young man became more and more frustrated. Finally, he threw up his hands and said, "You know what? If you're not going to listen to me, I'm leaving." He walked away. I looked around and the crowd slowly began to walk away as well, in awkward silence. One man came up to me and said, "Wow, you really blew it."

I was furious when he said that. I knew the facts and arguments about abortion inside and out—how dare he criticize my ability to debate and present a flawless argument!

And yet, I *had* blown it. I had become so caught up in mastering arguments that I missed the important skill of mastering *people*. That is why I teach pro-life ambassadors to follow these five ambassador rules when they engage in conversations on not just abortion but any controversial topic:[54]

1. Don't be weird.
2. Make your evidence bulletproof.
3. Use questions instead of statements.
4. Actually listen.
5. Agree whenever possible.

1. Don't be weird.

I understand that our culture often labels people who think abortion should be illegal as "weird." When I say, "Don't be weird," I don't mean do anything it takes to make pro-choice people like you. If that's your goal, then you should start paying for abortions! Instead, "Don't be weird" means don't engage in activities that will *unnecessarily* offend those who disagree. Consider the pro-life advocate who dresses up in a grim reaper costume, complete with skull mask and scythe, and holds an "I'll see you in hell" sign at an abortion facility.

Now, I bet this person cares deeply about the unborn, and I am glad he's at least outside an abortion facility.[55] But has he stopped to think of what the women going into this facility think when they see him? Instead of seeing someone who makes them feel safe and welcomed, those women see someone who makes them feel scared and uncomfortable.

When Abby Johnson served as a director of a Planned Parenthood in Texas and saw such protesters, she would think, "If they cared about these women, they wouldn't look so frightening."[56] Johnson later quit her job and became a pro-life advocate. She credits her conversion to the group 40 Days for Life, whose participants showed her genuine love and compassion while praying in front of her abortion facility.

As pro-life advocates, we become weird when we don't think about how our words and actions affect other people. St. Paul said, "Let your speech always be gracious, seasoned with salt, so that you may know how you ought to answer every one" (Col. 4:6). If I had been more understanding in my IVF conversation and less weird, I would have slowed down the pace and asked more questions. I would have known how to treat this young man like a person to be ministered to and not an enemy to be defeated. In fact, I was so focused on "winning" the conversation that I forgot to get from him the one thing that we use to dignify the person with whom we are speaking: his name.

Instead of going into a conversation with the attitude "I'm going to *win*," go into the conversation with the attitude "I'm going to be *winsome*," and the Holy Spirit will do the rest. Proverbs 15:1 reminds us, "A soft answer turns away wrath, but a harsh word stirs up anger."

2. Make your evidence bulletproof.

Does not being weird mean we should simply love other people and not try to prove they are wrong? If St. Paul were here, I'm sure he would say, as he often does in his epistles, "By no means!" In Ephesians 4:15 Paul says we must "speak the truth in love." The most loving thing we can do for someone is to tell him the truth and prevent him from being deceived. This doesn't mean that all pro-life advocates have to be walking encyclopedias, but it does mean that we must be committed to growing in our knowledge about the issues related to the abortion debate.

We must also acquire our knowledge from reliable sources or we might be embarrassed later. One of my pro-life friends gave a talk at a public university in which she claimed that an unborn child could feel pain at a very early point in pregnancy. When a pro-choice medical student challenged her claim with evidence from peer-reviewed medical journals, my friend admitted in front of the audience that the only source for her claim was a newsletter from a national pro-life group. Even if my friend had been correct when it came to fetal pain, the students she addressed would not have believed her, because she did not have adequate evidence to back up what she was saying.

What's the lesson? Just as one drop of cyanide can poison an entire glass of water, so too can one egregious error cause people to discount your entire argument. To keep this from happening, I do my best to make my evidence bulletproof.[57] This means using the most trusted, up-to-date sources and having responses to anticipated objections.

As I did earlier when I described abortion procedures, we should use sources that pro-choice advocates accept as being reliable so they have less excuse to dismiss our conclusions that are drawn from those sources. Of course, just as no amount of body armor can guarantee a person won't be injured, no amount of study can prevent us from occasionally being stumped.

Once while hanging out with a group of friends I was introduced to someone who volunteered for a euthanasia advocacy group. He found out I was pro-life and asked me, "Why won't you let people have dignity and be able to choose when they die?" His questions became more pointed, and I became flustered, because that year I had studied issues primarily related to abortion, not euthanasia. I felt almost naked at the lack of arguments I had to offer. I was so desperate that I opened my laptop while he was distracted and searched the Internet for anti-euthanasia arguments. Eventually, I just repeated the same weak assertions and evasions until the conversation switched subjects.

That is the wrong attitude to have. No one has the answers for every question. When someone asks us a question we don't know the answer to, we should just admit it. If the other person cares about truth, they should understand if you say, "You know, that's a really good question, and I'm not sure how to answer it at this moment. Would you mind if I do some research and e-mail you a more helpful answer, and you can let me know what you think of it?"

When people see that we genuinely care more about knowing the truth than winning arguments, it makes them more receptive to what we have to say. If we are honest and humble about our lack of knowledge, most people will not think we are ignorant. In reality, a person is more likely to sound ignorant when he pretends to be an expert in something he knows nothing about!

3. Use questions instead of statements. When we make statements in conversation, they can turn unintentionally into speeches that get ignored. A better approach is to ask questions, because this lets us steer our conversations toward the truth without having to "preach" the truth to anyone. I have found that there are four questions that are essential to any good conversation, including those regarding abortion:[58]

1. "What do you believe?" Too often we assume what someone else believes based on his income, his race, his gender, his religion (or lack of religion), or some other external factor. Never assume what someone believes. Instead just ask.

2. "Why do you think that's true?" or "How did you come to believe that?" How a person arrived at a belief, or why he thinks it's true, can be even more interesting than what he actually believes. It's vital to discover this so that you can help the person see where his thinking went wrong if he happens to have a false belief.

3. "What did you mean by [fill in the blank]?" If we don't stop and define the words in our conversations, we run the risk of misunderstanding the other person. Here are just a few words whose meanings can vary dramatically between people when they talk about abortion: *life, choice, rights, fetus, person, human,* and even *abortion.* By carefully defining the words being used, you will be able to talk to people you disagree with instead of talking past them.

4. "What would you say to someone who says [fill in the blank]?" After you learn what the other person believes and why he believes it, you may want to challenge his belief and show him it's false. It is not disrespectful to challenge the truth of someone's beliefs. You can respect a person and be kind to him without respecting any particular opinion he has.[59] By using a question from a hypothetical inquirer, instead of a direct accusation from yourself, the person with whom you're speaking is less likely to become defensive or take the challenge personally.

Asking a question is especially helpful when you have conversations with the two toughest audiences: family and people on the Internet. Conversations with family and close friends can be explosive, since they know us well and can push our emotional buttons. Conversely, conversations on the Internet can be explosive because those people don't know us well and can hide behind a veil of anonymity that emboldens their rude behavior. In both cases, a set of questions can lower the level of hostility. With enough practice, without having to make a single statement, you can help a person see that what he believes does not make sense.[60] One way to do this is to ask what I call "dumb questions."

One time a student told me that abortion wasn't a big deal because it just terminated a pregnancy. I asked him what a pregnancy was or what it meant when a woman was pregnant. He gave me a confused look, since it should just be obvious what pregnancy is. I pressed him to define it, and he said pregnancy meant a woman had a child inside her.[61] I then said, "Childbirth also 'terminates a pregnancy,' but would you agree that abortion is very different than childbirth? If abortion terminates a pregnancy without resulting in a live birth, then doesn't abortion terminate a child as well?" He was quiet and looked away until someone else started to talk to me.

To help your conversations on abortion, I recommend asking one of these ten "dumb questions":

1. What is abortion?
2. What is a child?
3. What is a human?
4. What is pregnancy?
5. What's wrong with being pro-abortion?
6. Why is it wrong to kill a newborn baby?
7. What does abortion do to the fetus?
8. Is there a difference between a condom and an abortion? (If so, then what is it?)
9. Why is abortion a sad or difficult choice?
10. What is so upsetting about pictures of abortion?

4. Actually listen.

My conversation at the University of Arizona went poorly because I was not practicing respectful listening. I certainly *heard* what this young man said, but I wasn't *listening* to him. We all fall into this temptation at some point. I remember once having a disagreement with my wife in which I calmly explained to her why I thought she was mistaken. I then asked her what she thought of my response, and she became startled and said, "I'm sorry! I wasn't listening. I was thinking of my next argument!" Of course, I have been guilty of doing the same thing to her. When it comes to being a better listener, my advice is to slow down the conversation and frequently paraphrase what you have heard.

Heated conversations are like ping-pong matches where arguments and rebuttals are traded back and forth in rapid succession. Sometimes there isn't a chance to catch your breath. In contrast, our conversations on abortion should feel more like a game of volleyball. When a volleyball is served or returned, it usually floats through the air for a few seconds before it is hit. The arguments we share with one another should "float" in a similar way.

To achieve this kind of dialogue, I recommend pausing to think after a person has finished speaking. Then paraphrase to the person what you heard him say. This reduces tension by slowing down the conversation and provides an opportunity for clarification of misunderstandings.

A good way to start a paraphrase would be to say, "Let me make sure I understand where you're coming from. You said [insert paraphrase of the argument]. Did I understand you correctly?" Psychologist Carl Rogers summarizes listening this way:

> Real communication occurs . . . when we listen with understanding. What does this mean? It means to see the expressed idea and attitude from the other person's point of view . . . to sense how it feels to him to achieve his frame of reference in regard to the thing he is talking about.[62]

Respectful listening also helps when dealing with the kind of person Christian apologist Greg Koukl calls a steamroller.[63] These people spew multiple, complex arguments while demanding simple yes or no answers. They're the kind of people who elevate the blood pressure of everyone around them. By not talking and instead listening intently to what the person is saying, you can let the steamroller just run out of steam. When he stops talking, simply say, "You've given me five arguments to answer. [If you're really good, paraphrase each argument.] I can't answer all of them at once, so which one would you like me to respond to?"

If he continues to interrupt, or is rude and disrespectful, you might leave the conversation by saying, "I'm interested in having a real dialogue, and I don't think we can with your at-titude." If someone is not willing to listen to you, you are not obligated to listen to him and can choose to talk to someone else who is more open to hearing the truth.

5. Agree whenever possible.

Some pro-life advocates think that if they agree with a critic on *anything*, then somehow they have hurt their defense of the pro-life position. In reality, if a pro-life advocate fails to agree with a critic on *anything*, he will come off as a walking agenda and not as an honest seeker of truth.

Pope St. John Paul II wrote in his encyclical *Redemptoris Missio*, "Dialogue does not originate from tactical concerns or self-interest, but is an activity with its own guiding principles, requirements and dignity. It is demanded by the deep respect for everything that has been brought about in human beings by the Spirit who blows where he wills."[64] One tool that moves our conversations forward and respects the dignity of each person is the use of common ground. Steve Wagner, author of *Common Ground Without Compromise: 25 Questions to Create Dialogue on Abortion*, defines the essence of common ground:

> [W]e should build common ground to begin a dia-logue at the beginning of an argument. We should also retreat to common ground frequently throughout the argument, not to give up on finding truth, but to gain necessary footing so we can move forward to a new consensus on what is true. If the argument we are hav-ing is like a car taking us to the beach of truth, then common ground is the fuel. Your argument will have to access common ground from the outset if it is to move forward. You will need to stop and refuel at times, too.[65]

Common ground allows people to focus on their agree-ments instead of their disagreements. In fact, it's so enjoyable the participants may be tempted to keep the dialogue *only* on common ground and avoid the heated topic of disagreement. That's why it's important to remember that common ground is not an end; it is a tool that helps us solve our disagreements. In a meeting with more than 200 representatives of other world religions, Pope Benedict XVI said that dialogue is not meant to create good relationships but that "the broader purpose of dialogue is to discover the truth."[66]

Here are some questions Wagner considers to be the most helpful when trying to find common ground on the issue of abortion:

1. "What do you think about late-term abortions?" (If you think they should be illegal, then where would you draw the line? Why did you pick that stage of development to outlaw abortions?)
2. "Do you believe men should have the choice to abort their fetuses?" (Do you think men should be charged with the murder of a human being if they kill a pregnant woman's fetus? Do you think the punishment should change if the fetus was unwanted?
3. "What do you think about aborting a fetus simply because she is female?" (Do you think a feminist can support abortion against female fetuses?)
4. "Would you prefer there were fewer abortions?" (Why? What is it about abortion that you find unpleasant?)
5. Should abortion be legal through all nine months of pregnancy for any reason? (If not, why not? Where do you think the cutoff should be, and why do you draw the line there?)

U.S. President Barack Obama broached what he considered common ground in his controversial commencement address at the University of Notre Dame in 2009:

[W]hen we open up our hearts and our minds to those who may not think precisely like we do or believe precisely what we believe—that's when we discover at least the possibility of common ground. That's when we begin to say, "Maybe we won't agree on abortion, but we can still agree that this heart-wrenching decision for any woman is not made casually, it has both moral and spiritual dimensions."[67]

This is actually great common ground and provides the opportunity for the pro-life advocate to move the conversation forward with a question like this: "Why is abortion a heart-wrenching decision for any woman to make? What are the moral dimensions that are involved in having an abortion?" For pro-life advocates, the fact that abortion ends the life of a valuable human being explains why abortion is "heart-wrenching" and has a "moral dimension." I'm curious to see how pro-choice advocates would explain these aspects of abortion without referencing the death of a valuable human being.

How an ambassador defuses an emotional bomb

The following real-life scenario shows how the tools of a pro-life ambassador, when used wisely, can help you engage even the most emotionally difficult conversations.

It was the middle of the afternoon at the University of Northern Colorado, and my stomach was annoyed with me. But as I opened my humble brown paper bag to take out a sandwich, I noticed some students looking at our exhibit. I set my lunch aside and said to myself, "One more conversation couldn't hurt." Three girls were loudly agreeing with each other that our exhibit was stupid and offensive. I walked up to them and one girl, whom I'll call "Annie," dropped a bomb on me. She said, "I used to prostitute myself for cocaine, and when I got pregnant I knew that I couldn't give birth to a cocaine-addicted baby. Are you going to tell me that my abortion was wrong?"

I said to Annie, "Wow. I'm so sorry for what happened to you. But it seems that you've really turned your life around. How did that happen?" I spent the next twenty minutes listening to how Annie traveled out of the country to kick her drug habit only to feel judged by her Catholic friends when she came home. I learned that her friends' actions were the reason she had stopped going to church. By asking questions and listening, I gained Annie's trust and could now drive the conversation back to Annie's original question: Is abortion wrong?

I said, "Annie, I think you and I can agree that abortion is emotionally and circumstantially complicated, and each woman's abortion experience is different. I think you have a good heart and you try to do what's right concerning other people. Can we also agree that doing the right thing can be very, very difficult, and it's sometimes understandable when people don't choose to do it? Think of the prisoners in a concentration camp who are bribed by the guards with food for their starving children if they just tell them which prisoners are planning to escape. It's wrong to betray your fellow prisoners, but doing so is understandable given the horrible circumstances involved."

Annie nodded in agreement as I continued, "I oppose abortion, but I also want to make sure women who've had abortions are cared for and listened to. But if the unborn are human beings like these women, then I want to treat them with the same dignity and respect these women deserve. Do you understand where I'm coming from?" At this point Annie had done an about-face. We were now calmly talking about the humanity of the unborn instead of fighting about circumstances that can lead to abortion.

Annie declined my offer to be introduced to a volunteer who specializes in postabortive counseling, but I was still able to encourage her to give God a second chance in her life. In these conversations you should not think your message was rejected just because the person did not convert right in front of you. Sometimes the words we say don't sink in until months or even years later. Eventually our conversation came to a close, and Annie and I parted ways. I picked up my lunch, which had been withering in the sun for longer than an hour. It was an hour well spent.

PART II

People Who Avoid the Main Issue

3

The Pragmatists

When most people are asked why abortion should be legal, their first answer isn't "Because a fetus is not a human being." Instead, most pro-choice advocates bypass this issue and simply say abortion should be legal because women need abortion for some important reason. I call these reasons "what abouts," and you've probably heard them before. "If you make abortion illegal, then what about women who are too poor to take care of a child? What about the children who will be abused? What about the right to choose? What about respecting privacy and religious freedom? What about overpopulation? What about rape?"

The people who ask these questions are *pragmatists* who believe abortion is the most practical solution for the hardships involved in an unintended pregnancy. When some pro-life advocates engage pragmatists, they turn into insufferable optimists. They hope to deflect every pessimistic reason offered in defense of legal abortion with a solution that makes abortion unnecessary. Their conversation might go like this:

> Pro-choicer: What about women who are too poor to take care of a child?
>
> Pro-lifer: There's always adoption.
>
> PC: But foster care is a terrible system. Do you want kids to have to grow up being unloved and abused? Do you care about children at all?!
>
> PL: The rate of abuse in adoption is actually very low; the vast majority of children are fine. And there are no circumstances where a mom couldn't take care of her child. In America there are resources available to help these women.

PC: Not when pro-life conservatives cut funding that is needed for social services.

PL: Maybe if liberals like you didn't spend us into oblivion then we wouldn't have such economic instability in the first place.

PC: Well, what about the financial crisis caused by deregulation?

PL: Deregulation isn't the problem! It's the liberal need to subsidize unqualified lenders.

PC: You're an idiot!

PL: You're a communist!

What happened here? How did we get from discussing abortion to accusing people of being communists? Although this dialogue is fictional, I have heard real conversations proceed in an almost identical manner. These failed conversations happen when the pro-life advocate doesn't stay on the one question that matters most: "What are the unborn?"[68]

In order to avoid this kind of exchange, I use a tool created by pro-life apologist Scott Klusendorf called Trot Out a Toddler (TOAT). Of all the ways to present the pro-life message, Scott's method is my favorite. While the ideas behind his approach are implicit in other works, I appreciate how Scott organizes his approach and how easy it is to teach to others.[69] My favorite articulation of TOAT was created by my former JFA colleague Steve Wagner, which he calls "the four A's." They are *Agree*, *Apply*, *Ask Why*, and *Ah!* Here's how they work.

Step One: Agree

Whenever possible, agree with the sentiments behind the reason being given to keep abortion legal. Some pro-life advocates think that agreeing to anything is a sign of weakness, but pro-choice advocates see it as a sign of compassion and understanding. For example, when poverty is mentioned, you can agree that caring for an impoverished child is difficult. When the "right to choose" is invoked, you can wholeheartedly agree that women should be able to choose all sorts of things. Invoking many areas of agreement at the beginning of the conversation will create rapport and a sense of good will that can help ease tension when you discuss areas of disagreement. But your agreement should not be merely used as a strategy to win the argument. Instead, genuinely show concern for the lives of both the born and unborn people who are affected by an unintended pregnancy.

Step Two: Apply

Next, take the reason being given to justify abortion and use it to justify killing a two-year-old. This takes practice, and I recommend that when you describe the TOAT example, extend your hand two or three feet off the ground, as if you were touching the top of a two-year-old's head. If you get stuck, remember that the "apply" always starts the same way: Extend your hand and say, "Imagine I have a two-year-old here, and his mother . . ."

This works for almost any reason that does not answer the question "What are the unborn?"[70] For example, regarding poverty, you might say, "Imagine I have a two-year-old here, and his mother is poor and feels like she cannot care for him. Should she be allowed to kill him?" This may seem like a silly question, but that is precisely the point. If unborn children are as human as toddlers, then it should be just as silly to ask the question, "Imagine I have a poor pregnant woman who feels like she cannot care for another child. Should she be allowed to have an abortion?" The only difference is the age of the child who is being killed.

After using the pragmatist's reason for abortion as a justification for killing a two-year-old, it's important to resist the temptation to say, "Obviously, it's wrong for a woman to kill her two-year-old. Therefore, abortion is wrong, because the unborn is as human as a two-year-old." No matter how silly it sounds, ask the person only if the reason women need legal abortion (poverty, choice, women's rights, and so on) would also be a good reason to kill a two-year-old. Then be quiet. Just let the question hang in the air until the pragmatist responds.

Step Three: Ask why

When the pragmatist responds to your question and says that it is wrong to kill the two-year-old, ask "Why is it wrong?" You can even preface this question by saying, "I know this is a stupid question, but humor me. Why is it wrong for the woman to kill her two-year-old?" Sometimes the pro-choice advocate will answer, "Because it's illegal." You can then ask if killing two-year-olds should be illegal. If he says yes, ask, "Why do you think killing two-year-olds should be illegal?"

A pragmatist might argue that the reason it is wrong or illegal for a woman to kill her two-year-old is because she could always place that child for adoption. Since the fetus cannot be adopted, it's not wrong to kill a fetus through abortion. The pro-lifer can respond by saying the woman in the TOAT example lives in another country where poverty is rampant and adoption is simply not a feasible option. You might say, "Imagine I have a two-year-old, and his mother lives in the slums of another country where children can't be adopted, and she is too poor to care for him. Should she be allowed to kill her two-year-old?"

We can also argue that wantedness can't be the reason it is wrong to kill the two-year-old. If I decide to turn a beautiful mahogany dining room table into firewood because I'm bored with it, I'm sure there are many people who would *want* that table. However, that fact would not make it wrong for me to destroy my table. Likewise, there must be something about the two-year-old other than whether he is wanted (such as his humanity) that makes it wrong to kill him. If the unborn possess this trait as well, then it would be equally wrong to kill them.

In rare cases you may encounter a pro-choice advocate who says that it would not be wrong for a mother to kill her two-year-old. There are two reasons people say this. The first is they don't want to have a real conversation. They don't actually believe in killing two-year-olds, but they will say they do to provoke you. Don't fall for it. Simply say, "Well, if you don't have any respect for human life, then why should I have any respect for what you believe?" You can also ask, "Do you want to have a serious conversation or do you just feel like wasting my time?"

The other reason people say it's not wrong to kill a toddler is because they actually believe it. Such people may be genuinely disturbed individuals or philosophy majors (sometimes it's hard to tell the difference). If you feel that they have no respect for human life, then I recommend keeping your safety paramount and avoiding conversation with such people. If they hold a philosophical belief that justifies the killing of born children, consult the appendix that deals with answering infanticide.

Even though a few odd people will answer otherwise, this step is the easiest of the four A's. Most people agree that killing a two-year-old is wrong, because two-year-olds are innocent human beings, and it is wrong to kill innocent human beings. The pragmatist may even anticipate where your questions are leading and say it is wrong to kill a two-year-old because he is a *person*, or a *born* human, or he is *breathing*, or he is in some way different from an unborn child, whom we are allowed to kill. This is exactly where you want the conversation to go.

Step Four: Ah! (That's the issue!)

The last part of Trot Out a Toddler is the most complicated but also the most important. It narrates the epiphany the pro-choice person should be having in relation to the pro-life position. In this step, the pro-life person responds to the answer to Step Three and says, "Ah [or "Oh," or any other appropriate exclamation], so *that's* the issue. The issue is not about poverty [or choice, or age, or health, or whatever original reason was offered as to why abortion must remain legal], because you wouldn't justify killing a two-year-old for that reason. If the unborn are just as human as a two-year-old, then we shouldn't kill them for that reason, either. You and I just disagree over whether unborn children should have the same rights born children possess."

Let's apply the four steps of TOAT to the previous dialogue about abortion:

> Pro-choicer: What about women who are too poor to take care of a child?
>
> Pro-lifer: I agree that it's hard to care for a child when you are poor. Any woman contemplating abortion in such a situation must be agonizing over it. (Agree) But may I ask you a question?
>
> PC: Okay.
>
> PL: Suppose a woman has a two-year-old and just lost her job. She now feels that she can no longer care for her child. Should she be allowed to kill him? (Apply)
>
> PC: What? No, of course not!
>
> PL: I know this may seem like a dumb question, but why can't she kill her two-year-old? (Ask why)
>
> PC: Because the two-year-old is a human being.
>
> PL: (Ah!) I see where you're coming from. I think this shows that poverty, while important, is not the main issue. If it is wrong to kill an impoverished two-year-old, and the unborn are just as human as a two-year-old, then wouldn't it also be wrong to kill an impoverished unborn child?

PC: But they're different. A two-year-old is a human, but a fetus isn't.

After you've trotted out enough toddlers, you'll be able to use other examples of born people besides toddlers in order to make the same point. For example, in response to the argument that abortion should be legal because some children are unwanted, the pro-life advocate could apply this pro-choice reason to justify killing other unwanted born people such as the homeless or people who talk in movie theaters. If it were wrong to kill those unwanted people because they are human beings, then wouldn't it be wrong to kill unwanted unborn children who are also human beings?

Remember that TOAT does not constitute the entire pro-life position. That is why the preceding conversation ends abruptly with what seems like the pragmatist turning the tables on the pro-lifer. In reality, this is exactly where the pro-life advocate wants the conversation to go, to the one question that matters most: "What are the unborn?" In the following chapters I will explain how to defend the view that an unborn child is just as human, and therefore just as valuable, as a toddler. Before we examine those arguments, let's take a look at some examples of how to use Trot Out a Toddler.

Forced to have children?

In response to the argument that outlawing abortion forces women to have children, I would say that I agree that no one should be forced to have a child. What I mean is, no one should be forced to have sex and *conceive* a child. However, choosing to "not have" a child after the child is conceived means choosing to expel a dead child from the womb as opposed to a living one, which is a serious moral wrong.

A related argument claims that outlawing abortion forces women to be parents, but what's wrong with that? Several

years ago in South Korea, a young couple became so addicted
to video games that they stopped feeding their child and
spent all their time playing with a virtual child online while
their real child starved to death.[71] I'd ask a pragmatist, "If this
couple simply didn't want their two-year-old anymore, then
why shouldn't they be allowed to stop feeding him?" The
pragmatist could respond by saying, "They should not be allowed to starve their child. They could have given that child
to someone else, so that's why killing *that* child is wrong but
abortion is okay."

In that case I'd reply, "If no one was willing to adopt this
child, would it be okay to kill him? Your answer still forces
this couple to be parents against their wills. Even if the parents
place their child for adoption they are still *biological* parents
to the child as long as the child is alive (even if they are no
longer the child's *legal* parents). By making it illegal to kill this
child, aren't you forcing them to be biological parents against
their will?"

"That's different, because this child is already born," the
pragmatist would say.

"Okay, so that's the issue. It's not about being forced to have
children, because we don't think laws forbidding infanticide
force people to be parents against their will. If the unborn are
just as human as born children, then shouldn't we grant unborn
children the same legal protections born children receive?"

Child abuse

James Prescott argues in *Humanist* magazine, "Given the alternative to abortion—that is, the birth of unwanted children,
with all the adverse implications—it is clear that abortion is a
beneficent and humanitarian act that values the *quality* of future human life more than the *quantity* of future human life."[72]
Prescott augments his argument with gruesome images of a
baby whose parents scalded him with milk. The implication is

that if women are not allowed to have abortions, then those children who are unwanted will be abused after birth, and therefore it would have been better to abort them.

Of course, this argument bizarrely assumes that abortion prevents a child from coming into existence who will be abused later in life. In reality, abortion ends the life of a child who only *might* be abused. The blindness to abortion being the ultimate form of child abuse is like someone saying, "Since we really want to go out of town this weekend, we better let Uncle Chester watch the children. Sure, he's a convicted pedophile, but if we let the children stay here by themselves, they might get into a car with a stranger." In both cases, the solution is worse than the problem.

I sometimes tell the following story to help pragmatists see the flaw in their reasoning on this point. I say, "Where I come from in the Southwest, we have a lot of problems with meth labs.[73] Sometimes when people are arrested for running these labs, it turns out they also have children who are sick and even addicted to meth. These children will just be bounced around the foster care system until they are released when they turn eighteen and begin a life of crime or prostitution. Would you be in favor of euthanizing these kids while they are two or three years old so that they won't have to suffer later?"

Most people, even though they abhor the suffering the child may endure at a later time, don't think killing born children in those circumstances is an acceptable solution. But if the reason it is unacceptable to kill these born children is because they are human beings, it follows that if the unborn are human beings then no matter what difficult situation they will be born into, it would be wrong to kill them.

Overpopulation

At Pasadena City College, a student named Victor told me, "We need abortion. I mean, how are we going to care for these children when the world is so overpopulated?" I replied, "Let's say you're right—the world is overpopulated."

Now, pro-life advocates who think the world is not over-populated may be tempted to argue the point. Don't. You have enough to argue about without bringing up another topic of disagreement. On the other hand, don't say you agree with the person on overpopulation when you actually don't (that's called lying). Instead, *agree for the sake of the argument*. You can say something like, "I personally don't think the world is over-populated. But for the sake of the argument, let's say I'm wrong and you're right on that point . . ."

"You know," I continued, "some people like scientists or political leaders contribute knowledge or ingenuity that could help us solve the overpopulation problem. They are what you would call *givers*. Other people such as the homeless, the se-verely disabled, or people in prison only consume our resources and don't contribute anything to society. They are what some people might call *takers*."

"Sure," he said.

"If that's the case, shouldn't we kill the homeless, the se-verely disabled, prisoners, and other takers who only consume resources and give nothing back? Then, only after we've killed them, we can decide if we need to kill the unborn. After all, they are innocent and could grow up to be either givers or takers."

Victor smiled as he understood where my argument was headed and remarked, "But you can't do that, because . . ." As his voice trailed off I replied, "Because we shouldn't kill human beings just to ease overpopulation. If a baby in the womb is as human as you or I, doesn't he deserve the same protection you and I receive?"

It's also worth mentioning that overpopulation doesn't justify a pro-*choice* position but a pro-*abortion* position.[74] What if abortion is kept legal only in order to ease overpopulation, but women as a whole don't choose to abort? Would the pro-choice advocate argue that women should be *forced* to have abortions in order to reduce population levels? I doubt most people (at least in America) would argue for that solution. If it would be wrong to force women's bodies to have abortions in order to ease overpopulation, then wouldn't it be just as wrong to force the bodies of unborn humans to be aborted for the same reason?

The right to choose

When students ask me if I believe in the right to choose, I just stop, turn my head to the side like a confused beagle, and say, "The right to choose . . . what?" I believe people should have lots of choices in life, and I especially believe women should have lots of choices that they were denied in the past. Women should be able to choose the college they want to attend, the business where they want to be employed, the husband they want to marry, and the religion they want to follow. Women should be able to do so because, while all *people* are equal and deserve equal respect, all *choices* are not equal, and some choices should not be respected.

In fact, some choices are evil and should be outlawed. We stop people from choosing to hire only people of certain races or from choosing to pollute public areas (even with cigarette smoke). In a civilized society we don't allow one human being to exploit or harm another human being in the name of "choice."

Pragmatists may respond that abortion is a *private* choice, and so it is different than choices that might harm other people. The Supreme Court used the so-called "right to privacy" in its *Roe v. Wade* decision to argue that abortion should be legal because it is a private medical decision between a woman and her physician.[75] But when our choices affect other people, privacy is no longer a viable defense. Could we imagine the

Supreme Court upholding a right to give your child plastic surgery or euthanize an elderly relative in the "privacy" of your own home?

Sometimes the pragmatist will throw an effective piece of rhetoric into the previous argument and ask, "Don't you trust women to make private choices that are best for their families?" Answering yes implies that you trust and approve women choosing abortion. Answering no makes you look like a misogynist. I hedge the answer and say, "I trust women as much as I trust men, and I can't trust either men or women when they say it's okay to hurt innocent human beings. If the unborn are not human, I don't need to trust women, since they hurt no one by having an abortion. If the unborn *are* human beings, then we must pass laws to protect these children from the men and the women who might hurt them."

Stay on target

We must get pro-choice advocates to answer the question "What are the unborn?" and the best way to do that is to use some form of Trot Out a Toddler. It is perhaps the most important tool a pro-life advocate can learn. If pro-lifers start arguing about poverty, or the Constitution, or sex education, or contraception, or any other irrelevant issue, they will lose. In the next chapter we'll see how TOAT can be applied to other more sophisticated yet equally irrelevant arguments in defense of legal abortion.

Engaging the pragmatist

A pragmatist's main concern: Women need abortion for important reasons.

Your objective: Use TOAT to show that because these reasons would not justify killing a two-year-old, they would not justify killing an unborn child who is as human as a two-year-old.

★ ★ ★

Pro-lifer: What do you think about abortion?

Pro-choicer: I don't know. I mean, if a woman already has three kids and can barely feed them, I don't see why she has to be forced to bring another child into the world.

PL: I agree it would be really tough to not know how you are going to provide for your children. I don't know how I'd handle that situation. But can I ask you a question?

PC: Sure.

PL: Let's say this woman knows she can take care of three children and she actually wants a newborn. Should she be allowed to kill one of her other children, such as her two-year-old, so that she can make ends meet?

PC: No! I mean, she could always adopt that one out.

PL: Yeah, but what if she doesn't want to worry about what will happen to that child after she adopts him out? Maybe she's worried about him being abused by a stranger. Why would you say she shouldn't be allowed to kill her two-year-old?

PC: Because the two-year-old is a living, born human being. It's completely different! Are you saying that a woman should be forced to drop out of school or lose her job just because she's pregnant?

PL: I don't think women should be fired just because they are pregnant—that's definitely unfair. But let's say a woman gives birth and finds that she can't finish school or keep her job because her baby demands too much of her. In fact, most moms I know find born babies to be harder to handle than unborn babies. Should women be allowed to kill their newborns if that will help their education or career?

PC: Of course not, but you're confusing the issue.

PL: How am I doing that?

PC: You're talking about killing babies, and I'm just talking about women's choice.

PL: A choice to do what exactly?

PC: To not be a mother if they don't want to be one.

PL: I agree with you that no woman should be forced to become a mother.

PC: You do?

PL: Of course. We also agree that it's okay to force a woman to stay a mother by forbidding her from killing her born children. She can put them up for adoption and give up being their legal mother, but she'll always be a biological mother as long as the children are alive.

PC: But that's because you can't kill people.

PL: Ah! So that's the issue. It's not really about poverty or choice, since you and I agree those reasons wouldn't justify killing born people like two-year-olds. But if the unborn are just as human as a two-year-old, then why not treat them like we treat two-year-olds and make it illegal to kill them just because they are unwanted?

4

The Tolerant

During one of my high-school presentations on abortion, a student named Kelsey consistently gave me the "evil eye." After my talk, she raised her hand and, instead of asking a question, she made this triumphal statement: "Look, I don't see what the big deal is. I don't like abortion, but I don't go around forcing my views on other people like you do." The other students waited for my reply. Instead of giving a lengthy rebuttal, I asked her a simple question: "Kelsey, why don't you like abortion?"

Everyone fell silent as Kelsey struggled to answer the question. She finally said, "Well, I know it kills babies and all that. But what about women who will die or be stuck in poverty and can't feed their children? I don't like it, but I can't take away someone else's choice."

I replied, "Kelsey, is this your position: You don't like abortion because it kills babies, and yet you think it should be legal for other people to kill those babies? Did I understand you correctly?"

Kelsey's face grew red. "Well, it sounds terrible when you put it that way."

"But Kelsey," I said, "I didn't put it that way—you did!" The other students began to smile as they saw that being personally opposed to abortion while at the same time supporting its legality created a devastating contradiction.

Kelsey's view is common among pro-choice advocates. It tries to be a middle ground that neither condemns abortion nor supports it. People like Kelsey *tolerate* abortion, and while they personally don't like abortion, they believe other people should be able to choose it. In the 2012 vice-presidential debate, both candidates were asked about their view on abortion and how it was informed by their faith. Vice President Joe Biden said that while as a Catholic he *personally* believed that life began at conception, he could not impose that article of faith on other Americans. An accompanying on-screen graphic, representing the approval of a group of undecided voters, shot through the roof with positive responses.

Tolerance and evil

The problem with the tolerant approach to abortion is that it fails to understand why pro-life advocates want to outlaw abortion. It's fine to tolerate things that merely irritate us, such as a screaming baby on an airplane. Tolerance doesn't mean approval, acceptance, or even indifference. To tolerate something means that we are willing to allow the thing that bothers us to exist. Tolerating a screaming baby on an airplane means that we won't demand that the baby be moved to the cargo hold of the plane. While it's okay to tolerate nuisances, it's wrong to tolerate grave evils. We may tolerate a crying baby, but we should never tolerate a baby being molested by someone.

If pro-lifers merely disliked abortion in the same way they dislike other nuisances, then it would make sense to tolerate abortion. This is the thinking behind the pro-choice slogan, "Don't like abortion? Don't have one!" However, abortion is not a nuisance to be disliked but an act of evil that dismembers tiny human beings. It must be stopped. To pro-life advocates, this slogan is as silly as saying, "Don't like slavery? Don't enslave anyone!"

Even most pro-choice advocates agree that there are things we should not merely tolerate. I remember once engaging a group of pro-choice students who said that the government should not take away the choice to have an abortion. I told them that I too believed that the government shouldn't be allowed to meddle with most of our private choices (agree).

I asked them if the government should take away an employer's choice to fire someone because of his sexual orientation (apply). They said of course, so I asked why the government should be allowed to do that. The students sensed where I was going with my argument and said, "Well, that's different because that choice harms someone. We shouldn't tolerate their intolerance." I smiled and responded, "Does the choice to abort harm the unborn child? I mean, isn't abortion the ultimate act of intolerance because it does not tolerate a baby's presence in the womb?" (Ah!)

"Forcing" morality

Relativists, or people who reject an objective moral code, say pro-life advocates shouldn't force one moral view on everyone else, because morality is relative to what an individual or society already believes. The problem with this view is that the relativist can't say that "forcing" morality, or anything else for that matter, just *is* wrong. He can say only that it is wrong from his or our culture's perspective. There are many books and resources that I recommend for refuting the pernicious doctrine of relativism, but one quick example collapses the entire belief system.[76]

Ask the relativist, "Is it wrong for me to outlaw abortion?" If he says it is wrong from "his point of view," ask him why his point of view should dictate your moral behavior. You wouldn't let his opinions about food or clothes dictate what you eat or wear, so why should his opinion on outlawing abortion change your behavior on that issue? The relativist may not like that I want to outlaw abortion, but why should I care about what he likes? I know outlawing abortion is the right thing to do!

If he says it is wrong because our culture supports abortion and abortion is legal, then ask him if what you are doing would become moral if public opinion changed and a majority of people thought outlawing abortion was the right thing to do? If he responds that it just *is* wrong to outlaw abortion, or it's something no one should do, then he has admitted that morals are not relative but objective. If there is one objective moral rule, then there could be other rules such as, "Do not directly kill innocent human beings."[77]

Furthermore, when someone says that pro-life advocates want to *impose* their views *on* the rest of society, I usually correct them and say we want to *propose* our views *to* the rest of society. In a democratic republic like the United States (and most other countries that permit legal abortion), laws can change only when a majority of citizens believe they should change. Even if a politician passes a restrictive law against abortion, if his constituents do not share his views he will be out of a job when his term expires, and the law he passed will probably be overturned. If pro-life advocates are persuasive enough to change the minds of the public, and the public chooses to pass laws that protect the unborn, then isn't that a fair, free, and—dare I say—"pro-choice" way to resolve the issue of abortion?

Settled law?

Some critics claim that pro-life advocates should not try to change abortions laws, even through a democratic process, because the law on abortion was "settled" by the Supreme Court.[78] But this neglects the numerous occasions when the Supreme Court has reversed its own decisions. For example, in 1954 *Brown v. Board of Education* overturned the Court's 1896 *Plessy v. Ferguson* case, which had supported racial segregation, and declared laws supporting this practice to be unconstitutional. In 2003, *Lawrence v. Texas* overturned the decision made a mere seventeen years earlier in *Bowers v. Hardwick* and declared that antisodomy laws were unconstitutional. Justice Kennedy said in *Lawrence*, "*Bowers* was not correct when it was decided, is not correct today, and is hereby overruled."[79] Pro-life advocates simply wish that the Supreme Court would view *Roe v. Wade* with the same attitude.

In fact, many pro-choice advocates want the Supreme Court's 2010 *Citizens United v. Federal Election Commission* ruling overturned (which itself overturned a previous Supreme Court ruling) because they say it promotes the incorrect view that corporations are legal persons.[80] If these advocates can challenge the Court's view, why can't pro-life advocates do the same?

Impossible neutrality

Like the relativist who says we should tolerate every view on the morality of abortion, some pro-choice critics say we should tolerate all the diverse and often religious views people have about when human life begins. While this approach sounds fair and practical, in reality it is neither. Upholding the right for individuals to define when life begins would lead to morally heinous consequences. Should the state allow some indigenous tribes or secular philosophy professors to practice infanticide in accordance with their belief that infants are not persons? In *Reynolds v. the United States* (1879), the Supreme Court held that religious freedom was not absolute if it undermined the common good. Chief Justice Morrison Waite wrote in the Court's unanimous opinion:

> Can a man excuse his practices to the contrary because of his religious belief? To permit this would be to make the professed doctrines of religious belief superior to the law of the land, and, in effect, to permit every citizen to become a law unto himself. Government could exist only in name under such circumstances.

The Supreme Court also ruled in *Prince v. Massachusetts* (1944) that a child's right to life and good health supersedes his parents' right to practice their religion. The Court said, "The right to practice religion freely does not include liberty to expose the community or the child to communicable disease or the latter to ill health or death." Pro-life advocates simply believe that the principle of protecting born children from the dangerous religious beliefs of their parents should also be applied to unborn children. These children should be protected from the dangerous belief of some adults that they are not persons until birth.

Finally, the state is clearly not neutral to the question of when life begins, having accepted "birth" as the correct answer (which is why infanticide is illegal). There is simply no way the state can be neutral on the question of when life begins, because if there can be any laws at all that protect human beings, the state has to make a decision on who counts as a human being and who doesn't under those laws. Pro-life advocates simply maintain that the state should endorse an answer to the question of when life begins, or who counts as a human being with a right to life, that is backed by science and common sense. The state should not support an answer to this question that is backed by convenience or a mere desire to keep abortion legal.

I can't impose my faith

Even if we can't tolerate every view of when life begins, is it fair to legislate the belief that human life begins at fertilization (or twinning, in the case of identical twins), when this is typically a religious belief? When he ran for president in 2004, Massachusetts Senator John Kerry said, "I can't take my Catholic belief, my article of faith, and legislate it on a Protestant or a Jew or an atheist."[81] A standard reply from pro-choice Catholics is that abortion is wrong for *them* because the Church forbids it, but they cannot in good conscience impose their faith on unwilling non-Catholics by making abortion illegal. By their reasoning, a Catholic can be pro-choice and allow other people to choose abortion while he personally opposes abortion.

Now, it is true that the state cannot, in the words of the Second Vatican Council document *Dignitatis Humanae*, "impose upon its people, by force or fear or other means, the profession or repudiation of any religion," but this is irrelevant to the issue of legal abortion. For example, a Catholic politician could not force his constituents to accept his views on racial equality that spring from his faith, but he could use the law to stop racist acts of violence such as lynchings. That is because his faith coincides with the common-sense view that human beings have a right to life regardless of their race, age, or level of development.

In fact, the Catholic faith demands that politicians protect the victims of lynching as well as innocent victims of other acts of violence by making such acts illegal. Pope St. John Paul II said, "[A] law which violates an innocent person's natural right to life is unjust and, as such, is not valid as a law. For this reason I urgently appeal once more to all political leaders not to pass laws which, by disregarding the dignity of the person, undermine the very fabric of society."[82]

The fact that a law—whether it is a ban on lynching or a ban on abortion—happens to align with a widely held religious belief does not mean that such a law is unconstitutional. According to pro-choice Harvard law professor Laurence Tribe, "The participation of religious groups in political dialogue has never been constitutional anathema in the United States. . . . [T]he theological source of beliefs about the point at which human life begins should not cast a constitutional shadow across whatever laws a state might adopt to restrict abortions that occur beyond that point."[83]

As long as nonreligious evidence can be provided from the science of biology to show that the unborn are humans, there is no political problem in advancing laws to protect those humans from being unjustly killed.

Is a compromise possible?

Some critics understand that pro-life advocates simply will not tolerate abortion, and in response they propose a compromise: Without outlawing abortion, why not reduce abortions to the point where they practically never happen?[84]

This proposal is tempting. I would almost be satisfied to live in a country where abortion was legal but no one chose to have an abortion, but this approach seems hopelessly unrealistic. We would never talk about reducing rape, robbery, or speeding without passing laws that forbid those things. In fact, in the absence of laws forbidding those actions, we would expect rates of these crimes to increase dramatically.

Justice demands that the unborn, as human persons with a right to life, be protected under the law. We would find it absurd if spousal abuse were not outlawed but only the "underlying causes" of abuse were addressed by providing free counseling to potential abusers. Common sense dictates that in cases involving born victims, there is no contradiction in working against the underlying causes of the violence against them while simultaneously working for laws that protect them from abuse. Why not have the same attitude for unborn victims of violence? There is no reason we cannot work to address the underlying social reasons, like poverty, that drive women to choose abortion while, at the same time, we outlaw the abortion procedure itself.

Even if a majority of people do not believe unborn children should be protected, the pro-life advocate must still work toward that goal. The proposal that pro-life and pro-choice advocates should work together to reduce unintended pregnancies is not a compromise. Compromise entails two sides giving up parts of their position in order to reach a middle ground. This is just asking pro-life advocates to give up fighting for the un-born child's right to live and to do what pro-choice advocates have always done: work to prevent unintended pregnancies.[85] In practice, this means promoting contraception.

At this point some critics say, "If pro-lifers really cared about ending abortion, they'd support the use of contraception to prevent unintended pregnancies. But they don't really want to do anything practical to help end abortion—they just want to punish women who have sex!" Of course, even if pro-lifers were hypocrites, their argument that abortion kills an innocent human being would still be correct. But are pro-life advocates hypocrites if they don't promote contraception? No, and here's why.

The pro-life endgame

The goal of the pro-life movement is to restore the right to life of unborn human beings. Does promoting contraception help or hinder that goal? I think it's safe to say contraception doesn't help that goal. Birth control pills and condoms don't teach people that unborn children are biological human beings who are entitled to the same basic rights you and I possess. To many people, contraception just prevents pregnancy, or it prevents a "potential person" (who will one day become a baby) from being created inside of a woman. There's nothing hypocritical about pro-life advocates not promoting contraception, because contraception doesn't do anything to reach our ultimate goal of changing public opinion and public policy to protect unborn children from harm. Promoting contraception may even detract from the goal of ending legal abortion.

In *Planned Parenthood v. Casey,* the Supreme Court said that *Roe v. Wade* "could not be repudiated without serious inequity to people who, for two decades of economic and social developments, have organized intimate relationships and made choices that define their views of themselves and their places in society, in reliance on the availability of abortion in the event that contraception should fail."[86] I'm all in favor of teaching people how to responsibly plan their families, but if contraception fosters the attitude that the interests of unborn children do not need to be taken into account when adults have sex, then contraception is a hindrance and not a help to the pro-life movement. If a child is conceived in spite of a couple's desire to stop him from coming into existence, then it is much more likely that child will be aborted to compensate for the failure of contraceptives. Pope St. John Paul II said in regard to this problem:

> It may be that many people use contraception with a view to excluding the subsequent temptation of abortion. But the negative values inherent in the "contraceptive mentality"—which is very different from responsible parenthood, lived in respect for the full truth of the conjugal act—are such that they in fact *strengthen this temptation when an unwanted life is conceived* [emphasis added]. Indeed, the pro-abortion culture is especially strong precisely where the Church's teaching on contraception is rejected.[87]

Promoting contraception may also reinforce attitudes toward sex and pregnancy that conflict with the goal of creating a culture of life. On one university campus, a group of students chastised me for not passing out condoms. I told them I didn't have to, because the campus health center gave condoms away for free. One man responded, "But the center is all the way on the other side of campus. I don't want to have to walk all the way over there just for condoms. You guys should be passing them out here." If this man was too lazy to walk a few hundred yards for condoms, why in the world would we expect him to work hard to provide for a child should the condom fail and his partner become pregnant?

Pro-life advocates should not be suckered into thinking that abortion is a public health problem that we have to alleviate by dispensing contraceptives as the cure. We must continue to teach our culture that abortion is a moral problem and that the unborn deserve cultural recognition and legal protection as a remedy to this problem. Granted, it will be easier to pass laws against abortion when fewer people seek abortion services, so there is value in developing strategies to reduce unintended pregnancies. But pro-life advocates should not have to compromise their belief that the unborn are human beings so that everyone can play nice together. Instead, we must refocus our strategy and find better ways to achieve the goal of restoring legal protection for unborn human beings and not become caught up in reducing the need for abortion.

Abortion is a necessary evil

Even if the pro-life advocate can show that the unborn is a human person with the value and right to life you and I have, there is another gambit for the pro-choice advocate. He could say that abortion is just a tragic and necessary evil that we have to live with. Pro-choice feminist Naomi Wolf writes, "[What] all of us deserve is an abortion-rights movement willing publicly to mourn the evil—necessary evil though it may be—that is abortion. We must have a movement that acts with moral accountability and without euphemism."[88] Other critics assert abortion ends a human life but ask, "So what?"[89]

To answer these critics, the pro-life advocate will have to revisit the pragmatist's arguments for abortion that have risen from the grave like decaying zombies. They need to show that there is no "necessity" or circumstance that can justify killing unborn children through abortion. They must show that our country is smart enough and strong enough to overcome abortion's blight on our nation's reputation for promoting justice and human equality.

Otherwise, why not publicly mourn hate crimes or spousal abuse as "necessary evils" that must occur as the by-product of a free society? If we don't tolerate the enslavement of African Americans (something people once said was a "necessary evil" that would never go away), why should we tolerate a similar attitude toward the unborn? As Elbert Hubbard once said, "The man who says it can't be done is generally interrupted by someone doing it."[90]

Some pro-choice advocates may accept that the arguments for the pro-life position succeed but nevertheless choose to ignore them. How should we respond to such apathy? Aside from prayer and God opening the person's heart to be receptive to truth, one way to convince others about the awful reality of abortion is by using images of embryos and fetuses that have been aborted. Some pro-choice advocates object that graphic images of abortion are just scare tactics used to manipulate people. To these critics I sometimes ask, "What's wrong with scare tactics if it turns out there is something to genuinely be afraid of?"

The power of pictures

For those critics who say it is disgusting for pro-life advocates to show graphic images of abortion, I would refer them Naomi Wolf's article, in which she candidly admits:

> The pro-choice movement often treats with contempt the pro-lifers' practice of holding up to our faces their disturbing graphics.... But feminism at its best is based on what is simply true. While pro-lifers have not been beyond dishonesty, distortion and the doctoring of images (preferring, for example, to highlight the results of very late, very rare abortions), many of those photographs are in fact photographs of actual D & Cs; those footprints are in fact the footprints of a 10-week-old fetus; the pro-life slogan "Abortion stops a beating

heart" is incontrovertibly true. While images of violent fetal death work magnificently for pro-lifers as political polemic, the pictures are not polemical in themselves: they are biological facts. We know this.[91]

Graphic images will not move everyone to accept the pro-life position (they clearly haven't moved Wolf), but they do cause many people to rethink abortion as an abstract "choice" or even a "necessary evil." Once at a JFA exhibit I saw a young woman who thought abortion was no big deal even when she was shown bloody images of aborted children. The director of Justice for All asked her if she would feel the same way after watching a video of an actual abortion procedure. She agreed, and her face drained of color after watching an actual child being aborted piece by piece. Trembling, she said she would really have to rethink the issue.

To those who say it is disgusting to show graphic images of abortion in public I ask, "What is it about abortion that disgusts you?" If they say it involves dismembered children, I reply, "That disgusts me, too. But do you think we should be more upset by pictures of dismembered children or by the fact that the children are being dismembered?" While I think graphic images are necessary in the fight to end abortion, there is a debate within the pro-life community about the role graphic images of abortion should have in the movement, or if they should have any role at all. I won't weigh in on that debate in this book, since my primary aim is to teach people how to talk about the issue of abortion.

However, I don't believe the pro-life movement can win without using images of any kind. We live in a visual culture, and I have found that most conversations about abortion that occur without pictures of either living or aborted unborn children proceed in a rather theoretical way. The images I prefer to use are of children in the first trimester of pregnancy, since that is when the majority of abortions take place. For pictures of living children I try to use neutral medical sources, and for pictures of aborted children I try to use sources that can prove the pictures are authentic images of abortion.[92]

When I use graphic images in a presentation, I always warn my audience of the graphic nature of the pictures, give them an opportunity to look away, and tell them that we in the pro-life movement do not condemn those involved in abortion but that we want to expose the truth about abortion in order to help others. When people do choose to view images of abortion in my presentations, I find that this opportunity amplifies the message I have spoken, and the audience is more likely to shift from apathy to action. Sometimes the pictures even change people's hearts by themselves. One woman at the Justice for All exhibit stopped, looked at the images of aborted fetuses, and told one of our volunteers, "I've had three abortions, and I had no idea it was like this. I'll never do that again."

Engaging the tolerant

The tolerant's concern: Making abortion illegal will impose one narrow view of morality and be intolerant of other views.

Your objective: Show that one narrow view of morality is already imposed and that if the unborn are human beings, we cannot tolerate them being killed by abortion.

★ ★ ★

Pro-choice: I'm personally opposed to abortion, but I don't have the right to take away someone else's choice.

Pro-life: Why are you personally opposed to abortion?

PC: Well, I know it's bad. I mean, nobody likes abortion, and that's why I'm for contraception, which is something I think everybody can agree on.

PL: Help me understand where you're coming from. What is it exactly about abortion that you don't like?

PC: Well, I mean, it is taking a life of some kind, so that's bad.

PL: Would you say that since the mother and father are human that abortion takes a human life?

PC: Sure, and like I said, I don't like it. I just don't have the right to tell other people what to do.

PL: Do you think I should work to make abortion illegal?

PC: No, you should respect other people's choices.

PL: So you do think you have the right to tell other people what to do in some cases, since you think I shouldn't work to outlaw abortion. Let me ask you another question. Some people choose to rob banks or fly airplanes into buildings. Should we make those choices legal, since we can't tell other people what to do?

PC: Of course not. But those are different, because those choices involve hurting people, and I'm talking about abortion.

PL: I think that's where you and I disagree. If abortion does end the life of a human being, then shouldn't we outlaw it like we outlaw other choices that end the lives of human beings?

PC: You can't, because in those other choices we know human beings are being killed, while the fetus's humanity is a religious belief we can't enforce by law.

PL: Why do you think opposition to abortion and the humanity of the unborn are religious beliefs?

PC: Well, whenever I see pro-life marches it's always people from churches who are marching with signs saying things like, "God hates abortion."

PL: Is it possible that a religious belief could be right? For example, large numbers of Christians were involved in banning slavery and segregation. Should we repeal those laws because religious people fought for them?

PC: No, but we can't prove the fetus is human like how an African American is human.

PL: Why not? If two African Americans conceive a child, what race would the child be while it was in the womb?

PC: That's not what I meant. Slavery involved real, born people. The fetus isn't like that, because it isn't born yet.

PL: Okay, if I could show you that there are only four differences between us and the unborn, and none of them show the unborn have any less value, would you agree that abortion should not be tolerated in the same way we don't tolerate child abuse?

5

The Distractors

While participating in a JFA outreach in Oklahoma, I watched a girl named Nikki march up to a table of pro-choice protesters and unleash a flurry of pro-life arguments. "How can you be for abortion?" she asked. "Don't you know that abortion causes depression and breast cancer?! And there are so many other choices, like adoption! One of these babies could grow up to be the next Einstein!"

One of the protestors responded, "Reputable, unbiased studies show abortion does not cause depression or breast cancer. Those are anti-choice lies."

Another protestor said, "Adoption is great for some, but many women and children regret it. It should be the woman's choice. Besides, how do you know that the baby won't be abused and grow up to be a serial killer?"

"Yeah, but it's still a baby!" Nikki fired back. What if *you* were aborted?!"

One of the men smiled and said, "If I had been aborted, then I would never know what happened, so it wouldn't matter." Nicki then threw up her hands and sighed loudly before walking away from the table in disgust. As Nikki walked by me I said, "I bet that was frustrating. Want to take a walk and tell me what happened?"

I admired Nikki's passion, but it was clear her arguments had not been persuasive. As we walked, I showed Nikki why.

What are the ineffective pro-life arguments?

There are some arguments that a pro-life advocate should not use, because they don't directly address the key issue in the abortion debate: "What are the unborn?" Greg Koukl writes in his book *Precious Unborn Human Persons*, "If the unborn is not a human person, no justification for abortion is necessary. However, if the unborn is a human person, no justification for abortion is adequate."[93] Koukl uses a story to illustrate the point that we can't answer the question "Can I kill this?" unless we know the answer to the prior question "What is this?" I usually paraphrase Koukl's story in this way.

Imagine you're at the kitchen sink washing the dishes. Your five-year-old child runs up behind you and says, "Mommy [or Daddy], can I kill this?" What is the first question you will ask? Probably, "What is it?" After all, if it's a cockroach, then it's time to get out a can of Raid. If it's a cat, some people who resent cats may waver on the answer, but most of us would say the answer is no. But what if it's his two-year-old sister? Along with saying no you'd better call a counselor!

We give different answers for each situation because the answer to the question "Can I kill this?" depends almost entirely on the identity of the thing being killed. Every honest person involved in the abortion debate admits *something* is killed during an abortion. If it is mere tissue, then abortion is no more immoral than clipping a toenail. But if a human being with the right to life is killed, then abortion is immoral.[94]

If we fail to answer the question "What are the unborn?" we will argue pointlessly about subjects that have nothing to do with whether abortion is right or wrong. That is why Scott Klusendorf's Trot Out a Toddler tool is so effective in our conversations: It gets us back to "the one question" in a concise and creative way. In order to stay on that one question, pro-life advocates must be wary of *distractors*, or people who want to move the conversation away from discussing what the unborn are.

During JFA outreach events, I often visited the tables of pro-choice student groups to see what their best counter-arguments were. I've rarely heard arguments that the unborn are not human beings. Instead, I've poured over countless pamphlets with titles like "Pro-Life Myths Exposed." These pamphlets argue that abortion does not cause depression, breast cancer, or any other negative side effects for women. The pro-choice advocates I encountered thought that as long as they could prove abortion was safe for the woman having it, their argument for legal abortion would be successful.

However, pro-life advocates can also be guilty of being distractors who turn the conversation away from the key question "What are the unborn?" Here are the top seven arguments pro-life advocates should *not* use as their main argument against legal abortion:

1. "Would you have aborted Beethoven?"
2. "What if you had been aborted?"
3. "Abortion tortures babies."
4. "The Bible [or the Church] says abortion is wrong."
5. "What about adoption?"
6. "Abortion hurts society."
7. "Abortion hurts women."

I understand that many pro-life advocates use these arguments, and I don't mean to impugn their intelligence by saying these arguments are ineffective. Rather, I hope these pro-life advocates will be as open-minded toward my assessment of these arguments as they wish pro-choice advocates would be toward their arguments against abortion. Moreover, I think that many of these arguments can be rehabilitated to serve the pro-life cause, so long as they serve to answer the question "What are the unborn?"

1. "Would you have aborted Beethoven?"

In this argument, the pro-life advocate describes a child enduring a miserable and impoverished life (they may even throw in a disability such as deafness for good measure). He then asks the pro-choice advocate if that child should have been aborted. If the pro-choice advocate says yes, the pro-life advocate says, "I just described the life of Ludwig van Beethoven. So you would have aborted the great Beethoven?"[95] Other famous figures can be substituted, but the idea behind this argument is that a woman should not abort her child, because even if the child will have a difficult life, that does not mean it will not be a good and productive life. Although the argument is true, it suffers from two problems.

First, this argument makes contraception, or even abstaining from sex, as bad as abortion, because those acts also potentially deprive the world of future Beethovens. If the pro-life advocate objects that abortion kills a future Beethoven while contraception or abstinence merely prevents that human from coming into existence, I would simply add that abortion is wrong not because it kills a future musical genius but because it kills a human being who could have any kind of future if he were not aborted. Second, this argument can be easily turned on its head. If we should not abort one child because he could become the next Beethoven, then perhaps we should abort another child because he could become the next Hitler.[96] The bottom line is that it is wrong to abort an unborn child because he *already* is a person in the womb who has a valuable future ahead of him that abortion unjustly takes away from him.

2. "What if you had been aborted?"

The question "What if you had been aborted?" is meaningless from the pro-choice perspective. If the pro-choice advocate had been aborted before birth, then he would never have existed in the first place. The pro-life advocate's question is on par with asking, "What if your parents had decided not to have sexual intercourse on the night you were conceived?" This argument is appropriately answered by saying,

"I wouldn't exist to miss the life I never had." This argument also fails to capture the moral gravity of abortion. After all, we wouldn't oppose infanticide by asking, "Well, what if you had been killed when you were a newborn?" We would just say, "What's the matter with you! You can't kill newborns. They're human beings!"

3. "Abortion tortures babies."

Pro-life and pro-choice advocates usually agree that it is wrong to cause living creatures unnecessary pain. If abortion caused an unborn child pain, this could offer common ground in the campaign to make abortion illegal. However, there seems to be little evidence at this time that abortion causes pain in unborn children who are younger than twenty weeks old (the time when 99 percent of abortions take place).[97] While it's possible these studies are flawed in various ways, most laws that aim to restrict abortions after the point at which an unborn child could feel pain set that mark at twenty weeks.

Even if the unborn felt pain from the moment of conception, this would not be an argument against legal abortion; it would only be an argument against *painful* legal abortion. This fact would force abortion providers to use anesthesia or other painless abortion methods, but it would not be a reason to outlaw abortion. After all, dogs and cats can feel pain, but it isn't illegal to kill them. If we fail to prove the unborn are human beings, then there is no reason not to kill unwanted human fetuses humanely in the same way we kill unwanted animals.

This does not mean pro-life advocates should give up their efforts to promote legislation that protects pain-capable unborn children. Banning abortion after the fetus can feel pain, or even requiring the use of anesthesia to ease the pain of dismemberment, could serve a useful educational purpose and cause people to oppose at least some abortions and be suspicious of abortion in general.

4. "The Bible [or the Church] says abortion is wrong."
There are two problems with the argument that abortion should be illegal because it is prohibited in the Bible or by Church teaching. The major problem is that civil law in the United States must be nonsectarian, i.e., not based solely upon the authority of one particular religion. Just as U.S. Catholics should not be forced to live under the teachings of Islam (such as Sharia law), Catholics should not impose aspects of our faith onto others through the law. An obvious example would be a requirement for all Americans to attend Sunday Mass. Of course, if a teaching of the Church benefits the common good, then it would be fine to legislate that teaching.

For example, paragraph 2356 of the *Catechism the Catholic Church* states that raping children is a sin. It would not be wrong for a Catholic lawmaker to outlaw child rape, even if he does so because the Church forbids it. That's because child rape can be shown to be wrong using secular principles of morality, and outlawing rape benefits the common good. In the same way, a Catholic legislator could argue that abortion should be outlawed because, like laws forbidding child rape, laws against abortion benefit the common good by respecting the rights of children. Also, like rape or homicide, the crime of abortion can be shown to be wrong using secular principles of morality.

The minor problem with the argument is that the Bible nowhere explicitly states that abortion is wrong. As pro-choice religion professor Roy Ward writes, "One thing the Bible does not say is 'Thou shalt not abort.'"[98] Of course, the Bible also nowhere states that airplane hijacking or Internet pornography are wrong, but we can reasonably infer those actions are wrong from explicit commands found in the Bible, such as "Thou shall not steal" or "Anyone who lusts commits adultery in his heart." In Chapter 12 I will show how pro-life Christians can make a compelling biblical case against abortion and answer objections like Ward's that claim the Bible is silent on the issue. But for now, keep the conversation focused on secular reasons to oppose abortion that all rational people can recognize and accept.

5. "What about adoption?"

Between 2006 and 2010, 2.5 million women had taken steps to adopt a child.[99] Many adoptive couples pay the birth mother for her pregnancy-related expenses, and some are willing to adopt children with disabilities such as multiple sclerosis. For some pro-life advocates, the answer to an unwanted pregnancy is simple: Give up your baby for adoption. Of course, while one might "give up" a beloved sweater at a garage sale, women don't "give up" their babies to anyone (it's more appropriate to say a woman *places* a child for adoption). Unfortunately, many women describe the experience of placing a child for adoption as a kind of death. Pregnancy resource centers routinely report that women fear adoption more than either abortion or raising their child themselves.[100]

Adoption is a good thing, but we should describe the choice to place a child for adoption as a heroic one. We should not casually suggest a woman choose adoption any more than we would casually suggest a woman choose to saw off her own leg if she were caught in a bear trap. It may be what she *needs* to do, but that does not make her decision any less heart-wrenching. The only thing that can motivate a woman to make this difficult choice (especially if raising the child is not an option) is to know that abortion ends a child's life and would be the worst choice of all.

Finally, even if a woman lived in a country where adoption was not available (or was illegal), this would not make it right to abort the child, since we don't support killing orphans no one wants to adopt. Rather than be our main argument against abortion, the availability of adoptive parents should be what we present as our practical response to abortion. After we've used science and philosophy to show that abortion is wrong because it ends the life of an innocent human being, we can suggest adoption as a nonviolent alternative.

6. "Abortion hurts society."

Pro-life advocates sometimes say that abortion has caused a "birth dearth," and declining birth rates in some countries will have dire consequences, such as a lack of young people that can pay into the Social Security system. Like the Beethoven argument, this argument assumes abortion is wrong because of its consequences on society and not because of what abortion actually is. It also proves too much and would lead to the same conclusion the Beethoven argument led to: that contraception or abstinence are just as wrong as abortion, because they too deprive the world of millions of human beings. A pro-life advocate might object and say, "Obviously abortion is worse than contraception because it involves killing children." If that is the case, then why even argue that abortion is bad for society in the first place? Why not say any society that allows the killing of helpless humans is an inherently bad one, regardless of whether or not Social Security is being funded?

Just as abortion's negative effect on society doesn't prove it is morally wrong, it's supposed positive effect on society doesn't prove it is morally right. In their bestselling book *Freakonomics*, economist Steven Levitt and journalist Stephen J. Dubner claimed that legal abortion reduces crime, eliminating unwanted children who would grow up to be criminals.[101] They maintained that the declining crime rates in the 1990s were proof of this, because that was when the "unwanted" children aborted en masse just after *Roe v. Wade* would have become adult criminals. Although this claim has been challenged by other economists, even if it were true, so what? It's probably also true that if we killed unwanted, impoverished toddlers, future crime rates would decline, but that wouldn't make it moral to do so.

7. "Abortion hurts women."

Some pro-life advocates say the movement has focused too much on the baby and that it should instead focus on the message that abortion hurts women, since our culture identifies abortion as being a "woman's issue."[102] These advocates say we should show abortion-minded women that abortion is not in their best interests—it allegedly increases their risk of developing breast cancer, infertility, and clinical depression.

Now, I've seen the devastating effects abortion has on women as well as men who were involved in choosing abortion for their spouses. As an observer at post-abortive retreats, I have listened to women describe how abortions they had *fifty years ago* still cause them anguish and heartbreak. While I agree abortion can have serious consequences for the woman who has one, I don't see how that fact justifies outlawing abortion. There are many things in life that have serious negative consequences: for instance, tobacco, alcohol, fast food, and impulsive weddings in Las Vegas. In spite of that, few think we should pass laws banning them. Showing that abortion hurts women does not show why we should *outlaw* abortion.

Advocates of the woman-centered approach may respond that abortion-minded women can at least be deterred from choosing abortion by being shown evidence of abortion's negative health effects. But proving abortion is, on the whole, worse for women than giving birth can be difficult and involves making sense of a bulk of complex medical research.[103] Relying on personal testimonies in lieu of academic studies won't help much, either. For every testimony pro-life advocates can offer that abortion has hurt a woman, pro-choice advocates can find someone who is adamant that she does not regret her abortion.[104] The woman-centered approach may indeed be successful in keeping some women from choosing abortion. However, I'm skeptical that this approach will, in the long-term, create a culture of life in which a majority of people believe unborn children have the same basic rights as born children.

The "woman-centered" pro-life strategy is like arguing that killing civilians in war is wrong because it results in post-traumatic stress disorder in soldiers. That's a relevant fact—as well as indirect evidence that innocent human beings are being killed—but it's not why killing civilians is wrong. The intentional killing of innocent civilians is an intrinsically evil act, and the negative side effects (such as PTSD) flow from the act's evil nature.

Pro-choice advocates could even admit abortion hurts women and address the issue by working to develop treatments to eliminate the negative effects of having an abortion. I once informally debated a pro-choice advocate who said women's negative reactions to abortions are caused by pro-life rhetoric. According to her, the best way to reduce the negative emotional effects of abortion is to stop saying abortion kills babies.[105]

The foregoing doesn't mean I think the woman-centered approach has no place in the pro-life movement. I encourage women to share their testimonies once they feel comfortable speaking publicly about their abortions. These gripping stories add a personal element to the discussion that makes the arguments for the pro-life position more persuasive.

So when a woman at a pro-life event holds up an "I regret my abortion" sign, she should hold another sign that says, "Ask me why." The woman-centered approach may not provide the complete case for why abortion should be outlawed, but it does provide a great opportunity to start a conversation about why women regret their abortions; namely, that they regret being accomplices to the death of their own children. If *that* is the reason women regret their abortions, then the case for outlawing the procedure becomes much stronger.

Stay on the one question

Rather than make ineffective arguments against abortion, pro-lifers must stay focused on the one question that matters most: What are the unborn? As Greg Koukl's dishwashing story shows, if the unborn are not human beings, then getting an abortion is little more serious than going to the dentist to have a tooth pulled. Since we would not outlaw tooth extractions in order to reduce the number of them that occur, we should not outlaw abortion simply to reduce the number of abortions that occur—if, that is, the unborn are not human beings.

But if they are, then abortion can't be justified any more than killing a two-year-old could be justified. If we wouldn't kill two-year olds because they were unwanted, and if the unborn are as human as a two-year-old, then it follows that we should not kill unborn children, even if they are unwanted.[106] Unfortunately, if you make this point in such a blunt way, opponents may feel lectured to or judged and ignore what you have to say. A more effective approach involves asking a series of questions that helps the person with whom you're speaking come to this conclusion on his own—which is exactly what we do with Trot Out a Toddler and why I consider it the best way to keep our conversation on track. In the next three chapters I'll explain what the pro-life advocate must do once our conversations reach the all-important question "What are the unborn?"

Engaging the distractor

The distractor's concern: Pro-life advocates have bad reasons to outlaw abortion.

Your objective: Direct the conversation from the less effective arguments for the pro-life position to the more effective ones.

★ ★ ★

Pro-choice: I've heard the arguments people make against abortion, and I don't think they're very good.

Pro-life: Which arguments have you heard?

PC: Well, for starters, I always see pro-lifers holding up images of fetuses with signs that say things like, "Don't kill me, Mommy!" But that's really misleading because fetuses can't say that or even feel anything.

PL: I'll grant you that fetuses can't ask their moms not to abort them, but I don't see how this refutes the pro-life view. I think that unborn children should be treated with the same respect we give to newborns, even though neither can beg their mothers not to kill them.

PC: But it's different, because you can always place newborns for adoption.

PL: Well—

PC: I know what you're going to say: you can always wait and place a fetus for adoption once it's born. But adoption is not always the best option for women with an unplanned pregnancy. People always say, "Choose adoption, not abortion," but do you know how many kids don't get adopted?

PL: The adoption system in our country is not a monolithic system, so we have to make sure not to oversimplify what we're talking about. And I wasn't going to suggest that. Even though you have a dim view of adoption, you think it's better for newborns to be adopted instead of being killed. I just have the same attitude toward unborn children.

PC: Well . . . I really don't see what the big deal is. Pro-lifers say abortion is this bad thing that causes breast cancer and depression, but I know women who've had abortions, and they're totally fine.

PL: Can we both agree that drawing conclusions from just a few people we know isn't an accurate way to determine the long-term effects of abortion? But I do have a question for you. Why do you think some women legitimately regret their abortions? Why do you think abortion, out of all surgeries, would cause them grief?

PC: I don't know. Maybe because pro-lifers make them feel bad.

PL: Well, I'm not sure I can make you feel bad about something that you believe isn't wrong. But let's say I agree with you that abortion does not cause severe side effects for the *mother*. What do you think abortion does to her child? If abortion ends the life of a woman's child, do you think that would explain why many women regret their abortions?

PC: But it's not a child yet.

PL: I think that's our main issue. If the unborn are not human beings, then abortion really doesn't matter. It would be important to tell women abortion has negative side effects, but that would be no reason to outlaw abortion. But if the unborn *are* human beings, that fact alone justifies passing laws to protect their lives.

PART III

People Who Deny That the Unborn Matter

6

The Skeptics

I remember during my first years as a pro-life advocate arguing with a college student over the question of when life begins. As a crowd swelled around us, he said, "Look, no one knows when life begins. It's a religious question that can't be answered!" I was determined to prove that life began at conception, but without any data at my fingertips, I blurted out, "Everyone knows life begins at conception. I've read twelve embryology textbooks that say so!"

As people began to disperse, an older pro-life man came up to me and smiled. "Twelve books, eh?" he said. "That was quite a line." He had me. At that time I had read excerpts of one or two books, so, maybe I combined the numbers 1 and 2 and came up with 12. Regardless, I had become flustered in the face of the skeptic who denied that anyone can know when life begins.

The skeptic often shares the pragmatist's view that abortion resolves certain societal problems such as poverty or over-population. Although after the pro-life advocate "trots out a toddler" to show why these reasons fail to justify abortion, the skeptic responds, "That's completely different! A two-year-old is not like a fetus. We all know a two-year-old is human, but we're divided over whether a fetus is human. No one knows when life begins!"

Resolving the "difficult question"

The unwillingness to define when human life begins can be found in *Roe v. Wade*, where Justice Harry Blackmun wrote:

We need not resolve the difficult question of when life begins. When those trained in the respective disciplines of medicine, philosophy, and theology are unable to arrive at any consensus, the judiciary, at this point in the development of man's knowledge, is not in a position to speculate as to the answer.[107]

Why is there disagreement? The problem is that the question of when human life begins is actually two distinct questions. It can be a *scientific* question about the beginning of a human organism, or it can be a *philosophical* question about when a human organism has intrinsic value, a right to life, or becomes a "person."

Pro-life advocates generally see life as a simple concept and answer the question of when life begins scientifically. For them, a human being is either alive or dead, and each human being's life began at conception, case closed. Pro-choice advocates generally see life as a complex concept and answer the question of when life begins philosophically. For them, a two-celled embryo is insignificant life with the *potential* to become a human later in pregnancy. The failure to acknowledge these two different kinds of questions about the beginning of life can result in people talking past each other instead of talking to each other, as is demonstrated in the following dialogue:

Pro-lifer: Abortion kills a baby.

Pro-choicer: It's not a baby; a fetus can't even think or feel.

PL: But at conception, the twenty-three chromosomes of the mom and the twenty-three chromosomes of the dad come together and—

PC: Yeah, but—

PL: —they make a new being who has forty-six chromosomes and needs only food and nutrition to grow. It's a human being!

PC: A fetus is not a human being; it's a *potential* human being.

PL: If it's not a human being, then what is it? A dog? A cat? A turnip?

PC: It can't think or feel; it's not human.

PL: Of course it's human; it's got human DNA! It has human parents—

PC: You're not listening. Being human means—

PL: No! Look, it's a human being. Every scientist and abortionist knows it's a human being. It has forty-six chromosomes. It has human DNA. That's a fact.

PC: We're done here.

In this dialogue, the pro-life advocate is trying to defend the biological humanity of the unborn child, while the pro-choice advocate questions whether the unborn child is a person who has as much value as you or I have. I'll talk about defending the claim that an unborn child has the same basic human rights you and I possess, and therefore is a person, in the next chapter. For now, let's focus on answering the skeptic who says no one knows when life begins biologically, or no one knows if the unborn are members of the species *homo sapiens*. I sometimes say at my training seminars, "You can't have human rights unless you are a biological human being."

Making the biological case

How can pro-life advocates prove the unborn are biological human beings? It may be tempting to use in utero images, or ultrasounds, of children as our sole evidence of their humanity. While this tactic is useful in some cases, it has the potential to reinforce the idea that our human value comes from what we look like instead of what we are. It's not a good way to demonstrate the humanity of a four-week-old child who resembles a tadpole.

Pro-life advocates should also avoid making simplistic claims such as "Abortion kills a life" or even "Human life begins at conception." This leaves them open to a rebuttal such as this one from atheist Carl Sagan:

> Despite many claims to the contrary, life does not begin at conception: It is an unbroken chain that stretches back nearly to the origin of the Earth, 4.6 billion years ago. Nor does human life begin at conception: It is an unbroken chain dating back to the origin of our species, hundreds of thousands of years ago.[108]

While it is true that living cells or human cells have a long history, the same is not true for individual human beings. Sagan's criticism is overcome if we drop the assertion "Life begins at conception" and say instead "A human organism begins to exist at conception" or "The life of an individual human being begins at conception." This may seem like semantics, but it is important to use this vocabulary with pro-choice advocates who may think an embryo is alive in the same sense that sperm and egg are alive. This mistaken set of assumptions may cause the pro-choice advocate to think that an embryo's life never really began at conception. He might instead think that at conception life in the form of sperm and egg was rearranged and became life in the form of an embryo that has the same value as egg or sperm until the embryo becomes a human being later in pregnancy.

When it comes to defending the claim that an individual human being begins to exist at conception, I don't recommend appeals to authority such as "Science says life begins at conception" or "All scientists agree life begins at conception." The members of your audience may simply not believe you, or they may think the authorities you are citing are simply wrong. Instead, I recommend using a simple argument that shows that at conception two body parts (sperm and egg) recombine and form an entirely new *body* that is a living, whole, human organism who is growing and developing into adulthood.

My favorite argument for the humanity of the unborn is based on Steve Wagner's "10-second pro-life apologist."[109] Steve was once flustered that he could not defend his pro-life beliefs in a conversation that took him by surprise, so he went home and crafted a 10-second sound bite that goes like this:

> If it's growing, isn't it alive?
>
> If it has human parents, isn't it human?
>
> And human beings like you and me are valuable, aren't we?

Sometimes, Steve's sound bite will do the trick, and the person with whom you are talking will accept that the unborn are biological human beings. Other times you may have to use more evidence to prove that the unborn are (1) alive, (2) human, and (3) whole organisms. Let's examine each one of these points in the argument.

Are the unborn alive?

Some skeptics will say that we can't know if the unborn are alive because we can't know if anything is alive. Scientists generally agree that if something is growing by cellular reproduction, converting food into energy (metabolism), and responding to stimuli, it is alive. However, there are certain entities that possess only some of these traits, and so we aren't sure if they are alive.

The most common examples are viruses that reproduce by hijacking living cells in order to create copies of themselves. This makes viruses seem more like molecular machines than living creatures. In any case, it doesn't follow that because there are *some* cases in which we can't tell if something is alive (such as with viruses), we can't know if *anything* is alive. That is like a painter saying that since it is sometimes difficult to distinguish between light blue and light green, we can never tell if something is blue or green (or any color for that matter). Hard cases that confuse us do not negate simple cases that don't.

Clearly, the unborn are alive, because they are receiving nutrients from the mother that cause the fetus to grow via cellular reproduction. I've heard some students argue that the unborn are not alive because they can't survive without the mother, or they can't survive outside of her body. The problem with these objections is that they prove only that the unborn are alive in a certain place, not that they aren't alive at all.

The critic even concedes this when she says that unborn children can't live on their own or they can't live outside of the womb. This is just a roundabout way of saying that unborn children live with the assistance of their mothers (just as newborns can live only with assistance from their mothers or another human). If the fetus is growing, has a heart that is pumping blood through a circulatory system, and is sending electrical signals through a nervous system, how could it not be alive?

Another simple way to show that the unborn are alive is to ask the question, "What does abortion do to the fetus?" Most people will say that abortion kills the fetus, while some stubborn pro-choicers will say abortion removes the fetus from the womb. You can ask these stubborn people what happens to the fetus after it is removed. The critic must admit that the end result of these actions is the death of the fetus. But in order for something to die, wouldn't it have to be alive at some point?

Of course, so what if the fetus is alive? Bacteria and oak trees are alive, and we kill them all the time. To answer this objection, we must show that the unborn are not just alive but that they are a special kind of living thing.

Are the unborn human?

Remember that when some people say the unborn are not human, they are usually using the word *human* in a philosophical sense to mean *a valuable human being* or *a person*. I will answer the question of whether the unborn are human in that sense in the next chapter. When it comes to demonstrating that the unborn are *biologically* human, or members of our species, there are two kinds of evidence the pro-life advocate can use.

First, we can ask what kind of animal the parents of the fetus in question are. If the parents are dogs, then the fetus will be a dog. If the parents are cats, then the fetus will be a cat. If the parents are human, then the fetus will be human.[110] The other way to show that the unborn are biologically human is to examine their genetic code, or DNA.[111] If the fetus possesses a human genetic code, with approximately forty-six chromosomes, then he is a human being.[112]

Some critics will make the bizarre objection, "It's not human. It's a fetus." When a pro-choice student tried to make this argument in front of a crowd of cheering protesters I asked in reply, "What is a fetus? Could you define what that word means, or what it refers to?" The protester became uncomfortable and fired back, "Well, if you're so smart, why don't you tell me what the word *fetus* means?!"

"I'd be happy to," I said. "*Fetus* is a Latin word that means *little one*. According to most medical dictionaries, among humans, *fetus* refers to a human being from the eighth week of life until birth. An *embryo* is a human being from conception until the seventh week of life. The words *embryo* and *fetus* are like toddler or teenager—they are stages of development in the life of a human being. So isn't a fetus by definition human?"[113]

The protester looked down at the ground until one of his comrades came to relieve him. She was a petite, blond girl carrying a large white poster board. "This will be interesting," I thought. She flipped over the poster to reveal four pictures of early embryos that looked nearly identical.

"If you're so sure about what makes us human," she said, "then surely, Mr. Horn, you won't have a problem identifying which of these embryos are human and which are not."

I answered, "Well, I can't, because I need more data—" This young woman interrupted, "Ha! See, he can't even do it. Pro-life is a lie, they let women die!" She turned and gave a thumbs-up to the other protesters.

As she walked back to her smiling friends, I said into the microphone, "Nice try, but just because I can't see if something is human doesn't mean it isn't. If I showed you a picture of a dead person and a picture of a sleeping person, I'll bet you couldn't tell the difference, but that wouldn't show there's no difference between being dead and being asleep. I can't tell with my eyes which of these embryos is human, but scientific analysis would have no problem identifying the human embryo." My voice began to rise. "Our eyes can deceive us, but science sets it straight, and you know what, ma'am? I'll go with science every time!"

The pro-life members of the audience began to applaud, and the pro-choice spectators realized that it was useless to argue that the unborn were not biologically human. The terms *embryo* and *fetus* describe an organism's stages of development in the same way the terms *infant*, *toddler*, and *adolescent* describe stages of development. It would be nonsensical to define these terms without referencing the organism they describe, which brings us to our final question.

Are the unborn organisms?

Many skeptics try to take the evidence that the unborn are alive and human and use it to make the pro-life position look absurd. They will say, yes, the fetus is alive and human, but every cell in my body is alive and human. Is every cell in my body a human being? The cruder critics say things like, "If abortion is murder, then is masturbation genocide?" They say this because when sperm is released from the male body it results in the death of millions of male sex cells. If sperm and egg are alive and human, and fetuses and embryos are also alive and human, then are embryos and fetuses as well as sperm and egg all human beings?

This false argument confuses parts and wholes. Saying, "A fetus is alive and human. Sperm and egg are alive and human. Therefore, a fetus is a body part like sperm and egg" is as fallacious as saying, "A truck is made of metal. Nuts and bolts are made of metal. Therefore a truck is a car part like a nut or a bolt." Because two things have traits in common does not mean they are the same kind of thing. Sperm, egg, and other body cells are parts of a human body. In contrast, a fetus is a whole human body that is able to develop itself over time.

Sperm, egg, fetuses, and toddlers are all *human* in the adjective sense of the word, since they possess human DNA. Unlike sperm and egg, however, fetuses and toddlers are also *human* in the noun sense of the word. A fetus is a human and a toddler is a human, while an individual sperm cell or egg cell is not *a* human. This is similar to how we might say apple pie and the president are both American, while the president of the United States is *an* American, and the apple pie is not.

If a cell of a male gynecologist's skin, which has a complete set of human DNA, winds up inside a woman's uterus as the result of a medical procedure, we don't say that the woman is pregnant or that she is carrying a human being inside of her. On the other hand, if the human DNA inside of her is an *organism* that is using its genetic instructions to grow and develop, then the woman most definitely has a child inside of her, and she is (or soon will be) pregnant.[114]

The organism test

What do we mean when we say the unborn is an organism? An organism is a collection of biological parts, or organs, that function together to sustain the existence of a whole being that possesses the qualities of life.[115] Some critics will say that the unborn are clumps of cells and not organisms, but this objection reveals a mistaken understanding of biology. We describe loose collections of things as *clumps* when the parts do not interact for the good of the whole.

For example, a fistful of sand would be a clump, but a functioning watch is not a "clump of gears" (unless you smashed it with a hammer). An embryo is like a watch with parts that work together for the good of the whole and not like a pile of sand that has no interacting parts. I use the following simple test to show something is an organism and not a clump of cells:

> If I can give this living thing time, nutrition, and a proper environment, and it is able to develop toward becoming a mature member of its species, then it is an organism and not a mere body part.

Because body cells such as skin, sperm, and egg can never —even given time, nutrition, and a proper environment— develop into an adult human, they fail the organism test.[116] When removed from the human body, they are clumps of cells, or tissue, that will quickly die. In contrast, you and I are organisms, because if we are given time, food, and the proper environment (i.e., not on the moon or at the bottom of the ocean), we will continue to develop into mature members of the human species.

Likewise, an unborn child, when given time, nutrition, and a proper environment (i.e., not outside the uterus) will develop into a mature human being if he does not die prematurely.

Embryologist E.L. Potter points out, "Every time a sperm cell and ovum unite, a new being is created which is alive and will continue to live unless its death is brought about by some specific condition."[117]

The unborn are not mere tissue or body parts like sperm, egg, or skin cells. They are also not like cancerous tumors that can grow and even sprout body parts such as hair or teeth but have no potential to develop into an adult human.[118] The fact that some embryos and even other born children die before they become adult humans does not negate the fact that they are human beings. They still are human beings because they have the intrinsic capacity to develop into mature human beings even if their development is tragically cut short.

Pro-choice bioethicist Peter Singer agrees. "[T]here is no doubt that from the first moments of its existence an embryo conceived from human sperm and eggs is a human being," he says, "and the same is true of the most profoundly and irreparably intellectually disabled human being, even of an anencephalic infant—that is, an infant that, as a result of a defect in the formation of the neural tube, has no brain."[119]

Some skeptics say the early embryo's ability to twin during the first two weeks of its life counts against considering it a distinct, individual organism.[120] However, when a flatworm is cut in half, it will continue to develop as two distinct flatworms. This fact would not cause us to think that no flatworm existed prior to the split.[121] We're not sure if prior to twinning two organisms share one cellular body that later splits, or if one organism dies and gives rise to two new organisms in its place. Regardless of what happens, each outcome presupposes that some organism exists prior to the twinning event, because the pretwinning embryo still satisfies the definition of an organism by being able to mature into an adult human being. In the case of twinning, the embryo just matures into multiple adult human beings.

Just a parasite?

Some critics argue that an organism has to exist independently of other organisms. Because an unborn child requires his mother's body to live, these critics maintain he isn't independent and so is not an organism. Some people will say the child's dependence makes him a parasite, and that is why abortion is not wrong.

This type of critic almost always neglects the fact that parasites *are* a kind of organism that lives off another organism's body. To say an organism exists independently of another organism simply means it can't be a literal part of another being, such as an arm or a leg. It has to be able to develop itself apart from any other organism's DNA.[122] But it doesn't mean the organism survives without interacting with or depending on any other organism in order to survive. There are hardly any organisms like that!

Saying an unborn child is a parasite does not mean it is okay to kill an unborn child. After all, a parasite is a kind of organism, and we know unborn children are human organisms. We normally do have the right to kill parasites, but that is true only because parasites usually belong to species that have no right to live.[123] Since the unborn are human beings, calling them parasites because of how dependent they are is as offensive as calling a mentally handicapped person a "retard" because of how less developed he is.

A student of history will remember that, during the Holocaust, Jews were called parasites, and this was used as a rationale for exterminating them.[124] Does the critic really want to invoke this same kind of argument against another group of human beings?

Call in the experts

Once you have defended the claim that from conception the unborn are biological human beings by using the 10-second pro-life apologist, it is more than appropriate to augment that argument with appeals to relevant authorities. For example, in *Planned Parenthood v. Rounds* (2008), the Eighth Circuit Court of Appeals found that requiring abortionists to say that the fetus is a "living, separate, whole human being" does not force an abortionist to espouse an unconstitutional religious viewpoint. The Court ruled that this statement was a biological fact that even physicians affiliated with Planned Parenthood accept! The ruling declared:

> Planned Parenthood's evidence at the preliminary injunction stage does not demonstrate that it is likely to prevail on the merits. . . . The State's evidence suggests that the biological sense in which the embryo or fetus is whole, separate, unique and living should be clear in context to a physician. . . . Planned Parenthood submitted no evidence to oppose that conclusion. Indeed, Dr. Wolpe's affidavit, submitted by Planned Parenthood, states that "to describe an embryo or fetus scientifically and factually, one would say that a living embryo or fetus in utero is a developing organism of the species Homo Sapiens which may become a self-sustaining member of the species if no organic or environmental incident interrupts its gestation."[125]

Distinguished scientists and philosophers back up the Court's opinion. The standard medical text *Human Embryology and Teratology* states, "Although human life is a continuous process, fertilization is a critical landmark because, under ordinary circumstances, a new, genetically distinct human organism is formed."[126] (Among embryologists, the preferred term for the beginning of life is *fertilization*, especially since, as I discussed earlier, fertilization and conception sometimes have different meanings.) Keith Moore and T.V.N. Persaud's textbook *The Developing Human* states, "Human life begins at fertilization," and *Langman's Medical Embryology* also states, "Development begins with fertilization."[127] Finally, the fourth chapter of Scott Gilbert's textbook *Developmental Biology* is titled, "Fertilization: Beginning of a New Organism."[128]

Leading pro-choice philosophers agree that human fetuses are human beings. David Boonin, author of *A Defense of Abortion*, writes, "Perhaps the most straightforward relation between you and me on the one hand and every human fetus on the other is this: All are living members of the same species, homo sapiens. A human fetus after all is simply a human being at a very early stage in his or her development."[129]

Peter Singer holds the same view: "It is possible to give 'human being' a precise meaning. We can use it as equivalent to 'member of the species homo sapiens.' Whether a being is a member of a given species is something that can be determined scientifically, by an examination of the nature of the chromosomes in the cells of living organisms. In this sense there is no doubt that from the first moments of its existence an embryo conceived from human sperm and eggs is a human being."[130]

After reviewing medical and embryology textbooks, I have yet to find a single book that denies that a human embryo or fetus is a human organism, and since by definition a human fetus is a stage of development for a human organism, I doubt I ever will find such a claim in a serious textbook.[131]

When "experts" disagree

In 2014, U.S. Senator Marco Rubio said on a cable news program that it is a "scientific fact" that "human life begins at conception."[132] In attempting to "fact-check" Senator Rubio's statement, the *Washington Post* asked the American College of Obstetricians and Gynecologists (ACOG) when human life begins. ACOG replied, "Government agencies and American medical organizations agree that the scientific definition of pregnancy and the legal definition of pregnancy are the same: pregnancy begins upon the implantation of a fertilized egg into the lining of a woman's uterus."[133] Some pro-choice advocates claim that life can't begin at conception because pregnancy begins when the embryo implants in the uterus. How can a woman have a "life" inside of her before she is even pregnant?

But pregnancy is a condition associated with the woman's body, not the unborn child's. This reply doesn't answer the question of when the child comes into existence. Even pro-choice philosophers such as David Boonin admit that defining pregnancy as beginning at implantation does nothing to disprove the pro-life advocate's case that human beings begin to exist at conception. He writes, "If we agree that pregnancy begins at implantation rather than at fertilization, this is only because we are distinguishing pregnancy as a state of the woman's body from pregnancy as the condition in which a new individual member of our species has come into existence. To say that a given method of birth control prevents pregnancy in this sense, then, does not entail that it prevents a new member of our species from coming into existence. The use of such methods will still result in the death of such an individual."[134]

In addition, ACOG's fields of expertise are pregnancy and childbirth, not necessarily embryology. When experts in the fields of embryology and human development testified before a U.S. Senate Judiciary Committee, the committee reached the conclusion, "Physicians, biologists, and other scientists agree that conception marks the beginning of the life of a human being—a being that is alive and is a member of the human species. There is overwhelming agreement on this point in countless medical, biological, and scientific writings."[135]

Construction vs. development

With the evidence for the biological humanity of the unborn so simple and abundant, why do so many pro-choice advocates think we can't know when life begins? A helpful answer comes from law professor Richard Stith, who says that many pro-choice advocates (and even some pro-lifers) mistakenly think that an unborn child is constructed in the womb like an object and does not develop like an organism.[136]

Pro-choice advocates who think the embryo is "constructed" believe that the philosophical concept of a "person" or a "human being" emerges once the unborn child reaches a certain level of biological complexity. This is similar to saying that a car begins to exist once its construction reaches a certain level of complexity, such as when you can drive the finished product. Although people may disagree on when a car becomes a car during construction (Does it need an engine? An outer body shell? An air freshener?), hardly anyone would say that when the first nut and bolt are screwed together a "car" exists. The concept of a car includes things like "capable of being driven" or "a metal vehicle with four wheels." Nuts and bolts make up a potential car, not an actual one.

Likewise, pro-choice advocates usually don't consider a two-celled embryo a human being, because for them the concept of a human being includes things like "being born" or "capable of thinking or feeling." In their view, a two-celled embryo is a potential human being, not an actual one. Stith argues in response to this view that human beings are not objects that are constructed but organisms that develop and retain their identity through change.

A human being doesn't emerge when different body parts get snapped together and are complex enough to be called a human. Instead, humans retain their identity through development and grow their own parts. Stith uses the example of a Polaroid picture to illustrate how humans develop in the womb and are not objects that become human after a lengthy construction process but remain human throughout their entire growth process.

The camera analogy

In the twentieth century, Polaroid cameras took pictures and then printed the pictures on the emulsified paper that was stored inside the camera. When the paper emerged from the camera after the photos were taken, the images looked like brown smudges. After several minutes they emerged slowly as the film paper developed.

Now, imagine you took a Polaroid picture of something rare, like you standing with the president, and you show your friend the freshly printed Polaroid (which looks like a brown smudge). What if your friend proceeds to tear up the picture? I imagine you would be furious. But what if he said, "Chill out. That wasn't a picture of you and the president. It was just a brown smudge that had the *potential* to become a picture of you and the president. Any Polaroid picture has that same potential, so what's the big deal?"

You would rightly respond, "No! That was an *actual* picture of the president and me; it just looked like a brown smudge at that stage of its existence. Everything that was the picture of the president and me was fully there; you just couldn't see it. You destroyed it before it developed into a picture you could recognize."

In the same way, when the pro-choice advocate says, "Chill out. That wasn't a human being that was aborted. It was just a bundle of cells that had the *potential* to become a human being," you would rightly reply, "No, that was an *actual* human being who was aborted. He just looked like a bundle of cells at that stage of his existence. Everything that was that human being was fully there; you just couldn't see him. You destroyed him before he could develop into a human being that looks like other born humans."

From a biological perspective, a human being is a member of the species homo sapiens. An embryo or fetus does not become human as it gets older any more than a Polaroid picture becomes more of a Polaroid picture as it gets older. Rather, it just *develops*, or unveils what it was from the beginning of its existence.[137] The pro-life position merely adds one philosophical truth to the biological claim that the unborn at every stage are human beings. That truth is, "All biological human beings should possess equal rights and be treated equally under the law."

The skeptic strikes back

Even after all the evidence that the unborn are biological human beings is put forth, the skeptic may accept none of it. He might claim that there's no unanimous way to define the words *life* or *human*. How do you know scientists aren't all wrong? How can we be absolutely certain the embryo is human?[138] There's no way to know with 100 percent certainty which actions are right and which are wrong!

Although credulity is a good thing, a hyperskeptic is going too far, and you should respond by simply saying, "Alright, I guess I can't convince you. I'm just going to try and persuade other people to make abortion illegal—unless you can give me a reason to think I shouldn't."

If the skeptic gives any reason to show that you *should not* outlaw abortion, this proves there are some things he is not skeptical about. The burden of proof is now on him to show that the unborn are not alive, are not biologically human, are not organisms, or that unborn children don't deserve to be treated equally with other human beings.

If he defaults to his skepticism and says that we should keep abortion legal because we don't know if the fetus is human, you should say that this is actually a very good reason to make abortion illegal! After all, we wouldn't blow up a building if we thought there could still be people inside of it. Likewise, we should not destroy the contents of the womb if there could be a person in there as well.

You should then remind the skeptic that nearly all professional advocates of abortion in law, medicine, and philosophy do not doubt that the unborn are biological human beings. The real debate lies in whether the unborn are persons who have a right to life.

Engaging the skeptic

The skeptic's main concern: Outlawing abortion is wrong because no one can agree on whether the unborn child is a human being.

Your objective: Show that there is no doubt the unborn child is a biological human being and that the debate over the status of an unborn child involves philosophy, not science.

★ ★ ★

Pro-choicer: Abortion should be legal because no one knows when life begins. It's a religious question.

Pro-lifer: Okay. I agree with you that we shouldn't make laws that have only a religious basis, but I don't think it's true that no one knows when life begins.

PC: What do you mean?

PL: Well, is it okay for me to kill a six-year-old? I mean, since no one knows when life begins, you can't say with 100 percent certainty that it's wrong for me to kill him.

PC: That's dumb. We know *his* life has begun. I'm just saying no one knows when life begins before birth.

PL: Why do you say no one knows when life begins before birth?

PC: Well, because everyone disagrees about it.

PL: Sure, but people used to disagree about slavery and the shape of the Earth, and that didn't mean there were no right answers. Would you mind if I gave you some evidence to show that an unborn child is as alive as a six-year-old?

PC: You can try.

PL: Okay. Well, if something is taking in food and using that to grow, wouldn't we say it is alive?

PC: Okay.

PL: Then isn't an unborn child alive, since throughout the pregnancy he's taking in food from his mother and growing? I mean, if the fetus wasn't alive, then why would we need to abort it?

PC: I'll give you that it's a "life" or a clump of cells, but it isn't human. Or at least no one agrees that it's human.

PL: What do you mean by human?

PC: You know, like a baby. Someone who can feel and be human like you and me.

PL: Okay, I think our definitions may be confused. From a scientific perspective, *human* means belonging to the human species, and that's easy to prove. What you're talking about is being a person or being "fully" human and having a right to life. You're right that people are divided on that question, because it's philosophical and not scientific. But can we agree that if a fetus has human parents and human DNA, then, biologically, it has to be human?

PC: But it's just a clump of cells. How is it different than a clump of cells on my arm?

PL: Well, for starters, the cells on your arm are a part of your body. If we took those cells and gave them food and the right environment, they could never develop into a fully grown human being. But a fetus can. It's a small human being that, like you and me, can develop into an adult human being when given food and the right environment. I just think we should treat these humans like we treat other humans.

PC: I still think it is just a potential child.

PL: Okay. If something is *potentially* one thing, it has to *actually* be another thing. For example, if I am a potential corpse, then what does that make me right now?

PC: Alive?

PL: Right. So if the fetus is a potential child, then what is it actually?

PC: A fetus.

PL: But what does that word *fetus* actually mean? What does it refer to?

PC: I don't know. I don't think we can know when a fetus becomes a baby.

PL: *Baby* is word that carries a lot of emotion, while *fetus* is merely a scientific term. But a fetus is a human being at a certain stage of development, like a toddler or an infant. If these fetuses have human parents, and they are organisms at a certain stage of development, then can we at least agree that they are biological human beings? I mean, what else could they be?

PC: I'll agree they have human DNA, but being human is more than just about having the right kind of DNA.

PL: Okay, now we're talking about philosophy, or "valuable" humans. My position is that all biological human beings, the kind we can identify with scientific tools, are equally valuable. Can you tell me what's wrong with my view?

7

The Disqualifiers

When I was nine, I remember learning there were people who might hate me because of something I had no control over. I was in the grocery store with my dad, and it was a few days before Hanukkah. Even though my mom is Christian, my dad is Jewish, so in our house we got to celebrate the holidays of both religions. I said to my dad in an excited plea, "Can we get some latkes?" (Latkes are potato pancakes Jews eat at Hanukkah.) My dad turned to me and with a serious look said, "Shh. We don't need anyone to know we're Jewish."

This confused me. Why would it matter if someone knew I was of Jewish ethnicity any more than if they knew I liked potato pancakes? I was then given a lesson about anti-Semites. My grandfather was assaulted in the navy because he was Jewish. After the war he changed his name from Hornstein to Horn so as not to arouse any suspicion regarding his heritage.

It crushed me to learn that some people would say that while I was certainly a *biological* human being, my ancestry lessened or even voided my human value. I couldn't believe there were people who thought I wasn't a *person*.

What is a person?

When faced with the stubborn facts of science, honest skeptics will admit that the unborn are at least individual members of the human species. What these skeptics will not admit is that each individual member of our species deserves the same basic rights. In order to bear that burden of proof, skeptics become *disqualifiers* who claim that unborn children do not have a right to life. They claim that because the unborn are different from born humans, they are not persons.

Isn't this kind of argument familiar? Every time in history a group of human beings has been disqualified from being considered people (e.g., blacks, women, Jews, the mentally handicapped), the reason for the disqualification turned out to be bogus. Of course, the experiences of these groups differ dramatically from the experiences of aborted unborn children (who are usually not self-aware when they are aborted), so it isn't wise to say that abortion is "just like" slavery or the Holocaust. However, it should be noted that the process of stripping the unborn of their personhood because of morally irrelevant biological traits does parallel previous oppression of born people.

Since all human beings differ in size, intelligence, skin color, gender, and physical ability, we must ground human equality in the one thing that is truly equal about all of us: our human nature. Otherwise, if a person's right to life is based on a property that comes in degrees, such as his level of intelligence, then the right to life itself would come in degrees. For example, smarter people would have more of a right to life than the less smart. Even pro-choice philosophers who are sympathetic to this view, like Jeff McMahan, recognize it "rest[s] on distressingly insecure foundations" and seems to conflict with society's cherished belief that all human beings should have equal rights.[139]

It makes more sense to associate our right to life, a property you either have or don't have, with something a human being either does or doesn't have—in this case, being a member of a rational kind like the human species.[140] The sixth-century philosopher Boethius said that a person was "an individual substance with a rational nature."[141] What this means is that a particular being is a person, or has basic rights, if it is a member of a rational kind.[142] But this definition of personhood is not "human-centric," because even intelligent aliens or other rational beings such as angels would be persons under such a view.

Even if we can't function rationally (such as when we were infants), we were still members of a valuable kind that deserves respect and protection under the law. Since we remain members of the human kind throughout our entire existence, it follows that through every stage of our existence we deserve the respect and protection humans normally receive.

Use your SLED

After you've presented your view that all human beings should be given equal rights (which is hopefully common ground), it is up to the disqualifier to show why unborn humans should be disqualified from having those rights. In order to disqualify the unborn from being considered persons, the critic has to know what a person is. After all, we disqualify squares from being considered triangles because we know the definition of a triangle is having three sides, and we know that a square has four.

If the disqualifier doesn't know what a "person" is except that fetuses aren't people, then his view is as bigoted as the racist's view that the only thing he knows about black "persons" is that they don't have the same basic rights he has. In order to justify their position, disqualifiers usually pick a difference between born and unborn humans and say that until the unborn grow enough to overcome this crucial difference, they are not persons with a right to life.

The philosopher Stephen Schwartz has argued that there are only four differences between born and unborn humans, and none of the differences justifies depriving unborn humans of the right to life.[143] Schwartz uses the acronym SLED to summarize these differences:

- Size
- Level of development
- Environment
- Degree of dependency

Just as we would ask a racist why skin color makes someone less valuable, we should ask disqualifiers why SLED differences make someone less valuable—or not a someone at all. We must make disqualifiers defend their view of personhood and show why it is superior to the pro-life view based on universal human equality. The SLED critique follows the same basic pattern:

1. Affirm the difference illustrated in the SLED acronym exists.
2. Ask the critic what a person is or why this difference is what makes someone a person.
3. Show that this difference has nothing to do with being a person, because some born people also differ in one or more of these ways.

Size

Atheist Richard Dawkins says, "A certain kind of religious mind cannot see the moral difference between killing a microscopic cluster of cells on the one hand, and killing a full-grown doctor on the other."[144] It seems Dawkins believes it is wrong to kill the abortionist but not the embryo, because the abortionist is much larger and can be seen without the aid of a microscope. But I would condemn the murder of an abortion provider even if he were very small, because in the pro-life view, all humans have the right to life, regardless of their size.

Daniel Maguire ridicules an embryo's size to discount its humanity and says, "I have held babies in my hands and now I held this embryo. I know the difference."[145] Of course there is a difference in size between newborns and embryos, but the key issue is this: "Does that difference matter?"

I clearly know the difference between an adult woman who I can talk to and a premature infant who is smaller than a football and can't even recognize me. But neither the premature infant nor the human embryo can be rightfully disqualified from being considered a person simply because it is smaller than I. Size is irrelevant to the issue of human value.

Level of development

Dawkins goes on the say, "An early embryo has the sentience, as well as the semblance, of a tadpole. A doctor is a grown-up, conscious being with hopes, loves, [and] aspirations."[146] Other people make this argument by saying that a woman's rights take precedence over any rights the unborn child might have. That is because the woman has relationships with other people and has a rich "intellectual life" full of hopes and dreams for herself that an unintended pregnancy will ruin. The child, on the other hand, has no interests because he cannot think or feel. Therefore, his lack of development means he is not a person like you or me.

Now, Dawkins and critics like him are correct that the unborn cannot think or feel at the same level you and I can, but why does being able to think or feel at a certain level make someone a person? After all, infants cannot function like adults in the sense of being able to think rationally, but we don't say they have the "sentience of a cow" (even though they have about the same level of brain development as a cow). We don't say a mother, by virtue of being older and more developed than her infant son, has the right to kill her infant son or that her rights "trump" his. Why shouldn't we treat all human beings equally, regardless of how developed they are?

Pro-life advocates should remember that when critiquing the disqualifier's definition of a person, it's important to use noncontroversial examples. For example, if the critic says that a person is anyone who can feel pain or think like he can, it's not wise to ask in response, "But what about comatose human beings who will never think or feel again? Are they not persons?"[147] The disqualifier might reply, "No, the irreversibly comatose are not persons."[148]

That's why in nearly all my examples I use newborn infants, because they are close in age and level of development to fetuses, and almost everyone agrees it is wrong to kill newborn infants. If we can show human embryos and fetuses do not differ in any relevant way from human infants, then we can redirect people's natural moral outrage against infanticide toward abortion (or should I say feticide?).

Another argument related to the level of development criterion is found in the statement, "A newly fertilized ovum (or a newly implanted clump of cells) is no more a person than an acorn is an oak tree."[149] However, while an acorn is not a tree, it is a tiny oak in the first stages of its life. In the acorn stage the oak starts out as a plant embryo within the acorn and then grows into a sapling before it becomes a tree many years later. All this statement proves is that an embryo is no more *an adult* than an acorn is an oak tree—and that's right!

The difference is, trees aren't persons, so it doesn't matter how old they are when we kill them. Human beings *are* persons, and the pro-life view holds that we should not kill persons just because they are very young, because all humans have an equal right to life.

One variant of the acorn argument is the egg argument, which is embodied in the phrase, "The egg you had for breakfast is not a chicken, just as the embryo in the womb is not a human." However, this objection misses the fact that the eggs you buy at the grocery store are unfertilized eggs. These eggs don't have the genetic information to develop into chickens.

You could incubate a grocery store egg all you want, and no chicken will ever hatch. (Unlike those eggs, boiled duck eggs, or *balut*, as they're called in Asia, are fertilized eggs, and their crunchiness will alert you to the presence of an *actual* duck at a lower level of development and not a *potential* duck.)

The pro-life advocate can respond to these kinds of arguments in this way: "Yes, acorns are not oaks, and eggs are not chickens. All this means is that embryos are not adults. But it's not okay to kill human embryos, human fetuses, human toddlers, or human teenagers just because they aren't adults yet. A human being's level of development is irrelevant to the issue of human value."

Environment

Disqualifiers sometimes say the unborn aren't "in the world yet" (i.e., they aren't born), and so it's not wrong to abort them. But why does living in a certain environment make someone a person? Now, I'm not saying women are "merely" an environment, location, or vessel that carries an unborn child. Instead, I am saying that a woman's body represents intimate space that is shared with another human being. If moving from one place to another outside of the womb does not negate our personhood, then how could moving from inside the womb to outside it cause someone to become a person?

If the disqualifier is stubborn and says that birth just *is* what makes a human a person, ask him to refute you when you say that having a Y-chromosome just *is* what makes a human a person. After all, a Y-chromosome makes a human a man, and women just aren't persons. If the disqualifier says that "having a Y-chromosome," "being a man," and "not being a woman" all mean the same thing and you are arguing in a circle, point out that "being in the world," "being born" and "not being a fetus" all mean the same thing, and he, too, has been arguing in a circle. By saying birth is what makes someone a person, he is merely asserting the unborn are not persons. He has not proven the unborn are not persons.

Peter Singer summarizes the absurdity of placing value on the location of an organism: "[P]ro-life groups are right about one thing: the location of the baby inside or outside the womb cannot make such a crucial moral difference. We cannot coherently hold that it is all right to kill a fetus a week before birth, but as soon as the baby is born everything must be done to keep it alive."[150] This shows that environment is irrelevant to the issue of human value.

Degree of dependency

A disqualifier could respond to the last argument and say that at birth what changes isn't the unborn child's location but the fact that he no longer needs the woman's body in order to survive. This is not entirely accurate, because a fetus can survive outside of a woman's body at an age several months before the traditional time of birth. The earliest time a newborn can survive outside the womb is called *viability*, and it is usually dated in the United States at around twenty-four weeks after conception.[151]

But newborns cannot live on their own outside of the womb; they would be dead in a few hours or days if left on a hospital table. If the disqualifier says that a person is someone who can survive outside the womb even with assistance, then he is blindly asserting that the unborn are not persons. Why not say that a person is anyone who can survive outside of either a womb *or an incubator*? If he believes that premature infants who can survive only in what are essentially low-grade, artificial wombs are persons, then why not extend that same belief to unborn children who reside in natural wombs?

The entire idea that the unborn are not persons because they are dependent is opposite to our cultural intuition. Crimes against adults are wrong, but nearly everyone thinks those same crimes, such as rape or abuse, are even worse when committed against infants. This intuition comes from the fact that infants are utterly dependent and cannot protect themselves. If we consider it worse to harm an infant because he is so helpless, then wouldn't it be worse to kill a human being who is even more helpless than an infant, such as a fetus or an embryo? This shows that degree of dependency is irrelevant to the issue of human value.

Countering SLED

A critic might argue that all four SLED criteria are necessary for personhood, and since the unborn do not possess the necessary size, level of development, environment, and degree of dependency, they are not persons. But if each of these criteria is invalid on its own, adding them up does not make the critic's case stronger. Philosopher Christopher Kaczor writes, "An invalid or unsound argument counts for nothing. Such an argument is a philosophical zero, and even an infinite number of zeros never adds up to more than zero."[152] The critic has to present a good argument against the personhood of unborn children, not just many bad arguments.

It's also important to remember that when a disqualifier brings up reasons that relate to environment or degree of dependency, he may not be trying to disqualify the unborn from being considered a *person*. He may instead be arguing that women have a right to remove the children who are so dependent on their bodies from their wombs, even if the children are persons with a right to life of their own. These are called *bodily rights arguments* for abortion, and I'll examine these arguments, as well as how pro-life advocates sometimes misunderstand them as SLED arguments, in Chapter 8.

Another way a disqualifier could respond to SLED would be to argue that a fetus becomes a person gradually.[153] Smaller or less developed embryos are less human, but as those unborn humans become older, they gradually become more and more human until they are "fully" human at birth. But the problem with the gradualist thesis is twofold.

First, even if our humanity or personhood were a degreed property, there is no reason for the gradualist to maintain that the fetus gradually becomes a person until birth. Why not say fetuses gradually become persons until they reach their complete humanity at age two or even twenty-two? According to the description for the book *The Fourth Trimester: Understanding, Protecting, and Nurturing an Infant through the First Three Months,* "The fourth trimester has more in common with the nine months that came before than with the lifetime that follows."[154] The gradualist has no reason to affirm that the gradual process of becoming human ends at birth as opposed to several months after birth when distinctly human traits like self-awareness emerge.

Second, the gradualist has simply assumed that "humanity" is a degree property like color that can come in various "shades." If, on the other hand, humanity is a categorical property like the properties of "being alive" or "being pregnant," then you either have it or you don't. While it's true that humans gradually gain other rights after birth, such as the right to vote or the right to choose a certain religion, most critics agree that humans don't gradually gain basic rights after birth.[155] For example, we don't say nine-year-olds are halfway to having the right not to be tortured, because all human beings, regardless of their age, have the same *intrinsic* value.[156]

If it's absurd to believe that born humans gradually acquire basic rights such as the right to life and don't possess them in equal amounts after birth, then isn't it equally absurd to say that unborn humans gradually acquire those same basic rights before birth? It makes more sense to say that our intrinsic human value is a categorical property and that one can no more be "half human" than one can be "half pregnant."[157]

A disqualifier could admit that the SLED tool does show that generic statements such as "The unborn are too small" or "The unborn are too dependent" are not good arguments against fetal personhood, and he could also concede that the gradual thesis proves too much. He may instead try to argue that there is a nonarbitrary moment before birth when the human fetus becomes a person. Let's examine a few of those potential moments and see if they make sense.

How could you be so heartless?

An unborn child's heart starts to beat about three weeks after he is conceived.[158] Some people think this is when personhood begins, because if our lives end when our heart stops, then wouldn't our lives begin when our hearts start? While it's true that older humans with complex circulatory systems would die without a heart to pump blood, the same is not true for very young humans. Embryos less than three weeks old do not need to circulate blood in order to live. When their bodies become complex enough to require a heart, they grow one.

I should also correct a misunderstanding that some people, including pro-life advocates, have about the heartbeat criterion. I sometimes ask students, "How do you know the fetus is alive?" to which they respond, "Because it has a heartbeat." Now, a heartbeat is a *sufficient* condition for life (if something has a heart then it is alive), and so this is something you can bring up to the pro-choice advocate in order to prove the unborn are alive in the biological sense of that word.

However, a heartbeat is not a *necessary* condition for life, because bacteria, plants, and early embryos are alive even though they do not have hearts. Pro-life advocates should point out that the unborn meet all the *necessary* conditions for a thing to be alive, including growth by cellular reproduction and response to stimuli.

Aside from being alive or being a person, some people mistakenly say the reason a fetus is human is because it has a heartbeat. However, my parent's dog, Champy, has a heartbeat, and he is definitely not human. Our heartbeat shows only that we are a certain kind of living thing. In order to show a being with a heart is human, we must examine either its DNA or the species of its parents. If those are human, then the animal with a heartbeat is a human being.

A face only a mother could love

"How can a bunch of cells that have come into existence right after conception be a human being? They don't even look human!" This objection assumes that humans must look a certain way in order to be human. But what does it mean to "look human"?

You might say something looks like a human being if it has two arms, two legs, two eyes, and is of a certain height and shape. While human fetuses do begin to possess a human appearance by the eighth week of life, there are other humans who have lost all their limbs or have been horribly disfigured in accidents. They don't look human, but that doesn't mean they aren't human.

The idea that humans must look a certain way in order to be considered persons is a bigoted idea. For example, in the early twentieth century, diminutive African pygmies were put on display in human zoos.[159] This was considered acceptable, because pygmies did not look "human" (in other words, they did not have white skin and European facial features). They were considered some kind of advanced apelike creature and not human beings worthy of respect. Of course, African pygmies look just like humans are supposed to look in a certain geographical region of the world. Likewise, a one-celled zygote looks just like a human is supposed to look at a certain stage of development.

Another reason that human appearance is a bad criterion for personhood is that robots and mannequins can be designed to *look* human even though they are neither humans nor persons. Aliens or angels may not resemble human beings, but we would not deny they are persons simply because they look different from members of our species. All these reasons show that human appearance is irrelevant to being a person.

And yet it moves

Quickening refers to a time in pregnancy during the second trimester when a pregnant woman can feel her unborn child move inside of her (although the child was already moving long before that moment). However, the fetus's ability to move does not prove he is a person any more than a slug's ability to move proves slugs are people.[160]

In the past, some people mistakenly thought that at quickening the fetus became a person because that was the moment when the fetus's soul entered his body and transformed the body from lifeless matter into a moving human being. But with the advent of modern embryology, we know that a human fetus is a living organism that guides its own development long before the mother can feel it move inside of her.

If I only had a brain

One of the biggest differences cited by disqualifiers between born and unborn humans is the possession of a brain. A healthy adult has a developed brain, a fetus has an undeveloped brain, and an embryo does not have a brain. In one pro-choice documentary the interviewer asks a neuroscientist, "Can there be a person without a brain?" The doctor responds, "No, no way. You can't be a person without a brain, you can't be a dog without a brain, you can't be a cat without a brain, or a chicken without a brain."[161] Most people agree that we stop being a person at "brain death," so doesn't it make sense to say that we become a person at "brain life," or when we develop a brain?[162] To answer the question "Does having a brain make someone a person?" we must answer a more basic question: "What does the brain do?"

When our brain isn't performing complex tasks (such as when we sleep), or when it hasn't developed the ability to do so (such as when we are infants), our brain simply keeps our bodies alive. At brain death we lose our "organic unity," and we become a corpse. Our body parts no longer function together to keep us alive.[163] If a person stops existing not when the brain dies but when his body parts no longer function together to keep him alive (or when he no longer has organic unity), then it makes sense to say that a person begins to exist when his body achieves this organic unity.[164]

When does this occur? At fertilization a person begins to exist, because at that time the unborn child's parts work together to keep the child growing and living. When the child becomes so complex that he needs a brain to survive, he will simply grow one, because he is a person who can continue developing new organs and new abilities over time. A brain-dead person cannot do this, and that is why the brain-dead are no longer persons, while the unborn, even without a brain, are persons who are merely immature.

Stephen Schwartz says that the brain-dead and the unborn are not similar in any relevant way, because the brain-dead are former persons who are "no more," while the unborn are actual persons who are "not yet" fully developed. He writes, "We throw out food that has lost its nourishing power, that has it 'no more': we do not, however, throw out food that has 'not yet' developed its nourishing power. We wait, and give it a chance. This is what we must do with human beings in their embryonic stage."[165]

The disqualifier may respond that having a brain isn't important just because it's the organ that keeps us alive (otherwise any animal with a brain would be a person). Having a brain is important because the brain allows us to do specifically human things, such as thinking rationally or thinking at a level that surpasses other animals. Therefore, any being without a brain capable of rational thought, whether it's a cow or a twelve-week-old fetus, is not a person.

The problem with this response is that the brain of an infant is nowhere near complex enough to think rationally. From birth until nine months later, the number of synaptic connections in a human brain increases from 56 trillion to 1,000 trillion.[166] Most child psychologists agree that human children do not outperform other animals cognitively until they are at least twelve to twenty-four months old.[167]

Does this mean we should treat infants like animals and send them to kennels instead of day care? A disqualifier could say that infants aren't disqualified from being persons, because they have brains that, while they can't function rationally now, will be able to do so in the future.

The obvious problem with this response is that if infants are persons only because they possess brains that will eventually let them "act human," then unborn children must also be considered persons, because they, too, possess brains that will allow them to "act human" in the future.

To summarize, if the disqualifier says that a person is the kind of creature that can function rationally *now*, then he can't consider infants to be persons.[168] If he says that a person is the kind of creature who can function rationally *later*, then he must include fetuses and embryos in the category of beings who are persons.

What a pain

Some disqualifiers will try to save their position and say that adults and infants are not disqualified from being considered persons because they can feel pain, while most unborn children cannot feel pain. A protester at a school in Oklahoma once said to me, "I don't think abortion is a big deal, because a fetus can't even feel anything. It doesn't even know it's been aborted. That's why I'm pro-choice." This protester mistakenly assumed that hurting someone means the same thing as harming someone.

Hurt refers to those acts that cause pain, such as physical assault or even emotional attacks that might "hurt someone's feelings." *Harm* refers to anything that makes another person worse off. Not everything that hurts someone is harmful. A dentist who painfully drills a tooth hurts the patient, but he does not *harm* him, because the dentist's act makes the patient better off by treating a medical problem. Likewise, some acts can harm a person without hurting him.

If I steal an inheritance from someone who didn't know it existed, I haven't hurt him (he isn't sad about the lost money), but I have harmed him. [169] If a male nurse fondles an unconscious female patient, he hasn't hurt her, but he has harmed her, because she is worse off by having her body violated by a stranger.

These cases help us see that while abortion may not hurt the fetus (or cause him pain), it does greatly *harm* the fetus by making the fetus worse off than if the abortion had never happened. Instead of being deprived of an inheritance or bodily integrity, the aborted fetus is deprived of the greatest earthly good of all: life. [170]

Blast from the past

A disqualifier could object that the unconscious woman could feel pain *in the past* and would not have wanted to have been molested in the future. This is what makes it wrong to violate her, whereas the fetus never had any desires at all, and so it is not wrong to abort him. [171] The fetus never wanted anything in the past, so he can't be harmed.

There are two problems with this "desire account" of harm. First, most people consider it wrong to kill someone, even if that person does not have a desire to live. Imagine if we genetically engineered fetuses so that when they grew up they had no desire to live and enjoyed being slaves.[172] Would that make it right to own such slaves and kill them at our leisure? I think most people would agree that it would be wrong, because those fetuses had a right to grow up normally and not be turned into brainwashed slaves. But if those fetuses had a right to grow up normally, then it follows that they have a general "right to grow up," and so it would be wrong to abort them.

Or imagine a fetus that is born in a coma and has a 99 percent chance of awakening from the coma in one week. According to the disqualifier, because this born infant has never had any experiences (just like his fetal brothers and sisters), he would not have a right to life, and it would be acceptable to kill him during the week he slept in the hospital nursery. Our general intuition that it is still wrong to kill this infant counts against the view that only beings who have had experiences are worthy of the right to life.[173]

Finally, if the disqualifier argues that sentience, or the ability to feel pain, is what makes something a person, then in order to be consistent, he will also have to grant personhood to other animals that can feel pain, such as apes, dolphins, cows, dogs, cats, squirrels, rats, and possibly some birds, fish, and reptiles. The disqualifier cannot merely oppose cruelty to these animals but must consider them persons with a right to life. This means a cow, which is as sentient as a newborn, should be given the same legal protection a human newborn receives.[174]

I would ask the disqualifier this question: "Should people who eat cheeseburgers be given the same punishment as people who eat newborns?" Since most people would not consider cows to be persons simply because they can feel pain, this shows that the ability to feel pain is not what makes something a person.[175]

Does viability matter?

Along with the other problems I discussed in relation to the "D" in SLED, the viability criterion also proves too much. If surviving outside of the womb makes *anything* a person, then squirrels and pigs would be persons because they can survive outside of the womb. I brought up this example at a JFA exhibit, and an exasperated opponent yelled, "Pigs and squirrels aren't persons, because they're from the wrong species, idiot!" I replied, "What species does the human fetus belong to?"[176]

At Georgia Tech, a student named Ryan adamantly told me that the unborn are not "persons" because they are not viable (they cannot survive outside of the womb). Of course, the unborn certainly are "viable" when they live in the uterus, or the environment in which they were designed to live. They are not nonviable or dead like a stillborn child. Unborn children are as viable outside of the uterus as we are on the surface of the moon. In other words, both born and unborn humans are viable only in the right conditions.

Even after I pointed out to Ryan that some born people, such as infants or disabled adults, are also dependent on others and are thus "not viable" like the fetus, he still defended his claim. He said that viability is when a fetus can survive outside of the womb, and so that is when a fetus becomes a person. At this point I highlighted Ryan's circular reasoning.

> Ryan: The fetus isn't a person because it cannot sur-
> vive outside of the womb.
>
> Me: So you're saying that any human being who
> requires a womb to live is not a person, and
> since the fetus needs a womb to live, it is not a
> person. Do I understand your view correctly?

Ryan: Yes.

Me: But why are persons only those humans who can live outside of the womb?

Ryan: Because they can survive on their own!

Me: Why does it matter that they can survive on their own?

Ryan: Because that is what a person is; someone who can survive on his own.

Me: But you haven't given me a reason to think that's true. Saying a person is someone who can survive on his own is just another way of saying a person is not a fetus. Why should I believe persons have to be able to survive outside of the womb?

Many people who support the viability criterion generally make an argument like Ryan's:

Premise 1: A person is a human who can survive outside of the womb.
Premise 2: A fetus cannot survive outside of the womb.
Conclusion: Therefore, a fetus is not a person.

But notice that this argument is circular. A human who can survive outside of the womb is the same thing as a human who is not a fetus. This means that Premise 1 says the same thing as the Conclusion (or "a person can't be a fetus"), and therefore the argument fails. Knowing this, I challenged Ryan's reasoning: "Ryan, you're claiming that the fetus can be considered a person only if he or she can survive where you can. But what if the fetus demanded you prove your personhood by living where he or she does, in the watery environment of the womb? You wouldn't last more than five minutes. Perhaps from the fetus's perspective, you're not a person!" Ryan replied, "Wow . . . you got me . . . that's deep, man. I'm going to have to think this over some more."

How does it follow that just because the unborn cannot survive where born people live they are not persons? Suppose Martians abducted Earthlings and put them on Mars, where they would immediately suffocate. What if the Martians defended their actions by saying that humans are not "viable" and so are not persons?

Another example that disproves the notion that a person must be "viable," or not physically dependent on another person in order to live, is that of conjoined twins. In 2000, a British court had to decide what should be done with conjoined newborns named Jodie and Mary. Mary could not survive without being connected to Jodie's heart and lungs, while Jodie could survive without being connected to Mary. Unfortunately, Jodie's organs were expected to fail after a few weeks due to the strain of supporting both herself and Mary. The court decided that the most ethical decision was to separate Mary from Jodie so that at least Jodie could survive.

Now, if Mary had the same legal status as a cancerous tumor, then the decision to separate the girls would have been without controversy. But the court emphatically stated that Mary, in spite of her complete dependence on Jodie, was still a person with a right to live and so the courts were needed to decide how both of these persons should be treated. The court said, "All parties took for granted in the court below that Mary is a live person and a separate person from Jodie. . . . [I]n the face of that evidence it would be contrary to common sense and to everyone's sensibilities to say that Mary is not alive or that there are not two separate persons."[177]

When disqualifiers tell me, "I'm pro-choice because the fetus is not viable," I respond, "I'm pro-life for the same reason. If you take the unborn child out of the womb, that kills the child, and I don't think we should put human beings in places where they aren't 'viable,' or places that would kill them."

The born identity

The last marker in human development where a disqualifier can affirm abortion while denouncing infanticide is birth. There are even more problems with the birth criterion than the problem of arbitrariness I mentioned in relation to the "E" in SLED. For example, if a fetal dog or rat does not become a person through the process of birth, then why does a fetal human become a person by going through the exact same process? If humans are special and deserve rights that dogs and rats do not deserve, then why not give those basic rights to humans who are waiting to be born?

Furthermore, if birth is what makes someone a person, then when during birth does a fetus become a person? Is it when it is delivered halfway out of the body? If so, is it okay to kill the child when only 30 percent of the child's body is born? If a fetus is not a person until it is completely delivered, then would it be okay to kill a fetus whose foot was still inside the mother? For those who would not support "almost-entire-birth abortion" or infanticide, this should cast heavy doubt on the birth criterion.[178]

One argument in favor of the birth criterion is that most cultures celebrate birthdays as opposed to conception days. But birthdays don't commemorate the day we began to exist, since no one knows exactly when he was conceived.[179] Instead, birthdays celebrate when we met our parents, when other people could see us outside of the womb, and when our relationship with our mother changed.

Other disqualifiers say a fetus becomes a person at birth because that is when a child becomes a citizen and is issued official state documentation, such as a social security number. Aside from the fact that there can be delays of several weeks for this documentation (thus allowing for infanticide), I wonder if these disqualifiers also think the approximately 11 million undocumented workers who live in the United States who are not citizens are also not persons? This shows that birth is irrelevant to the issue of human value.[180]

Putting it all together

Most people you speak with on the issue of abortion will display a mix of pragmatism, skepticism, and disqualification. While still going into the conversation with the five rules of attitude I outlined in Chapter 2 (don't be weird, use bullet-proof evidence, ask questions, listen, agree when possible), try to keep the conversation on the following "game plan."

1. When any pragmatic reason to justify abortion is presented that does not answer the question "What are the unborn?" use Trot Out a Toddler to bring the conversation back to the main issue: "What are the unborn?"

2. If the person is skeptical that we can know if the unborn are "human," explain the difference between the scientific concept of human (species member-ship) and the philosophical concept (a being worthy of a right to life). Use the 10-second apologist to show that the unborn are biologically human, or members of our species.

3. If the person says the unborn are different and there-fore they are not people, identify which part of the SLED acronym the difference belongs to. Then ask him why this difference matters and provide ex-amples of born people who also differ in the same way. Make him defend his view of what a "person" is and show how his definition leads to absurd results.

4. Finally, share with the person how the pro-life view treats all human beings equally and is therefore su-perior to the pro-choice view.

As my friend Stephanie Gray, the executive director of the Canadian Center for Bio-Ethical Reform, says, "The pro-choice view of personhood is 'human plus birth,' or 'human plus consciousness,' or 'human plus viability.' But how is this different from those who say personhood is 'human plus white skin,' or 'human plus male gender,' or 'human plus an IQ higher than seventy'? Why not just say 'being human' is enough?"[181]

Engaging the disqualifier

The disqualifer's main concern: Fetuses don't deserve to be treated as if they were equal to born humans because they are different from us.

Your objective: Show that the differences between born and unborn humans are as trivial as racial or sex differences and therefore do not justify depriving these humans of the right to life.

★ ★ ★

Pro-choice: I just don't see how you can think a tiny embryo is a human being.

Pro-life: How would you define a human being?

PC: Someone who can think and feel and actually function in the world. Not some microscopic clump of cells.

PL: It seems that for you a human being has to act a certain way to be human. Would you agree that an unborn child is biologically human, or that he is growing and has human DNA?

PC: Sure, but being human is more than just having human DNA. Being human is about thinking and feeling. Embryos just sort of float there in the womb. They aren't people.

PL: Okay, you said that when a child is an embryo he is different. I agree he's tiny. But why does size make us valuable? Do you think a premature infant, who is probably 90 percent smaller than us, has only a 10 percent right to live?

PC: It's just that when an embryo is that tiny, it can't think or feel.

PL: What kind of feeling or thinking is required to be a "full" human, or a person?

PC: More than what an embryo does, that's for sure.

PL: Could you be specific? What level of thinking does a person have to exhibit?

PC: I mean at least some level. An embryo can't even feel pain or anything.

PL: That's true, but why does being able to feel pain make someone a person? There are animals like squirrels that can feel pain. Are squirrels persons?

PC: No, they're the wrong species.

PL: What species does the human fetus belong to?

PC: I see where you're going. I'm just saying that *humans* who can feel pain are persons.

PL: Isn't that self-serving? There are people in comas who cannot feel pain. How is your definition any better than "Persons are any human who can talk"? Isn't that what separates us from animals? You know, language and rational thought?

PC: Well, fetuses don't have those, either.

PL: You're right. Unborn children don't have reasoning skills, but why does that matter? Newborn infants don't have rational thought, and we consider them persons just because they are human. Can't being human be a good enough reason to value unborn children?

PC: Yes, but newborns are already born, so it's different.

PL: That's true. I mean that is why we call them "newborns." But why should I care about that difference? How does where someone lives change whether they are a person or not?

PC: When you're born, you're in the world.

PL: I'm having a hard time understanding what you mean. Are you saying that before birth we live on a different planet?

PC: No, I'm saying that after birth we are viable. We can live on our own in the world.

PL: Okay, so would you say squirrels are persons, since they can "live on their own" and survive outside of the womb?

PC: I meant a person is any human being who can survive outside of the womb.

PL: Why is that true?

PC: Because that's what a person is. Before birth the fetus is totally dependent on a woman's body.

PL: And?

PC: That means it's not a person.

PL: Would you say that a newborn infant, who is totally dependent on born people, or even his own mother's body, is not a person?

PC: No, because he's born.

PL: It seems that you are trying to find any way to disqualify the unborn from being considered persons. When I show you that your requirements are arbitrary, you just change them. As a pro-lifer, my view is simply that all biological human beings are equally valuable, and they all have a right to life. Why can't we just treat all humans as equals regardless of how they function? Unless you can find a problem with my view, why shouldn't it be the view we put into the law?

8

The Autonomists

During a JFA outreach at the University of Northern Colorado, I watched a conversation between one of our pro-life volunteers and a pro-choice student I'll call Carrie. They seemed to be discussing the one question that matters most: "What are the unborn?" Carrie said abortion should be legal because a fetus is totally dependent on a woman's body. The volunteer recognized the "D" in SLED and said, "Okay, so dependency is what matters to you. But what if a two-year-old fell into a swimming pool, and he was totally dependent on you to live? Would it be okay to kill him by not saving him?"

"That's different," Carrie said. "The two-year-old isn't inside your body."

"Okay, so it's environment [the "E" in SLED] that matters," the volunteer said. "But how can a change of location make you a non-person?"

"You're not listening!" Carrie shouted. "If it's in her body and needs her in order to live, then abortion is okay."

"But how can you say someone isn't human based on his environment or degree of dependency?"

After seeing Carrie's impatience turn into outright anger, I stepped into the conversation. While the volunteer was making good arguments, those points were not relevant to what Carrie actually believed.

"I think you may have misunderstood Carrie," I told the volunteer. "She never said the unborn weren't human, she merely said abortion was okay." I turned to Carrie and said, "Carrie, is this your argument? It doesn't matter whether the unborn are human or not. What matters is that women have a fundamental right to control what happens within their bodies, and therefore abortion should be legal for that reason."

"Yes!" Carrie said. "That's my argument."

Three pro-choice arguments

Up to this point we have examined three types of pro-choice people. First, there are the pragmatists who *assume* the unborn are not human beings. They argue that abortion should be legal, because women need abortion in order to resolve difficult life circumstances. But the pragmatic arguments for abortion fail, since we don't make it legal to kill human beings merely to satisfy other people's needs.

The second type of pro-choice argument actually *argues*, or uses evidence and reasoning, to show the unborn are not human beings. If the unborn are as human as sperm cells, then abortion would not be homicide, and there would be no reason to outlaw it. The skeptic does not take a position on the humanity of the unborn and thinks abortion should be legal since "no one knows when life begins." But the arguments from biology in Chapter 6 show there is no doubt the unborn are at least biological human beings. Even if we weren't sure if the unborn were human beings, that is an argument against killing the unborn, since we shouldn't kill something that could be a valuable human being.

In lieu of the skeptic's abstention, the disqualifier said we know the unborn are not persons because they don't have the qualities we associate with "persons." However, the differences summarized in the SLED acronym are as morally trivial as race or sex. As a result, the disqualifier's arguments fail to show the unborn don't deserve to be protected under the law like all other biological human beings.

But along with arguments that *assume* and *argue* the unborn are not human, there is a third type of pro-choice argument.

It *admits* the unborn are human beings with a right to life but claims it is not wrong to abort them. These kinds of arguments, called "bodily rights arguments," claim that even if the unborn had the same right to life as born people, a woman's right to control her body trumps or outweighs her unborn child's right to live. For the people I call *autonomists*, it doesn't matter whether or not the fetus is a human being, because a woman has a right to bodily autonomy. This includes the right to have an abortion.

Bodily rights arguments are powerful because they ground the pro-choice advocate's position on moral principles with which most people agree. In *McFall v. Shimp* (1978), a Pennsylvania District Court ruled that no one could be forced to donate an organ or bodily tissue in order to save the life of another person.[182] Indeed, most people would find it absurd to think that the government could treat our bodies like public property and donate them without our consent.

While bodily rights arguments may appear to be strong defenses of abortion, they rest on faulty premises. Typically, either they rely on principles about bodily autonomy that are controversial or they treat pregnancy like an ordinary case of organ donation, ignoring key differences between the two cases. In this section I identify two different bodily rights arguments autonomists use to justify abortion: the "sovereign zone" argument and the "right to refuse" argument.

The sovereign zone argument

When some autonomists claim women can "do whatever they want with their bodies," they may mean that to them the unborn child is literally part of a woman's body, like an arm or kidney. Linguist Noam Chomsky seems to endorse this view in a 2013 address: "There is a strong debate at the moment with regards to a woman's right to control an organ of her own body—namely, the foetus."[183] Just as you have the right to trim your toenails, the argument goes, so you have the right to "trim" or remove an unwanted fetus.

But if a fetus is a part of his mother, then all pregnant women have two brains, two hearts, four lungs—and, 50 percent of the time, male genitalia![184] Clearly the unborn have their own bodies, and are not part of their mother's bodies. Most defenders of body-rights arguments maintain that women have an absolute right to control their bodies, even if the fetus is a human being and not an organ. Feminist author Amanda Marcotte writes, "For our purposes . . . pregnancy is an event that happens inside a woman's body, and the right to abortion is a right that women have to control their own bodies."[185] Hence, the human body is a "sovereign zone" exempt from the normal moral constraints society places on people's actions. Only the owner of a human body can determine the morality of actions that happen inside his or her body.

When answering the sovereign zone argument, affirm that you, too, care about people's privacy and their right to bodily integrity. You could say, "I don't want the government treating our bodies like public property, but shouldn't the government have a say in what we do to *other people* who live inside our bodies?" You can then provide some arguments that show the sovereign zone argument does not prove abortion is moral or even that it should be legal.

First, the premise "A person can do *anything* she wants with her own body" is controversial, and there are good reasons to think it is not true. Pro-choice feminist Sally Markowitz calls this kind of argument "vaguely disturbing" and says that many feminists consider an unlimited right to bodily autonomy to be a characteristically male ideal.[186]

Philosopher Louis Pojman supports legal abortion but rejects bodily rights arguments. He gives the fictional example of an extremely large man who is sitting on my wallet and refuses to move because "he has a right to do what he wants with his body." According to Pojman, I have a right to retrieve my property, and the man has a duty to move his body and no right to be restricting my property. Pojman also uses the examples of men being drafted to use their bodies in war and parents being required to use their bodies to care for their children as evidence that "there is no such thing as an absolute right to do whatever we want with our bodies."[187]

Mary Anne Warren is another pro-choice philosopher who rejects this argument. She writes:

> ... the appeal to the right to control one's body, which is generally construed as a property right, is at best a rather feeble argument for the permissibility of abortion. Mere ownership does not give me the right to kill innocent people whom I find on my property, and indeed I am apt to be held responsible if such people injure themselves while on my property. It is equally unclear that I have any moral right to expel an innocent person from my property when I know that doing so will result in his death.[188]

The U.S. Supreme Court rejected this argument in *Roe v Wade*. Justice Blackmun wrote, "In fact, it is not clear to us that the claim asserted by some *amici* that one has an unlimited right to do with one's body as one pleases bears a close relationship to the right of privacy previously articulated in the Court's decisions. The Court has refused to recognize an unlimited right of this kind in the past."[189]

I can't think of any other right that is absolute in the way that defenders of the sovereign zone argument claim the right to control one's body is absolute. No one has an absolute right to free speech; we ban shouting "Fire!" in a crowded building when there is no fire. No one has the absolute right to engage in illegal religious activities under the guise of "freedom of religion." Laws against illicit drug use, prostitution, selling organs, public urination, and indecent exposure show there is no absolute right to do anything we want with our bodies. In fact, all it takes to refute this argument is *one* example that shows we cannot do whatever we want with our bodies. If that principle is refuted, then so is the sovereign zone argument. Here are just a few examples I would use to refute this argument:

- Intentionally causing birth defects: The drug thalidomide was once used to ease nausea during pregnancy. After researchers discovered that it caused children to be born without arms or legs, it was withdrawn from the market. If the sovereign zone argument is correct, then women have the right to use thalidomide, even if it harms the child in their womb. If bodily autonomy doesn't justify hurting children with drugs like thalidomide, it doesn't justify killing them through abortion.[190]

- Intentionally causing multiple abortions: In 2008, Yale University student Aliza Shvarts allegedly impregnated herself multiple times in order to have multiple abortions and use the fetal remains for her senior art project.[191] If women have complete bodily autonomy, then Shvarts' actions would not be morally objectionable.

  Yet even NARAL Pro-Choice America condemned Shvarts's actions: "This 'project' is offensive and insensitive to the women who have suffered the heartbreak of miscarriage." If women do have absolute bodily autonomy, then Shvarts's actions are no more offensive than the bulimic who vomits food instead of digesting it. We might condemn bulimia for health reasons (something abortion advocates will rarely do when it comes to abortion), but we wouldn't say bulimics are "insensitive" to people who cannot digest their food.

◆ Deadly transfer: If it is possible to remove a late-term fetus and keep him alive in an incubator, then, theoretically, if the technology existed, one could take a premature infant from an incubator and transfer him into a woman's uterus. Nearly everyone agrees that it would be wrong to kill the child in the incubator. But according to the sovereign zone argument, it would not be wrong to kill that child after he was transferred back into the sovereign zone of the womb. It is ridiculous that an infant could be treated like a human being in one location (the incubator) and like disposable property in another (the uterus).

This particular example also answers the autonomist's objection that perhaps people may not be allowed to use their bodies for any purpose (such as urinating in public), but they can do whatever they want to anything *inside* their bodies. But if that were true, then as soon as the fetus was placed back inside the uterus, it could be killed for any reason, because it would be in the sovereign zone of a woman's body. Since most people reject this as barbaric, we can reject the sovereign zone argument for the same reason.

Sovereignty does not justify tyranny

"Sovereignty" has also been used to defend injustice in the past. For instance, proponents of racial segregation maintained that store owners had a right to control what went on in their stores and, as a result, a right not to serve blacks.[192] In the nineteenth century it was legal for a man to beat his wife as long as he did not cause her permanent injury. In 1864, a district court in North Carolina ruled, "A husband is responsible for the acts of his wife and he is required to govern his household, and for that purpose the law permits him to use towards his wife such a degree of force as is necessary to control an unruly temper. . . . [T]he law will not invade the domestic forum, or go behind the curtain."[193]

While the sovereign zone argument claims that the unborn are human beings, in reality it treats them like disposable property. Pro-life advocates should either ask the question, "Is it ever okay to treat people like property?" or "Does owning a place give us the right to hurt people who live there?"

Furthermore, the argument admits that the fetus is a person and by the argument's own logic has a right to bodily autonomy. If we would respect the bodily autonomy of a sleeping or unconscious born person by not killing him, then wouldn't we be bound to treat an unborn child in the same way? Regardless of the status of unlimited bodily autonomy, the sovereign zone version of the bodily rights argument fails to support legal abortion.

The "right to refuse" argument

In the bodily rights conversation on the Colorado campus, when I shared sovereign zone counterexamples with Carrie, she was taken aback by the gruesome consequence of her belief. She said, "Well, no. Maybe you can't do *whatever* you want with your body. All I'm saying is a pregnant woman doesn't have to keep the fetus alive. I know this will sound weird, but what if you were hooked up to someone that needed your body to live? Should you be forced to keep him alive?"

I smiled and said, "You mean a famous . . . unconscious . . . violinist?"

"You know where I'm going with this," Carrie said.

Maybe *you're* wondering where I'm going with this. The sovereign zone argument holds that pregnant women can do anything with their bodies, which is a very broad and indefensible claim. The second type of bodily rights argument, which I call the "right to refuse" argument, makes the more defensible claim that just as I have the right to refuse to let a stranger use my organs to survive, a pregnant woman has the right to refuse to let her unborn child use her organs in order to survive.

This argument has its origins in a famous thought experiment proposed by Judith Jarvis Thomson in 1971 that has come to be known as the "Violinist Argument."[194] Thomson rejected a version of the sovereign zone argument and wrote, "No doubt the mother has a right to decide what shall happen in and to her body; everyone would grant that. But surely a person's right to life is stronger and more stringent than the mother's right to decide what happens in and to her body, and so outweighs it."[195]

In place of this crude bodily rights argument, Thomson argued that a right to life does not include the right to be kept alive by another person. Here is a paraphrase of her famous thought experiment that allegedly proves this point:

> Imagine you wake up one morning in a hospital bed and your kidneys have been connected to a famous unconscious violinist. It turns out the Society of Music Lovers has kidnapped you and has connected you to this violinist in order to filter the rare blood type you both share. They must do this for nine months and only then will the violinist recover and no longer need your assistance. The hospital director apologizes for what the Society of Music Lovers has done to you, but insists that the violinist is a person with a right to life and therefore you cannot unplug yourself from him without killing him and violating his right to life.

Nearly everyone agrees that in the above situation it would be very kind of you to stay plugged in and let the violinist use your body for nine months. However, most people would also agree that no one should be forced to do such a thing, even if the violinist dies as a result of you "unplugging" from him. Defenders of the right-to-refuse argument claim that just as we cannot compel people to donate the use of their organs or body tissue in order to save the life of another person, we cannot force pregnant women by law to donate the use of their bodies to sustain the life of their unborn children.

In the face of the violinist thought experiment, pro-life advocates should resist the urge to say, "That could never happen!" It's only an analogy, and it could be restated with the more mundane example of being forced to donate blood to someone who has a rare blood type. We also should not casually dismiss Thomson's argument, since it is reputedly the most reprinted essay in the history of philosophy.[196] I can almost guarantee that if you take an introduction to philosophy or ethics course at a public university this argument will be discussed.

One quick response to Thomson's argument is to simply ask, "What if you were the violinist?" This shows that Thomson's analogy works only when viewed in a way that allows us to identify with pregnant women, but not with the dependent unborn child.

But pro-life advocates should point out to autonomists that we, too, believe in the right to control our bodies. We also believe in the right to refuse to donate organs or tissues to other people. After building common ground with these statements, the pro-life advocate must show that the moral rules surrounding the right to refuse to donate one's body as life support for a sick human do not apply to the case of aborting a healthy human being in the womb. It's helpful to highlight the following differences between Thomson's violinist thought experiment (or other cases of organ donation) and cases of pregnancy.[197]

- The "responsibility" objection
- The "parental obligation" objection
- The "organ use" objection

The "responsibility" objection

In the case of a stranger who will die unless I donate blood or bone marrow, I am not obligated to help him, because I was not involved in how he became ill. Likewise, if I'm the one who's been kidnapped in Thomson's violinist scenario, the reason the violinist is dying has nothing to do with me.

He has been connected to my body by the plotting of the Society of Music Lovers. But why is the fetus connected to a woman's body in pregnancy? Ninety-nine percent of the time, it is because the woman engaged in sexual intercourse, which is known to create dependent people (i.e., unborn children). In normal cases of pregnancy, both the mother and father more resemble Thomson's Society of Music Lovers than they resemble the kidnapped kidney donor, because they created an innocent child and caused that child to be dependent on a woman's body. If I freely engaged in an activity that I knew had the possibility of creating a helpless human life, I am responsible for creating that life, and I owe her whatever assistance she needs to survive.

One way to illustrate the responsibility objection is to invite the person to take part in a thought experiment first devised by my friend Tony George that could be called the "Reverse Violinist."[198] Imagine you wake up in a hospital to discover that your kidneys have been connected to Thomson's unconscious violinist. You decide that the violinist has no right to use your kidneys, and you unplug yourself and start to walk out of the room. The director of the hospital sees you and shouts, "Oh, no! You have to plug yourself back in or you will die!"

Feeling lightheaded and nauseous, you struggle back to the bed and replug yourself into the violinist. The hospital director explains to you that the violinist is a member of the Society of Musical Pranksters. The pranksters go around plugging their members' kidneys into sleeping or unconscious innocent people for the "thrill" of the experience. They take precautions to make sure no damage is done and that the members can be unplugged in a few minutes, but every now and then the bond sticks and the connection damages the innocent person's kidneys. This forces that person to rely on the use of the prankster's body for nine months until his own kidneys heal.

After hearing this, the stress of the situation causes you to pass out just as the violinist wakes up. The violinist decides that you have no right to use his body without his consent, and he unplugs from you. He walks out of the hospital, you die from kidney failure, and your lifeless body is disposed of in the hospital incinerator.

Surely this situation is terribly unjust. The violinist engaged in an activity he knew could cause someone like you to need the use of his body. Therefore, it seems outrageous to say he has the right to withhold the support you need to live, when he is responsible for placing you in need of his support in the first place.

Burglars, people seeds, and replicators

Thomson attempts to rebut this objection in her original paper with two counterexamples. The first involves a burglar who enters a woman's house because she left the window open. According to Thomson, the responsibility objection holds that the woman must let the burglar stay, since "she is partially responsible for his presence there, having voluntarily done what enabled him to get in, in full knowledge that there are such things as burglars, and that burglars burgle."[199] But the woman is not responsible for the burglary; the burglar is, because he is a moral agent and chose to commit a crime. The unborn child does not "invade" the uterus in the same way, so the woman—and the man she had intercourse with—are responsible for the child's presence in her body.

Thomson's second example is more promising and involves small "people seeds" that float through open windows and burrow themselves in one's carpet until they grow into children. In her example, some people even buy mesh screens (i.e., contraception) to keep the people seeds from floating through their windows, but every now and then the mesh fails. According to Thomson, just as the people seeds have no right to live in your home, even if you are "responsible" for them being there, an unborn child does not have a right to use a woman's body, even if she is "responsible" for the child being there. After all, why should any of us have to tolerate a life without "fresh air" (i.e., sexual intercourse) just to avoid having to take care of people seeds?

But the analogy doesn't hold. First, I'm not confident one is justified in killing the people seeds any more than one is justified in killing a toddler who wandered through your unlocked front door. Second, the act of opening a window is causally related and naturally ordered toward letting in fresh air. While the air may be refreshing or noxious (i.e., sexual relations may be pleasurable or unpleasurable), there is no mistaking the fact that opening a window is done with the intent of letting air into a room. Even if you weren't intending to let air in but just wanted to feel the breeze, you are still responsible for the immediate consequences of letting the air inside (such as if it comprised odorless, toxic gas). Even if you aren't responsible for the burglars or people seeds that float through the window, you are responsible for that toward which your act is naturally ordered.

Likewise, sexual intercourse is causally related and naturally ordered toward the creation of new human life.[200] Opening a window does not begin the burgling or people-seed-drifting processes, but sexual intercourse does initiate the process of reproduction. Therefore, a person who engages in an activity that not only has a good likelihood of creating human life but is *ordered toward* that purpose, is responsible for the life that is created. This is why the "Reverse Violinist" story is more analogous to pregnancy than Thomson's examples. In that story you engage in an act ordered toward being plugged into helpless people. Perhaps by taking some precautions and relying on sheer luck you can engage in the prankster's activities without being plugged into someone; but should that happen, you are responsible for the poor soul you have caused to be dependent on you to survive.

Now, a critic could object that the "Reverse Violinist" thought experiment involves taking someone who already exists and making him worse off by plugging him into the prankster violinist. In pregnancy the fetus comes into existence already dependent on someone's body, and so it's not wrong to deny the fetus assistance.[201]

However, imagine a replicator machine that can create any kind of object. If I activate the replicator, there is a high chance that the machine will dispense $10,000. There is also a chance that along with the money the machine will dispense a healthy newborn infant.[202] If you could find no one else to care for this child, you would become the guardian or "parent."

Why? Because you engaged in an act that you knew was ordered toward creating a helpless human being, and now that human being stands in need of your assistance. Abandoning this infant to die would simply never be tolerated. Michael Tooley says in his book defending the morality of abortion:

> . . . the anti-abortionist can argue that although people in general may be under no moral obligation to allow the foetus the use of their bodies, even when it is necessary if the other individual is to survive, a pregnant woman is, in general, under a moral obligation to allow

the foetus the use of her body, since she is morally responsible for there being a foetus that stands in need of a life support system."[203]

While the replicator is a science fiction example like Thomson's violinist, we can also use the rare though real example of women who do not know they are pregnant until they give birth. If the autonomist believes that we have no obligation to the children we create, then there is no reason a mother who unexpectedly gives birth to a child in a field could not simply leave the child there. Suppose a woman lived in a country where abortion was illegal, or she could not afford to pay for an abortion. Upon giving birth at home could she simply abandon the child or "refuse to provide life-giving bodily aid" in the form of breast milk? If this woman does have a responsibility to care for this child because she was responsible for his existence, then it follows she would be responsible for that same child when it came into existence at conception, and abortion would be morally wrong.[204]

The "parental obligation" objection

Defenders of right-to-refuse arguments sometimes concede that their argument justifies abortion only in the case of rape, or in cases where the mother is not responsible for the fetus that needs her body in order to live. Because she did not freely take part in causing the pregnancy, the woman has no duty to continue a pregnancy that results from rape.

Pro-life advocates, while sympathizing with the horror of rape and the injustice of any pregnancy that follows from it, must show that violence is still not an acceptable solution to the situation. What's the difference between pregnancy resulting from rape and the woman who is kidnapped so her kidneys can be used to help the violinist? The cases seem on the surface to be exactly parallel.

On further investigation, though, the two cases are different in two important ways. First, the woman who was kidnapped for her kidneys is not the *parent* of the stranger who is in need. The woman pregnant from rape, however, is the parent of the fetus who is in need.

Similar to the responsibility objection, the parental obligation objection states that parents have greater duties toward their children than I have toward an unrelated violinist. When a man fathers a child, he is expected to care for the child even if he no longer wants to be a father. The man is expected to use his body to work and earn money in order to make child-support payments. This is the case even if he openly claims he no longer wants to be a parent to the children he has created. Simply put, he is a father whether or not he wants to be.

The courts have ruled that even fathers who are sexually assaulted and never consent to sex must still pay child support for the children they help create.[205] If fathers are expected to shoulder significant burdens to provide for the children they create, shouldn't mothers be expected to provide child support in the form of maintaining a safe environment in the womb, even if they do not cause the children to come into existence?

Imagine a woman is kidnapped and taken to an isolated cabin where she is held against her will and raped. She becomes pregnant, and the kidnapper gives her food and medicine to facilitate the pregnancy, because it is his child. When she is nine months pregnant, the woman manages to escape, but as she flees through the wilderness she gives birth.

Does this woman have any obligation to this child?[206] She did not choose to create this child, and we might understand if she abandoned the child for fear of being recaptured. (Although, as I discussed in Chapter 2, an excusable action isn't necessarily a moral one.) However, sometimes in life we are confronted with dilemmas that force us to make either a difficult, heroic choice or a gravely evil choice. In these cases there is no "easy" middle ground.[207] If a madman threatens me with torture unless I torture someone else, I am morally bound to submit to being tortured. If I give in and torture someone else, that is morally wrong, but it's understandable that not everyone feels capable of making such a sacrifice. Likewise, a woman faced with pregnancy caused by rape should choose, and be supported by her friends and society as a whole in choosing, to heroically give birth to this child and to refrain from the evil choice of violently ending the child's life.

Finally, when we say infants or fetuses have a right to life, what does that mean? For adults like you or me, a right to life usually means a right to be left alone and not to have anyone try to hurt or kill us. But children are different. Leaving an infant or fetus "alone" actually violates its right to life, because such an act kills it. If young humans such as infants and fetuses have a right to life, then which born humans have the corresponding duty to take care of them? The logical conclusion would be the parents, who created those children whether or not they willed to.[208]

The "organ use" objection

One key difference between the violinist case and pregnancy is that in the former you are a stranger and have no obligations to the violinist. Pregnancy involves one's own children, who do have a right to their parents' assistance. An autonomist could object that because we would never legally mandate men to donate their body parts as a form of child support (such as donating a kidney or bone marrow), we should not legally mandate women to provide child support through pregnancy.

On one campus in Colorado a woman presented this objection to me, which I at first found compelling. She said, "If you have sex and know that the conceived child will need you to donate a kidney ten years later, are you obligated to donate your kidney?"[209]

Along with parental obligation and responsibility, this brings us to the other key difference between the violinist case and pregnancy. In the violinist case, I use a part of my body that was not made for the violinist in order to keep this person alive. I am going to extraordinary means to save him, since the purpose of my kidneys is to filter my own blood and not anyone else's. By my withdrawing the use of my kidneys, the violinist dies. I am not the cause of his death; I have merely chosen not to save him. Is abortion a similar act of withholding an extraordinary use of an organ?

Even in a nonreligious framework it makes sense to say things like, "The purpose of the heart is to pump blood" or "The purpose of the lungs is to absorb oxygen." Some people may deny that our organs have any "purpose" or are "for" anything, but I don't think they would hold that attitude should their own organs become damaged or infected. Saying an organ isn't working properly would seem to imply that the organ has a proper way of functioning, or a "purpose" or "end" in its operations that is not being achieved.

The uterus's purpose seems clear: to support the life of an unborn child. Otherwise, why is it even inside the body at all? If the uterus is designed to sustain an unborn child's life, don't unborn children have a right to receive nutrition and shelter through the one organ designed to provide them with that *ordinary care?*[210]

Unlike in the violinist case, where I fail to save someone who is dying, abortion involves separating a healthy child from what it requires to live. Abortion is not an act of "failing to save" but is an act of killing that deprives a child of its right to live safely.[211] It is on par with putting your infant out in a snowstorm that directly kills him, not just "fails to save (him) from an environment in which (he) cannot survive."

An autonomist may object that pregnancy is not "ordinary care," because it causes the woman's body to undergo extraordinary and uncomfortable transformation. But it is a transformation toward which women's bodies are naturally ordered. Puberty also involves large-scale and uncomfortable changes to the body, but no one says puberty is an "extraordinary" event on par with organ donation.

Likewise, throughout all of human history, fertility and pregnancy were considered ordinary events, and anyone reading this page was involved in such an event. Providing shelter and nutrition in the womb is simply an ordinary amount of care (even if at times it can be painful or uncomfortable) that we expect parents to provide to their unborn children.

The consent argument

In her book *Breaking the Abortion Deadlock: From Choice to Consent*, Eileen McDonagh argues that the only issue that matters in the abortion debate is consent. Just as a woman may let a man initiate sex with her, and then refuse him midway through the act—and even use force to remove him from her body—a pregnant woman may allow a fetus to reside in her body; but if she rescinds the use of her body, she may remove the fetus with lethal force. If you think I'm being hyperbolic by comparing rape to pregnancy, don't blame me—blame McDonagh. She writes, "Nonconsensual pregnancy, like nonconsensual sexual intercourse, is a condition that must be stopped immediately because both processes severely violate one's bodily integrity and liberty."[212]

There are two fundamental problems with McDonagh's argument. First, we *consent* to *actions* such as buying a lottery ticket or engaging in sexual intercourse, while we *accept* the *consequences* of those actions, such as winning the lottery or becoming pregnant. We can consent to actions, because they are within our control, but the consequences of those actions lie outside of our control and so don't involve consent.[213] True, we might engage in actions based on those consequences, such as giving away our lottery money or having an abortion, but those actions can then be judged as being right or wrong. I might consent to drinking and driving, and a consequence of that action may be that I hit a pedestrian. I can't say, "Well, I never consented to helping this poor fellow, so I'm just going to drive away now." My duty to help him is a consequence that followed from the drinking I consented to. Likewise, when a man and woman consent to sexual behavior, their duty to help the child they create is a consequence they either rightfully accept or wrongfully reject.

Second, if McDonagh is right about pregnancy requiring consent, it follows that pregnancy that occurs without consent would be an evil, like rape, that should be stopped. Imagine doctors are attending to an unconscious woman and discover she's pregnant. Let's say neither the woman nor her friends or family knew she was pregnant. In this case, it seems that in the absence of consent, the doctors should abort the child. After all, if we found a man having sex with an unconscious woman, we would stop him, since the woman is incapable of consenting.

Most pro-choice advocates would agree that an abortion should not be done without the woman's consent. If these advocates were consistent, it is not abortion that should require active consent but pregnancy itself. It makes more sense to say that pregnancy is not an activity to which women consent but a duty to which they are obligated, just as the law obligates a father not to abandon his children, at least not financially.[214]

Final thoughts

What makes right-to-refuse arguments such as the kind used by Thomson so appealing is that assumptions about the human person with which many people disagree are artfully concealed within their premises. Thomson portrays a "person" as an individual who is not morally obligated to anyone he does not explicitly choose to be obligated to. This may be Thomson's idea of a person, but it is a very controversial view that not everyone accepts.

Many people support an alternative account of the human person that is summarized by Francis Beckwith: "[H]uman beings are persons-in-community and have certain natural obligations as members of their community that arise from their roles as mother, father, citizen, child, and so on."[215] Since children are helpless, their well-being is possible only if adults—making sacrifices if necessary—ensure it. This should be no different for unborn children, created in a consensual act designed to bring about their existence, who have a right to live in the wombs of their mothers, which are naturally designed to accommodate them.

Engaging the autonomist

The autonomist's main concern: If abortion is outlawed, people will lose the right to control their bodies and will have their autonomy violated.

Your objective: Show unborn children have rights to their own bodies that abortion violates. Highlight the difference between prohibiting abortion and requiring organ donation.

★ ★ ★

Pro-choice. It's the woman's body. She can do what she wants.

Pro-life: Do you mean that the unborn baby is a part of her body, like an arm or leg?

PC: No, that's not what I mean. Of course the unborn isn't an extra arm.

PL: So do we agree that the unborn is a separate human organism?

PC: Sure. But she should still be able to do what she wants, because it's in her body.

PL: Are you sure? Thalidomide was a drug prescribed
        in the late 1950s and early 1960s for women ex-
        periencing morning sickness during pregnancy.
        The drug is now known to have caused thou-
        sands of deformities in unborn children. Do you
        think pregnant women should have the right to
        take drugs like thalidomide that can cause their
        children to be born without arms or legs?

PC: No, I think you've misunderstood me. What I'm
        trying to say is that no one can force me to use
        my body to keep someone else alive. Can you
        make me give you a kidney to save your life? I'm
        personally opposed to abortion, and I would keep
        the baby. But I can't force other women to use
        their bodies in that way if they don't want to.

PL: Well, I'm glad to hear that you wouldn't support
        aborting your child; do we also agree that if a
        woman chooses to engage in sexual intimacy, she
        is responsible for the new life she's helped create?

PC: Yes, but it's still her body. It's her uterus, and she
        should have the right to refuse to let the fetus use
        it.

PL: I agree that her uterus is part of her body. But
        I think using one's uterus to sustain the fetus is
        different than donating one's kidney to help a
        sick person. Would you agree that the woman's
        kidneys were made to circulate and filter her own
        blood and not someone else's?

PC: Yes.

PL: For whom was her uterus designed?

PC: For the child—but not if the woman doesn't want
        the child.

PL: I see. Do you think that if a man has sex and fathers a child he should have to pay child support, even if he doesn't want the child anymore?

PC: That's different.

PL: Why do you think that it's different?

PC: He doesn't have to get pregnant.

PL: That's true, but he is legally required to give child support, even if he doesn't want to be the father of the child. Why shouldn't a woman be expected to provide child support in the form of a safe environment in the womb before birth, just as men are expected to provide financial support for children after birth?

PC: But what if the woman used contraception and didn't intend to get pregnant?

PL: I can see how that appears to change her responsibility, but I don't think it does. Let's say that I let my child go skateboarding and give him a helmet and every pad imaginable to protect him, because I never intend for him to get hurt. But somehow he still manages to break his arm while skateboarding. Am I still responsible for his care and recovery, even though I took what I thought were the necessary steps to make sure he would not get hurt?

PC: But that's different; he's your child.

PL: You mean he's my "born" child?

PC: Yes.

PL: Then isn't that the issue? If parents are responsible for caring for their children after their birth, why are they not equally responsible before their birth?

PART IV

People with Tough Questions

9

The Concerned

At a university in Colorado, one protester was enraged that the JFA exhibit contained large, graphic photos of aborted children. He claimed we were "shoving aborted fetus photos" in people's faces, even though JFA posts warning signs to give people an opportunity to look away from the exhibit if they choose. This protester returned the next day with a picture of a woman who had died from an illegal abortion. He shoved the photo within a few inches of the faces of the JFA staff members.

"What does this woman's death have to do with whether or not abortion should be legal?" I asked him.

"Because," he said, "if you make abortion illegal, women will die from back-alley abortions just like she did!"[216]

Back-alley abortions

While the pragmatist thought abortion could help women achieve the best outcome from an unintended pregnancy, *concerned* pro-choice advocates believe that legal abortion keeps the worst outcomes from occurring. They worry that if abortion is made illegal women will still have abortions, but instead of going to hospitals they will go to untrained abortionists who will injure or kill them. Other women, they believe, will try to perform their own abortions with things like coat hangers, maiming or killing themselves. Since this is essentially a pragmatic argument for abortion, we can use Trot Out a Toddler to get the conversation back on the one question that matters most: "What are the unborn?"

First, we *agree* with them. If someone expresses concern about women dying from back-alley abortions, you should be a normal human being and be concerned, too. You could say, "I'm worried about anyone dying from an abortion procedure, whether it's an unborn child or a pregnant woman. I'm worried about them dying from either a legal or an illegal abortion. I don't want anybody to die!" Some pro-life advocates believe their position suffers if they admit to any more common ground than this. They sometimes argue that back-alley abortions are a myth created by pro-choice advocates, but this is unhelpful.

If abortion is made illegal, some women may still choose to have an abortion, regardless of the risk involved. There is a place to correct people on the facts about illegal abortion (and I'll get to that shortly), but for now I would simply say, "For the sake of the argument, let's agree that if abortion were made illegal, some women would still choose to have abortions, and they might be harmed in the process of doing that."

After agreeing, we must *apply* the argument to a born person. Remember the argument is, "Women should be allowed to legally kill their unborn children because they may hurt themselves if they try to kill those children illegally." Our "apply" should include a hypothetical case in which we make it legal so that it is safer for one born person to hurt another born person. You can use simple examples such as, "We don't legalize bank robbery to make it safer for bank robbers," or "We don't legalize terrorism to make it safer for terrorists," but these examples might make your audience think you are comparing post-abortive women to bank robbers and terrorists (you aren't; it's just an analogy).

A gruesome example

One example that I find particularly compelling is the practice of female genital mutilation. Female genital mutilation (FGM), also known as female genital cutting, is a cultural practice in Africa and the Middle East whereby young girls, including infants, have their genitals surgically removed or damaged in order to satisfy cultural purity requirements. This brutal act leaves women physically and emotionally scarred for life and is condemned by nearly all human-rights organizations.[217]

Now, imagine someone makes the following argument: Some immigrant communities in the United States still practice female genital mutilation, and since it is illegal, it doesn't happen in sanitary hospitals. Instead, family members take these girls to back alleys where untrained mutilators cause more injury or even kill the girls. Shouldn't we keep FGM legal so that it is safer for these girls who have to undergo it?

For most people the answer is, "No, we should not allow female genital mutilation to be legal. Women shouldn't be mutilated in either sterile or unsterile facilities." So we've agreed, applied, and now we *ask why*. "Why shouldn't it be legal?" Most people, especially feminists and human-rights advocates will say, "Because it's a brutal act of violence. It harms young girls for life. It's degrading and disgusting!"

We agreed, applied, asked why, and now *ah!* We might say, "Okay, so it isn't about safety, since we would never legalize a medical procedure designed to mutilate an innocent girl so that it is 'safer' to perform. If these little girls are human beings, then we can't make it legal to 'safely' mutilate their genitals. In the same way, if unborn children are human beings, we shouldn't make it legal to 'safely' mutilate their entire bodies by abortion."

When people ask whether abortion should remain legal so that it is "safe," I ask in response, "Safe for whom, the mother or child?" Shouldn't we promote nonviolent solutions that are good for both mother and child?

My friend Timothy Brahm offers another simple counterexample for this objection. Imagine a woman wants to kill her ten-year-old but is worried that her fairly large child will hurt her as she is trying to kill him. Should we make it legal for a woman to have others kill the child so it is safer for her? The concerned pro-choicer may object and say, "That's completely different. The fetus is not a child!" But that returns us to discussion of the one question that matters most in the abortion debate: "What are the unborn?"

The pro-choice philosopher Mary Anne Warren agrees that the back-alley objection is irrelevant. "The fact that restricting access to abortion has tragic side effects does not, in itself, show that restrictions are unjustified," she says, "since murder is wrong regardless of the consequences of prohibiting it."[218] The main question we must focus on when pro-choice advocates bring up this objection is, "Should we make it legal to kill an innocent person so that it is safer for the killer?" If the answer is no, then we must reject the argument from unsafe abortions.

Getting the facts right

Pro-choice advocates sometimes say, "Even if you outlaw abortion, it will still happen but just be more dangerous." First, as we've seen, abortion is equally dangerous for the child whether it's legal or illegal, and so justice demands the child be protected from this procedure. Second, any activity that is banned will still happen illegally, be it abortion, rape, robbery, or any other crime. Laws can't stop all crime, but they can reduce the frequency with which these crimes are committed.

Sometimes pro-choice advocates say this does not apply to abortion and that 1.2 million illegal abortions occurred annually in the United States before *Roe v. Wade*.[219] But a 1981 study found the average number of illegal abortions in the U.S. during that time was about 98,000, or about 10 percent of what the rate became shortly after *Roe v Wade*.[220]

The number of U.S. women who died from illegal abortions prior to *Roe v. Wade* is also exaggerated. I once attended a debate at which the pro-choice advocate used the well-worn statistic that, prior to *Roe v. Wade*, 5,000 to 10,000 women in the U.S. died every year from illegal abortions.[221] During the question and answer period, I said, "According to the Centers for Disease Control, only 39 women in the U.S. died from illegal abortion deaths in 1972, and 24 women died from legal abortions in that year.[222] Yet you claimed that, prior to *Roe v. Wade*, 5,000 to 10,000 women died every year from illegal abortions in the United States. Do you have a source for this exaggerated claim?"

"It's called 'Google,' young man," she said. "I don't have time for any more of your questions." I never was able to "Google" or find her source online. If she had not cut me off, I would have also quoted former Planned Parenthood President Mary Calderone, who said in 1960:

> Abortion is no longer a dangerous procedure. This applies not just to therapeutic abortions as performed in hospitals but also to so-called illegal abortions as done by physicians. In 1957 there were only 260 deaths in the whole country attributed to abortions of any kind. . . . Second, and even more important, the conference estimated that 90 percent of all illegal abortions are presently being done by physicians.[223]

Pro-choice advocates sometimes cite studies claiming that thousands of women die from illegal abortions annually in other countries around the world. But these studies usually describe impoverished nations where surgery, legal and illegal, is dangerous due to a lack of emergency rooms and modern medical care.[224] To be fair, we should compare legal and illegal maternal abortion deaths among *developed* nations. In 2010, the United States had a maternal mortality rate of 21 deaths per 100,000 live births. In Ireland and Poland, where abortion is illegal except in rare cases, the maternal mortality rate per 100,000 live births was 6 deaths in Ireland and 5 deaths in Poland.[225]

Any death from abortion is tragic, whether it's a woman or her child, regardless of whether the procedure was legal. But the answer to these tragedies is not to make it legal to kill certain people. There is no reason to think that a developed country cannot protect the health of unborn and born human beings by outlawing medical procedures that are designed to kill both.

Finally, every year thousands of women in the United States are unable to get an abortion because it is too expensive. Sometimes abortion providers simply refuse to perform abortions for women who are too far along in their pregnancies.[226] But the vast majority of these women do not break the law in order to pay for their abortions, nor do they try to perform an abortion on themselves.[227] Instead, they give birth to their child. If most women do not break the law to obtain expensive or hard-to-get abortions, then shouldn't we expect that, in general, women would not break the law in order to obtain illegal abortions?

How much time should she get?

In a 2007 video that was uploaded to YouTube called the *Libertyville Abortion Demonstration*, various pro-life demonstrators were asked, "If abortion were illegal, what should the punishment be for a woman who has an abortion?"[228] Many of the protesters seemed confused and didn't know how to answer the question. Some said that the woman is punished enough by the abortion process and were reluctant to say she should also be punished legally. Pro-choice advocates use this hesitation to show that if even pro-life advocates don't really react as if abortion is homicide, abortion should remain legal.

But even if pro-life advocates did not believe women should be punished for choosing abortion, that would not disprove the pro-life position. Inconsistent people can still be right. Prior to the Civil War, states that outlawed slavery still did not give African Americans the same legal protections whites had (e.g., blacks could not use white public facilities).

But the fact that some laws failed to treat African Americans as equals did not invalidate other laws that *did* treat them as equals (such as bans on slavery). Likewise, laws that fail to treat the unborn as equals in one respect (such as laws that do not severely punish people who kill the unborn) would not invalidate other laws that did treat the unborn as equals (such as abortion bans).[229]

How would I answer the question, "What punishment should a woman who obtained an illegal abortion receive?" I would say, "It depends." I don't think we can simply say the woman has suffered enough from the abortion itself and doesn't need to be punished. We would never say a mother who drowned her children in the bathtub had suffered enough from watching them die and so didn't need to be punished. If she knew it was wrong and chose to do it anyway, then a punishment would be deserved.[230]

After all, isn't it unfair that in many states men and women who kill a *wanted* fetus are legally punished? Most people did not consider it outrageous when Scott Peterson was convicted in 2004 of two counts of murder for the death of his wife, Laci, and their unborn son, Conner. So why wouldn't we charge Laci with committing a crime if she were to kill her own child under the same circumstances? It is precisely the question of circumstances that makes it difficult to answer whether or not women should be punished for obtaining illegal abortions.

Does infanticide deserve punishment?

When I am asked about how women who choose illegal abortions should be punished, I reframe the question in order to get at the moral logic that hides behind our conflicting emotions. The larger question we should ask is, "What punishment should women receive when they kill any of their children, born and unborn?"

One example I use comes from Virginia, where in 2009 the local district attorney refused to prosecute a woman who gave birth to her child in a hotel room and then smothered the child. An investigator from the local sheriff's office said that, because the umbilical cord was still attached, what the mother did was no different than a late-term abortion. She said:

I believe everyone was upset, except for the person who should have been upset, the mother. In the state of Virginia as long as the umbilical cord is attached and the placenta is still in the mother, if the baby comes out alive the mother can do whatever she wants to with that baby to kill it. And in the state of Virginia, it's no crime. . . . Simply because the mother was there, and the baby had not taken its own identity allegedly at this point, it makes the baby not its own person.[231]

If we can agree that this woman should have been punished for what was undoubtedly infanticide, then we should ask, "What should the punishment be if she had killed the baby five minutes earlier while it was in her womb?" I don't think such a short difference in time and location would change our intuitions about the matter. What about five weeks earlier? Or five months earlier? What *should* the punishment be for a woman who chooses abortion?

The most honest answer is the same answer we give for every other crime: "It depends." In fact, if the pro-life advocate is stuck in a sound-bite situation, he can simply say that punishments for crimes are complex matters but protecting the innocent is simple, and the unborn should simply be protected under the law. Punishments for crimes are not uniform because they are based on the criminal's intent and the circumstances involved and not just on the kind of crime committed. Not every homicide is considered first-degree murder, and punishment for homicide can vary from the death penalty to probation.

For many women, abortion has been legal for their entire lives, and in the United States there are no public education campaigns to discourage them from having an abortion (unlike for other harmful things such as smoking). Professional medical organizations endorse abortion, and many women choose abortion when their partner, family, or health-care provider suggests or imposes it upon them.

Finally, most women do not intend to kill their child through abortion. They just don't want to be pregnant. They may even think abortion is a form of surgical contraception that keeps a potential person from becoming an actual baby.

Because of these factors, women may not be completely morally responsible for choosing abortion and so may not deserve as harsh a punishment as concerned pro-choice advocates think they would receive under an abortion ban. This reasoning is not a case of special pleading for the pro-life view; it is used to justify giving lighter sentences to women who kill their born infants.[232] Infanticide is considered less serious than first-degree murder, because the perpetrators of that crime are usually a danger only to their own offspring and are often under extreme emotional stress. Punishments for infanticide can be as light as one to two years' imprisonment, or even probation.[233]

If abortion were made illegal, "feticide" laws could be enacted that mirror current infanticide laws in language and range of punishments. That way, women who choose abortion, as well as the men who cooperate and the doctors who perform the procedure, would be appropriately punished based on each person's level of moral responsibility.

If fetuses are persons, then women are not

In 2008, Colorado became the first state where pro-life advocates attempted to amend the state constitution to define the word *person* to mean "a human being who exists from the moment of fertilization."[234] Instead of arguing that the unborn were not persons because they lacked certain criteria such as sentience or viability, opponents of the "personhood amendment" argued that the unborn could not be persons because such an idea leads to absurd consequences, including:

- Fetuses could be claimed as dependents on tax returns and counted in censuses.
- Pregnant women would be allowed to ride by themselves in carpool lanes.
- Pregnant women would be monitored by the state to ensure they did not over-exercise, miss their prenatal vitamins, or put their fetuses in danger in any way.
- All miscarriages would be investigated as the suspicious death of a child.
- All hormonal contraception would be banned, since it can prevent an embryo from implanting in the mother's womb.
- All in vitro fertilization would be banned, since surplus embryos are destroyed in the process.

Most of these objections can be dismissed when we recognize that making it illegal to kill the unborn would not entail giving them every imaginable social privilege. As long as the unborn have a right to live, and their mothers have social rights and privileges, then state benefits given to pregnant women will be passed on to their unborn children. Furthermore, there is no easy way to determine if a woman is or has been pregnant, making many of the supposed consequences of personhood amendments moot.

The idea that pregnant women would be monitored to make sure they are not over-exercising or eating poorly is just silly. No one monitors born children to make sure they are being given vitamins or proper exercise. We investigate born children only when there is evidence (such as bruises) to believe that neglect or abuse is taking place. Since the unborn can't be observed, we assume that as long as the pregnancy is continuing, the child is safe.

If a woman were to visit a known abortion provider, then an investigation may be warranted. Otherwise, we would treat the parent-child relationship in pregnancy with the same privacy we extend to parents and born children. If a pregnant woman does miscarry, we probably would not investigate the matter, because there would be no way to determine the cause of the embryo's death.

The second problem with these kinds of objections is that they operate on mistaken moral intuitions. If hormonal contraceptives (provided they are truly contraceptive in their intent) could indirectly kill an unborn child, they would not have to be banned any more than other poisons are banned that can indirectly kill children. Society may simply need to regulate and prescribe how they are used.

In regard to in vitro fertilization, if more people were aware that the embryos killed in IVF clinics are whole human beings, they may be more apt to want IVF banned, especially since it can contribute to an abortion mentality. In her *New York Times* article "The Two-Minus-One Pregnancy," Ruth Padawer interviewed a woman who aborted one of her twins in order to facilitate an IVF procedure. The woman says:

> If I had conceived these twins naturally, I wouldn't have reduced this pregnancy, because you feel like if there's a natural order, then you don't want to disturb it. But we created this child in such an artificial manner—in a test tube, choosing an egg donor, having the embryo placed in me—and somehow, making a decision about how many to carry seemed to be just another choice. The pregnancy was all so consumerish to begin with, and this became yet another thing we could control.[235]

Finally, concerned pro-choice advocates who claim that treating the unborn as persons would spell the collapse of civilization seem ignorant of history. Abortion was illegal in the United States through most of our history, and during that time there were no miscarriage investigation squads, no secret police monitoring pregnant women, and no government officials counting fetuses in censuses. There were only law enforcement officers who would arrest rogue abortion providers, which seems rational if the unborn are human beings whom abortion kills.

Engaging the concerned

The concerned's main concern: There will be widespread, disastrous consequences if abortion is made illegal.

Your objective: Show that abortion is already a disaster and that fears related to outlawing abortion are unfounded.

★ ★ ★

Pro-choice: So, if you're pro-life, does that mean you think abortion should be illegal?

Pro-life: I think humans, including unborn humans, should not be killed because they are unwanted or different from other humans. That means I think directly aborting a child in order to end its life should be illegal—and is in fact illegal if its parents want the child. I just think the unwanted ones should get the same treatment.

PC: So you're okay with women going into back alleys and dying because they have to get illegal abortions.

PL: No, that would be terrible. I'm certainly not okay with women dying from illegal abortions.

PC: Then why not keep abortion legal?

PL: It seems like you're allowing only two options. Women either get legal or illegal abortions. Why can't women just not get any abortions and we as a society take care of both mother and child?

PC: Because some women can't handle having a baby, so they will get an abortion even if it is illegal. Because of people like you, they'll die at the hands of untrained abortionists, or they will kill themselves trying to abort with a wire coat hanger.

PL: I agree it would be tragic if a woman and her unborn child died from an illegal abortion. But can I ask you a question? Should we make it safer for one person to kill another person by making homicide legal?

PC: What?

PL: People have always killed each other—shouldn't we make it legal? That way at least the murderers won't be shot by the police.

PC: That's absurd.

PL: Why?

PC: Because murder *should* be illegal.

PL: Why?

PC: Because it's wrong to kill people.

PL: Okay, so if the unborn are persons, then shouldn't we make it illegal to kill them?

PC: But they aren't persons.

PL: I think that's where we disagree. If the unborn are not human beings, then you're right—outlawing abortion is as silly as outlawing tonsillectomies. But if the unborn *are* human beings, it would be wrong to keep abortion legal so that it's safer for men and women to kill these human beings.

PC: So are you going to have police follow pregnant women everywhere to make sure they don't secretly have abortions?

PL: Do the police follow women around now with their born children to make sure they don't secretly kill them? All I'm saying is that we don't keep injustice legal. Even if it's hard at first to return to the way things were, justice demands that the law protect the innocent.

PC: The law also punishes people who kill the innocent. Should women who have abortions be given the death penalty?

PL: Of course not, but I also oppose the death penalty in general and believe the state should execute people only if that is the only way to stop them from killing again. But even if I did support the death penalty, that wouldn't mean I support its use for everyone who is convicted of killing a human being. Don't you think the punishment ought to fit not just the crime but the intentions and the circumstances?

PC: Sure, but I'm asking you what the punishment should be for a woman who has an abortion.

PL: Well, it depends. Do you think we should punish women who drown their born babies in bathtubs?

PC: If the woman isn't crazy, then yes.

PL: Why?

PC: Because it's wrong to kill human beings.

PL: Okay, then if the unborn are human beings and someone—whether a man or woman—chooses to kill them, shouldn't the punishment be based on how culpable he or she is?

PC: But a fetus isn't a human being. Abortion is not the same as killing a born baby.

PL: I agree born and unborn children differ from one another, but people of different races also differ from one another. Even if people are different, how does it follow that we should treat them differently or not protect them under the law?

The Conflicted

At one pro-life outreach, a short young woman with long auburn hair walked up to me and asked, "Are you with the pro-lifers?"

"Yes." I replied. "What can I do for you?"

"When I was thirteen I was raped and had to get an abortion," she said. "Do you think girls like me should not be allowed to get an abortion?"

Now, I could have glibly answered her question by saying "No" or asking, "Why would you punish the child for his father's crimes?" But this answer lacks compassion and empathy. When people ask about abortion in the case of rape, they usually don't want to know if the unborn are human; they want to know if *you* are human.[236] Do you actually care about women in these terrible circumstances or are you just out to win an argument?

I'm not encouraging pro-life advocates to fake compassion in these cases in order to win an argument. I hope they will be genuine and thoughtful human beings who are willing to open up their hearts and be compassionate for the sake of doing the right thing. I'll explain a little later on how I responded.

According to a 2011 Gallup poll, while only 36 percent of Americans support legal abortion for women who can't financially care for a child, 75 percent support legal abortion for women who are pregnant due to rape or incest.[237] Like the *concerned*, the *conflicted* are a kind of pragmatist. They generally don't like abortion and they may even believe some or most abortions should be illegal.

However, they are also torn over the so-called "hard cases," like pregnancy from rape. To them, abortion is the least-bad solution to a nightmare scenario. In order to respond to the conflicted we must use the tools that were effective with other pragmatists (such as Trot Out a Toddler) but with extra empathy in order to show we understand the emotional dilemmas inherent in these hard cases.

Fetal deformity

My friend Drew once told me about a condition called "Stone Man Syndrome" that causes a person's connective tissue, such as muscle and ligament, to turn into bone.[238] The person's joints freeze, and attempts to remove the bone through surgery cause even more bone to grow in its place. In severe cases, the victim chooses a position he wants his body to be in permanently.

Drew then asked me, "Trent, if we could detect this condition in a two-celled embryo, wouldn't it be better to just abort that embryo than to let the child grow up with a condition like that?"

I thought about it for a moment. "Wow, that's a really hard case. But let me ask you this question. Suppose we could not detect this disease until after birth. Do you think it would be okay to euthanize a healthy newborn that happened to have this disease?"

"I'm not sure," Drew said. "But I see your point."

If the unborn are as human as a two-year-old, then, just as we wouldn't kill a two-year-old because he had a debilitating disease, we shouldn't kill an unborn child because he has a debilitating disease.

When using Trot Out a Toddler, it's important to stress you agree that a negative prenatal diagnosis is devastating for parents. Many of these parents would never think of aborting their child and come to do so only after the "advice" of misguided doctors. As a result, they may think it is better to end their child's life in the womb than let their child suffer after birth. This is especially true for terminal conditions like anencephaly, a condition that occurs when the child is born without an upper brain and will die a few hours or days after birth.

Is it moral to abort anencephalic children? Consider the case of a two-year-old who tragically finds his dad's gun and blows off the top of his head.[239] As he lies in the hospital dying from his injuries (which would mirror the plight of an anencephalic child), we would certainly do everything we could to ease this child's suffering, but most people wouldn't condone killing the child.[240]

It's important to remember that many children who are aborted due to a "fetal deformity" actually have mild conditions (or are even healthy and the diagnosis was incorrect). These mild conditions can include cleft palate or clubfoot, both of which can be treated with surgery. Other abortions due to fetal deformity are because the child has Down syndrome. This condition is neither terminal nor debilitating, and people with Down syndrome are able to lead happy and productive lives.

Of course, raising a child with Down syndrome is not easy—but then again, what child is easy to raise? When this objection is brought up, I am reminded of my friend David, whose son Dylan has Down syndrome and is, well, strange. Unlike "normal" people who ignore others, Dylan says "hi" and "bye" to nearly everyone he meets. But the most dangerous place for someone like Dylan to live is not in a war-torn country or an impoverished ghetto—it's in the womb, since some U.S. studies have estimated that nearly 90 percent of unborn children diagnosed with Down syndrome are aborted.[241]

The desire to eliminate Down syndrome by eliminating the unborn humans who are diagnosed with it reeks of eugenic evil. The nation of Denmark has even instituted a program of free prenatal testing that has doubled the number of children with Down syndrome who are aborted each year.[242]

What about in the case of rape?

The year 2012 was a disaster for pro-life politicians. During a Missouri senate campaign, Republican Congressman Todd Akin was asked if he supported abortion in the case of rape. He evaded the question by claiming that most women do not become pregnant as a result of rape.

"From what I understand from doctors, that's really rare," he said. "If it's a legitimate rape, the female body has ways to try to shut that whole thing down."[243]

Aside from the fact that Akin seemed implicitly to subscribe to a difference between legitimate rape and illegitimate rape, pundits mocked Akin's apparent lack of knowledge about human biology. In fact, some studies seem to indicate that pregnancy rates may actually be higher from rape than they are from consensual intercourse (although abortions due to rape or incest account for less than 2 percent of abortions each year).[244]

But Akin's comment was far from the pinnacle of media gaffes made by pro-life politicians. In a debate two weeks before the November presidential election, Indiana senate candidate Richard Mourdock said in response to the same question, "Life is that gift from God, and I think even when life begins in that horrible situation of rape, that it is something that God intended to happen."[245]

What many people took from the comment was that Mourdock thought God intended certain rapes to happen. Mourdock later clarified that he meant God intended for a particular life to come into existence, not for the rape itself to happen; but the damage was done. The next night President Obama appeared on the *Tonight Show* and said, "Rape is rape. It is a crime. These various distinctions about rape don't make too much sense to me."[246] President Obama went on to receive the majority of the female vote, one key factor in his reelection to the presidency.

So how do pro-life advocates answer the question "Would you allow abortion in the case of rape?" without stepping on a verbal landmine? When the young college woman I described at the beginning of this chapter told me she had been raped and had chosen abortion, I engaged her in a form of non-confrontational dialogue.

"Wow, that's awful," I said. "I'm so sorry that happened to you. I'm guessing the guy who did it wasn't caught, either." She said he wasn't.

I continued, "Honestly, I think that is one of the things that makes rape such an awful crime. Not only does it hurt the woman, but the rapist usually gets away with it. Or if he's caught he gets a slap on the wrist. Sometimes we as a culture even blame women for being raped, and that's inexcusable. But I think that just as the woman who has been raped is an innocent victim who needs our help, the child who is created is also an innocent victim and needs our help. The only person who deserves punishment is the rapist.

Think about this: In 2008, the U.S. Supreme Court struck down the state of Louisiana's statute allowing the death penalty for child rape.[247] In our country it is illegal to kill the man who rapes a child, but the child conceived in rape can be killed. Shouldn't we overcome this unfairness and protect both the mother and child from harm and punish the rapist?"

Another way to empathize with someone who is concerned about abortion in the case of rape is to say that you believe rape victims should be able to prevent a child from being conceived. Even though the Catholic Church teaches that contraception is an intrinsic evil, faithful Catholic theologians have taught for decades that the use of contraception in the case of rape is a justifiable act of self-defense.[248] The United States Conference of Catholic Bishops states:

Compassionate and understanding care should be given to a person who is the victim of sexual assault. Health care providers should cooperate with law enforcement officials and offer the person psychological and spiritual support as well as accurate medical information. A female who has been raped should be able to defend herself against a potential conception from the sexual assault. If, after appropriate testing, there is no evidence that conception has occurred already, she may be treated with medications that would prevent ovulation, sperm capacitation, or fertilization.[249]

Although empathy is important and necessary, it can only get you so far. Some people demand a yes or no answer to the question "Is abortion okay in the case of rape?"

Now that you've laid the emotional groundwork of empathy, you are in a position to give a logical answer to the question. In order to do that, we use Trot Out a Toddler, because the awfulness of rape does not address the question "What are the unborn?" If abortion is a pragmatic solution to a rape pregnancy, Trot Out a Toddler is our way to show that this "solution" shouldn't even be on the table, because it involves killing an innocent human being.

Here's how I usually use TOAT in this case. Imagine a woman has sexual relations with her husband, and the next day a stranger rapes her. Several weeks later she discovers she's pregnant but doesn't know if her husband or the rapist fathered the child. A DNA test reveals the husband is the child's father. The woman gives birth, and three months later the doctors call back while she is home alone with the baby. They inform her that they made a mistake and that the rapist is actually the baby's father.

The woman is devastated and can't stand to have this "thing" grow up who one day might become a rapist himself. Should she be allowed to kill this product of rape while it sleeps in the crib? If not, then why not? Shouldn't we forbid killing the product of rape in the womb for the same reason we forbid killing the product of rape in the crib: that both are innocent human beings?[250]

Rape is a horrifying evil, but should our answer to the evil of rape be to commit further evil against an innocent person? If a woman's rapist was released from jail and she could not sleep at night knowing he was out there and might strike again, we would have compassion for her awful situation. But we would not advise her to kill her rapist just so she can sleep at night. If we can exercise compassion for a victim of rape without endorsing a lethal solution for the guilty party, surely we should be able to endorse a nonlethal solution for the innocent child who did not asked to be conceived.

The health of the mother

Preeclampsia is a condition in which the pregnant woman has high blood pressure and an increased amount of protein in her urine. If left untreated, this condition can cause damage to the kidneys and can even be fatal. How should doctors treat a pregnant woman whose health is deteriorating during her pregnancy?

In cases like this, we must remember that when we see a pregnant woman in a hospital we are actually observing two patients: one who hands over the insurance card and another who is hidden. According to the medical textbook *William's Obstetrics*, "[T]he status of the fetus has been elevated to that of a patient who, in large measure, can be given the same meticulous care that obstetricians provide for pregnant women."[251]

In any medical decision, doctors should observe the following maxim: "Kill the problem, not the patient." It is acceptable to kill a bacterium, a virus, or any other damaged tissue if it is threatening the mother or her unborn child. However, it is not acceptable to *directly* kill a human being such as the mother or her unborn child in order to improve the health of someone else. For example, imagine you were stuck on a life raft with someone who had a contagious disease. If you become infected you will develop a serious but nonfatal condition (such as blindness or the loss of a limb). It would certainly be difficult to endure such an affliction, but that difficulty would not make it moral for you to directly kill this other person to protect yourself from becoming sick.

Even though modern medicine can manage most pregnancy complications, there are still risks to mothers as they nurture their unborn children through pregnancy. These risks call us to be immeasurably grateful for the sacrifices pregnant mothers make for their unborn children. But those same risks do not justify medical professionals directly killing these unborn children.

But what if the threat to the mother's life is fatal? What if the other person in the life raft has a disease that is going to kill you, though he does not intend for it to do so? Is it okay to kill an innocent person in that situation?

The life of the mother

When people ask me about abortion to save a woman's life, I like to clarify their question by dividing pregnancy into the three stages in which this dilemma arises.[252]

First, if a woman's life is threatened late in pregnancy after the fetus is viable, since it takes longer than a day to stretch the cervix wide enough to abort such a large fetus, it makes more sense to simply deliver the child by C-section.[253] I ask prochoice advocates, "Wouldn't it be better to deliver the child whole and give him a chance to live (even if the chance is small) as opposed to delivering him in pieces with no chance to live?"

In the second case, in very early pregnancy when there is essentially no hope the child can be saved, it is permissible for doctors to perform a lifesaving operation on the mother with the indirect result being the death of the child. According to the U.S. Catholic bishops' directives for Catholic hospitals, "Operations, treatments, and medications that have as their direct purpose the cure of a proportionately serious pathological condition of a pregnant woman are permitted when they cannot be safely postponed until the unborn child is viable, even if they will result in the death of the unborn child."[254] The most notable example of this case is an ectopic pregnancy that occurs when the embryo implants in some place other than the uterus, which in almost all cases ends up being in the fallopian tube.

Unlike in late pregnancy, the child cannot be removed and safely placed somewhere else, such as in an incubator. Any removal of the child will result in his death. In these cases it is morally acceptable to remove the damaged section of the fallopian tube where the child implanted.[255]

This action is moral because the primary intention is to remove the damaged section of the fallopian tube that is a threat to the mother's health. The child's death is an unintended consequence of this morally neutral action.

What about a threat to a mother's life that arises after the stage when ectopic pregnancy is a concern but before the fetus is viable? Prior to *Roe v. Wade*, all states allowed abortions if there was a grave threat to the mother's life.[256] In all likelihood, this practice would continue if *Roe* were overturned and abortion could be made illegal again. However, Catholics would not take part in an abortion in which the child's death is *directly* caused as a means to save the mother's life, because we do not believe innocent people should be killed for that reason.[257]

For example, it would be wrong for a mother to kill her born child (even if that child were going to die anyway) because the mother needed a heart transplant, and her child had the only compatible donor match. In this case, the child's death is *direct* and serves as a means to save the mother and so is immoral; whereas, in the case of ectopic pregnancy, a doctor treats the damaged fallopian tube and the child dies *indirectly*, which is not immoral. The child's death is not used as a means to save his mother but is a side effect of removing some of his mother's damaged tissue.

This is similar to the cases of two pilots: One bombs a missile silo and indirectly kills children who live nearby, while the other bombs an elementary school in order to harm enemy morale. The former action is moral, because the children's deaths are unintended, and bombing a missile silo in war is not wrong. (If it were always wrong to indirectly kill human beings, then any army that used human shields could never be defeated in a moral way, which seems absurd.) The pilot who kills the children in the school does something directly immoral, because he uses the children's deaths as a means to discourage his enemies, and human beings should always be treated as ends and not means.

Since the unborn are human beings, they cannot be killed to save the life of the mother, but the mother may also not be killed in order to save the life of the child. Instead, doctors must do what they can to save both. This includes treating any disease affecting the mother (such as removing a cancerous uterus), even if it kills the child indirectly. Finally, remember that the vast majority of abortions are not performed to save the mother's life but to end the child's. According to Thomas Murphy Goodwin, professor of obstetrics, gynecology, and pediatrics at the University of Southern California, his medical service sees 15,000 to 16,000 births each year, and, excluding emergencies that occur in the third trimester, he sees no more than one or two cases per year that are life-threatening.[258]

Final thoughts on hard cases

Even if the arguments from hard cases were successful, they would justify only a very small percentage of abortions, and it would be disingenuous to use them to justify legal abortion through all nine months of pregnancy for any reason—or no reason—at all. Imagine if someone argued that speed limits should be repealed because in some rare cases they must be broken in order to get a dying person to the hospital.

While we understand that exceptions could be justified, the mere presence of an exception doesn't justify getting rid of the rule. Likewise, the possibility of rare cases in which we don't know the moral way to resolve a conflict between a mother and child during pregnancy does not negate the vast majority of cases where it is clearly wrong to kill the child.

When discussing hard cases, it's important to distinguish between a wrong action and an understandable action. If a maniac breaks into a home and threatens to torture the husband unless he shoots his wife, how should we judge the man if he chooses to do so? The husband has no right to shoot his wife, but we would have compassion for him if he did, understanding that he was in an awful situation with no "good" outcome.

That man is not as culpable as another husband who shoots his wife in order to collect on her life insurance policy. Both actions are wrong, but the man facing torture can be excused for his moral failing, while the greedy husband cannot.

Likewise, we can say that it is wrong for a victim of rape to kill her child through abortion while still being sympathetic regarding her difficult situation. Only insensitive pro-lifers think there is no difference in the moral culpability of a woman who aborts because she was raped and a woman who aborts out of convenience. Remember the first rule of being a pro-life ambassador: Don't be weird. We can refrain from condemning those who commit evil under coercion without condoning the evil they commit.

Finally, while some people who bring up the hard cases are genuinely conflicted, others are what Scott Klusendorf calls "crusaders."[259] They aren't conflicted at all; they think all or nearly all abortions should be legal. They merely bring up these cases in order to make the pro-life position look bad.

When talking to a crusader, Klusendorf suggests, you should say something like the following: "Let's say you're right about these hard cases. If I am willing to join you in making these abortions legal, will you join me in making the ninety percent of abortions that are done for social or economic reasons illegal?" The crusader will probably reject this offer, to which the pro-life advocate can respond, "So, you want all abortions to be legal and not just these hard cases? Then why don't we focus on the real issue at hand, which is whether abortion should, in general, be legal or illegal? Do you think we should kill unborn human beings just because they are unwanted?"

Crusaders should be careful, because abortion advocates have their own hard cases to defend.[260] Just as rape is an emotional issue that affects only one percent of pregnancies, abortions that are done after the fetus can survive outside of the womb (or late-term abortions) are emotional and affect only one percent of pregnancies.

If the pro-choice advocate says that late-term abortions are irrelevant because so few of them occur, then he will have to give up his arguments from the rape cases, because they are equally infrequent. Other "hard cases" for pro-choice advocates are repeat abortions, abortions done because of a fetus's sex or race, and the practice of prosecuting people for homicide when they kill a wanted fetus.

The bottom line is that both sides have cases that seem to contradict our gut feelings. What we must do in these cases is take a step back and see which side's general principles make the most sense. When we do this, I think it's clear that we should rely on the pro-life position, with its commitment to equality, justice, nonviolence, and compassion for the downtrodden.

Engaging the conflicted

The conflicted's main concern: Hard cases justify abortion.

Your objective: Empathize with their concern and show how both mother and child should be cared for in the same way one would care for a mother and infant in a similar circumstance.

★ ★ ★

Pro-choicer: I'm not saying I'm for all abortions. All I'm saying is that in the really hard cases we can't be absolutist. I mean, do you think a rape victim should be forced to carry the rapist's baby and always be reminded of what he did to her?

Pro-lifer: I think for women rape is a tragic crime that men will never understand. When a woman is raped, the rapist has assaulted her body and her mind—he's taken away her ability to feel safe, even in her own home.

PC: Right.

PL: And often when the woman reports the rape, people don't believe her. They sometimes say it was her fault.

PC: That's not fair.

PL: You're absolutely right. It especially isn't fair if the rapist impregnated her, which forces her to parent a child, place a child for adoption, or have an abortion. But it is the rapist, not the child, who has forced the woman into making one of these hard decisions.

PC: Yeah, that's why I'm asking you if she should be forced to be a mom because of what the rapist did.

PL: Do you see, though, that if she is pregnant then she already is a mother? Just as the woman was an innocent victim caught up in circumstances beyond her control, her child is an innocent victim caught up in circumstances beyond his or her control. If we wouldn't punish the mother, or kill even the rapist, why do we kill the innocent unborn child?

PC: It's just harder than that—

PL: You're right: It *is* hard. The rapist found a violent solution to his anger and lust. But I'm saying we can love both mother and child and advocate for a virtuous, nonviolent solution. We don't have to add any more violence on top of the violence of rape. Do you think abortion is an act of violence?

PC: Maybe . . . but what if a woman's life is in danger? I mean, I don't like abortion, but if the woman is going to die, I think we need to do what we can to save her.

PL: Would you agree that if the unborn are human beings we should do our best to save both mother and child?

PC: Sure, but like I said, if she's going to die, shouldn't we do what we can to save her?

PL: I agree with you that we should do what we can to save someone who is dying, as long as what we're doing is moral. For example, do you think it is okay to steal one person's organs to save your life because your organs are failing?

PC: No, but abortion is different.

PL: Why would abortion save a woman's life?

PC: Well, like if the pregnancy is causing her to die.

PL: If the problem happens when the child can survive outside of the womb, would you agree it would be better to just deliver the child by C-section and not kill him if we don't have to?

PC: Sure, but what about before that?

PL: Before that time doctors can treat both the mother and child as patients. We usually can't save the child in an early pregnancy, but we can save the mother by treating whatever condition is hurting her. So for example, if she has uterine cancer we might use chemotherapy or remove her cancerous uterus. If the child dies, that is an unintended consequence of treating his mom.

PC: But isn't it still killing the child?

PL: Not directly. The doctors are treating the mother's condition, and a side effect is the death of a child we can't save anyway. But the important point is, we are trying to save the mother, not trying to kill the child.

The Fighter

During one Justice for All outreach exhibit, we were interrupted by a group of pro-choice protesters. Rather than engage in dialogue, they spent the entire day using kazoos, conch shells, drum kits, and air horns to overpower our conversations with other students. Even worse, the university administration not only permitted them to do this, it denied us the opportunity to host a debate with amplified sound. Why? It was worried that *we* would be too loud. We were told that electronically amplified sound was forbidden, but since the protesters were using *mechanically* amplified sound, their actions were acceptable.

As I left the campus, I watched the protesters cheer in victory and bang on their noisemakers even louder. I shook my head and began to dwell on some uncharitable thoughts about these people. Later that night I was reading Scripture and came across the Sermon on the Mount, where Jesus told the crowd, "You have heard that it was said, 'You shall love your neighbor and hate your enemy.' But I say to you, Love your enemies and pray for those who persecute you, so that you may be sons of your Father who is in heaven; for he makes his sun rise on the evil and on the good, and sends rain on the just and on the unjust" (Matt. 5:43–45).

I felt bad. Too many of us give lip service to "loving our enemies," but when the time comes to love them, we let our anger fester inside of us. If you publicly stand up for an unborn child's right to live, get used to dealing with mean, rude people, or what I call *fighters*. While some pro-choice advocates enjoy a friendly dialogue, fighters don't want to have a meaningful discussion. They're out for a battle, and they're not afraid to use

dirty tricks. As pro-life advocates, we must graciously neutral-
ize these tricks without emulating the fighter's underhanded
approach.

Ad hominem attacks

At a pro-life outreach in Pasadena, California, I asked a passerby
what he thought of our exhibit. He shouted, "How many of
these children have you adopted?" I paused for a moment,
unsure how to answer. "I didn't think so!" he shouted.

This man was making an *ad hominem* argument, which in
Latin means "against the man." Instead of attacking an argument, an ad hominem argument attacks the person making
the argument. It's a logical fallacy. The man's implicit argument
was that abortion should be legal because those like me who
oppose it are bad people for not adopting unwanted, unborn
children.

Some other common ad hominem arguments used against
pro-life advocates include:

- You're a man (or you've never been pregnant), so
  you have no right to speak on this issue.
- Why don't you do something for the born children
  who are dying?
- Are you a vegetarian?
- Do you support war or the death penalty?

I recommend four steps for answering an ad hominem
argument. First, *correct misunderstandings* of the pro-life position.
Some people tell me that if I'm pro-life then I'm inconsistent
for not being a vegetarian. Or they say that if I think it's always
wrong to kill humans, then I should be against all wars.

But those positions are not essential to the pro-life worldview. The pro-life position is that all human beings are persons
with a right to life, and therefore it is generally wrong to kill
those human beings. However, cows and pigs are not members

of a rational kind (or persons), and so they do not have a right to life.

In regard to war, killing someone can be a moral act, even if the person has a right to life. The same applies to killing in self-defense. The pro-life position holds only that we must not *violate* someone's right to life. Since the unborn do not pose a threat to anyone's life, self-defense is not a justification of abortion.[261] By clearing up these misunderstandings you can make charges of inconsistency evaporate.

Second, *build common ground* so that you can overcome past negative encounters that may be fueling the pro-choice advocate's negative attitude. For example, if a critic says he can't stand pro-life moralizing, you could agree that you also don't like it when people hypocritically tell others what to do. Then ask a question to advance the common ground such as, "Is it possible that an obnoxious person could be right about the issue he is talking about?"

Third, *admit you're a bad person.* Ad hominem arguments are effective because they tempt the target to abandon his original argument and defend his reputation. But remember, an argument's truth does not depend on the character of the person making the argument. Sweet, kind people can be wrong. Mean, vicious people can be right.

To demonstrate this, admit for the sake of the argument that you are as bad as the fighter says you are. You can even maintain you are *worse* than what the critic claims. After admitting to being an awful person, simply ask how your badness justifies killing the unborn by abortion. For example, let's say I had a chance to stand up for myself against the man at the Pasadena college, whom I'll call John:

John: How many children have you adopted?

Me: How does that relate to whether abortion should be legal?

John: You say abortion should be illegal and people should adopt unwanted children, but if you haven't adopted any children, then you're a hypocrite.

Me: Let's say you're right that I am a hypocrite who will never adopt children. Let's say further that I hate children, and I'm just an all-around bad guy. How do any of these character defects justify keeping it legal to kill children through abortion?

John: They're not children, they're fetuses! (Now we're back to the one question that matters most: "What are the unborn?")

Finally, whenever possible you should *turn the tables* on your accuser who, while he accuses you of being bad or inconsistent, doesn't realize he suffers from the same problem. Take the case of a pro-choice advocate who opposes war and the death penalty because she believes these things violate human rights and criticizes the pro-life advocate who does not share her views:

Pro-choicer: So you say you're pro-life, but are you opposed to the death penalty?

Pro-lifer: What if I supported the death penalty? How does that relate to whether abortion should be legal or not?

PC: Because if you support the death penalty, then you're not truly pro-life.

PL: Do you support the death penalty?

PC: I'm against it.

PL: Why?

PC: Because every year innocent people are convicted of crimes they don't commit and are wrongfully executed.

PL: But isn't it inconsistent for you to oppose the killing
      of innocent people by capital punishment and not
      also oppose the killing of innocent people by abor-
      tion? More human beings will die from abortion
      by lunchtime today than have been killed by the
      death penalty since it was reinstated by the Supreme
      Court in 1976.[262] Doesn't that concern you?

PC: But that's different. I oppose the killing of born
      people. (Once again, we're back to the one ques-
      tion that matters most.)

If the unborn are human beings, then the fighter is inconsistent by not applying her moral principles to the welfare of
those children. By showing how claims of inconsistency cut
both ways, we can get our accusers back to the one question
that matters most: "What are the unborn?"

Do you see how these ad hominem arguments and their
corresponding moral principles could show an inconsistency
on the critic's part?

1. *Why don't you adopt unwanted children?* "Okay, you
    think we should help children who are in trouble.
    Then why don't you support helping unborn chil-
    dren by outlawing abortion?"

2. *You must be a Christian or a Republican.* "So it is unfair
    for one group of people to impose their personal
    beliefs on everyone else. Why is it okay for you to
    impose your personal belief that life begins at birth
    on unborn children?"

3. *You only care about fetuses.* "So it's wrong to care only
    about one group of people? Do you only care about
    born humans? Do unborn humans have the same
    value as medical waste?"

4. *You're a man; you have no say in this.* "You seem to be
    saying that unless a moral issue affects you directly,

you shouldn't comment on it. Many pro-choice advocates, such as men and post-menopausal women, will never be pregnant. Should they not comment on abortion? Should we throw out *Roe v. Wade*? Nine male judges decided it. Since I'm not a child, I'll never be a victim of child abuse. Does that mean I should not support laws that make child abuse illegal?

Pro-life advocates are sometimes also guilty of using ad hominem arguments. This happens when pro-life advocates point out that abortionists have been sued for malpractice, pro-choice students have vandalized pro-life displays, and Planned Parenthood's founder Margaret Sanger supported eugenics and wanted to keep minorities from having large families.[263]

These are all facts, but they do not prove abortion is wrong any more than Henry Ford's anti-Semitism proves it's wrong to buy Ford automobiles. Even if abortions were performed by the cheerful and polite staff of a place like Disneyland, they would still be wrong, because abortion unjustly ends the life of a human being. And just as inconsistent pro-life advocates do not disprove the pro-life position, inconsistent or even monstrous pro-choice advocates do not disprove the pro-choice position.

The only question that matters is: are the unborn human beings? The character of the person aborting these children doesn't change the wrongness of the act.

Pro-lifers care only about fetuses

Pro-life advocates are sometimes asked, "If abortion is made illegal, how are you going to care for all these children?" I have been told that if I stop a woman from having an abortion, I must personally pay for all her child-raising expenses until the child is eighteen. Some opponents have even told me I have to pay for the child's college tuition as well. Does this criticism of the pro-life movement show that abortion should remain legal?

If this were the nineteenth century, I would not have to guarantee slave owners that I could provide jobs for slaves in order to justify ending slavery. Slavery was wrong because it exploited human beings. Even if no abolitionists had hired ex-slaves, that would not mean it was okay to keep slavery legal.

Similarly, even if we could not care for children at risk of being aborted, it wouldn't follow that it would be okay to kill them. Imagine firefighters being dispatched to a house fire where a family is trapped inside and the town mayor asks the firefighters, "If you save these people, where are they going to live, and who's going to take care of them? If you won't take responsibility for them, then we should just let them burn."

But firefighters aren't responsible for feeding and sheltering fire victims; that is the responsibility of other groups like the Red Cross. Likewise, pro-life advocates are not responsible for feeding and sheltering children who would have been aborted; that is a job for social services and other charities that focus on providing people with a decent quality of life. Pro-life advocates have a responsibility only to ensure that people are allowed to live, though many pro-life advocates do support charities that help people attain a decent quality of life.

Even this kind of objection can be turned against pro-choice advocates. Imagine a group that wants to force women to have abortions because too many impoverished women are giving birth to drug-addicted babies. What if forced-abortion advocates said to pro-choice advocates who opposed them, "If you are not going to adopt these drug-addicted babies whom these poor women cannot afford, then you have no right to say I can't force them to be aborted."

Pro-choice advocates would rightly reply, "It doesn't matter if I won't care for these children. That fact doesn't give you the right to force a woman to have an abortion." Pro-lifers can use the same logic and say, "It doesn't matter if I won't care for these children. That fact doesn't give you the right to kill them by forcing their mothers to abort them."[264]

When people claim that as a pro-lifer I don't care about born children and my only goal is to "get the fetus born," I don't necessarily disagree with them. "Do anything to get the fetus born" is identical in this case to "Do anything to stop the fetal human from being dismembered." So even if this were true (which it isn't), I would have no problem saying my only goal is to "get the fetus born." After all, we wouldn't fault a firefighter who didn't provide free housing to fire victims because his only goal was to save lives and put the fire out.

Aside from being irrelevant, this argument assumes incorrectly that pro-life advocates don't care about born children. Many pro-life pregnancy centers provide parenting classes and baby supplies, and some have medical staff that can perform prenatal care. Pro-life advocates also operate maternity homes where poor or homeless pregnant women can stay for free, sometimes up to a year after the baby is born. As pro-life advocate Helen Alvaré points out:

> Pregnancy resource centers devote significant resources to supporting women who have already decided to have an abortion, but abortion advocates offer no similar support to women who wish to continue their pregnancies. Indeed, they often devote their resources to shutting down the services provided by pro-lifers. NARAL Pro-Choice America reports spending $20,000 on "crisis pregnancy centers" in Maryland in order to "investigate" and publicly smear such centers for demonstrating a bias for life.[265]

These smear campaigns are ironic, because abortion clinics often rely on pro-life centers to do the work they won't do. At a pregnancy center in Arizona I met a young woman who had just come from Planned Parenthood. She told me that she went there saying she wanted to keep her baby and asked them what resources they could provide her. Planned Parenthood personnel said they didn't have any and sent her instead to the local pro-life pregnancy resource center.

Unhelpful allies

Sometimes the complaint that pro-life advocates care only about unborn children comes from other self-described pro-life advocates. Cardinal Joseph Bernardin famously said that life issues such as abortion, euthanasia, the death penalty, and unjust war were like a "seamless garment" that should not be torn apart.

In a speech given at Fordham University in 1983, Bernardin, then archbishop of Chicago, said, "If one contends, as we do, that the right of every fetus to be born should be protected by civil law and supported by civil consensus, then our moral, political, and economic responsibilities do not stop at the moment of birth."[266] Many people have seized on Bernardin's praiseworthy call to consistency and said that the pro-life movement should be "for all life" and not just unborn life.

But being "for all life" is a vague and confusing concept. Even if these critics argue that we should be "for all *human* life," would that mean pro-life advocates are obliged to solve every problem that affects human life from conception to natural death? Do pro-life advocates have to solve hunger, war, disease, human trafficking, poverty, discrimination, illiteracy, and slow Internet connections? Self-described "pro-life" advocate Thomas Friedman thinks so. He writes in the *New York Times*:

> You don't get to call yourself "pro-life" and want to shut down the Environmental Protection Agency. . . . You

don't get to call yourself "pro-life" and oppose programs like Head Start that provide basic education, health, and nutrition for the most disadvantaged children. . . . [T]here is no way that respect for the sanctity of life can mean we are obligated to protect every fertilized egg in a woman's body, no matter how that egg got fertilized, but we are not obligated to protect every living person from being shot with a concealed automatic weapon.[267]

Friedman's article shows that the terms *pro-life* and *pro-choice* are hopelessly vague. The goal of the pro-life movement is to secure the right to life of all human beings from conception to natural death. That means it should be illegal to intentionally kill an innocent human being, regardless of that human being's level of function or location.

It's not the responsibility of the pro-life movement to stop crimes, even crimes that take human life, such as mass shootings. The victims of those crimes have a right to life, and it is the job of law enforcement to protect that right. The pro-life movement's job is also not to secure the best possible life for all humans, because such a goal is impossible for one movement. All movements that care about doing good limit their scope of activities, because if they try to do everything, they accomplish nothing.

Even the pro-choice movement doesn't try to protect all "choices." Many pro-choice advocates oppose the choice not to join a labor union, the choice to own a firearm, or the choice not to hire a person because of his sexual behavior. Just as pro-choice advocates can restrict their definition of *choice* to mean "access to legal contraception and abortion," pro-life advocates should restrict their definition of *life* to mean "the legally recognized right to life of all human beings."

I am sympathetic to Cardinal Bernardin's view, and during college I started a respect-life ministry at my parish called

"The Seamless Garment." We focused on opposing abortion, euthanasia, the death penalty, and unjust war, because I agree that pro-life advocates should not ignore these issues.

I've had my share of arguments with pro-life advocates who, while they oppose abortion, believe the general use of the death penalty and the atomic bombings of Hiroshima and Nagasaki were morally right. But that does not mean pro-life advocates are obligated to treat these issues as morally equivalent to abortion or as deserving the same response. The Catholic Church has held that under some circumstances the death penalty can be a moral choice, and war can be just.[268] These acts are evil in circumstance or degree but not evil in and of themselves. Other acts, such as rape or abortion, are intrinsically evil and can never be tolerated.

The seamless garment approach doesn't mean that pro-life advocates must confront these other issues with equal energy or resources. Cardinal Bernardin clarified this point in a later address: "It is not necessary or possible for every person to engage in each issue, but it is both possible and necessary for the Church as a whole to cultivate a conscious explicit connection among the several issues."[269]

You don't really think they're human

Some pro-choice advocates argue that pro-life advocates are hypocrites who *say* the unborn are human beings but don't act like it's true. If embryos really are people, then why aren't pro-lifers doing more to prevent the millions of miscarriages that take place each year? Why aren't they working to find out why millions of embryos—50 to 75 percent annually according to some estimates—fail to implant in the womb?

(As I discuss in more detail in Chapter 12, there is a genuine dispute over the humanity of fetuses and embryos that miscarry or fail to implant. It could be the case that the development of these entities ceased because they were not actual human beings but only a collection of tissue that reached the end of its developmental potential and died.)

Let's suppose that this objection is correct, and pro-life advocates simply do not care about unborn children who are miscarried. Even if pro-life advocates were massive hypocrites, that would not disprove the pro-life position. Imagine if the U.S. surgeon general launched a public campaign meant to expose how cigarettes cause lung cancer and then was caught smoking. Would his hypocrisy mean cigarettes *don't* cause lung cancer? Likewise, hypocrisy on the part of pro-lifers does nothing to refute the scientific and philosophical evidence for the humanity of the unborn.

Furthermore, this objection misunderstands the goal of the pro-life movement. It is not to save as many human lives as possible; it's to secure the right to life for all human beings. Pro-life advocates simply do not have the resources to provide medical treatment for embryos or to research ways to reduce miscarriages. If pro-life advocates could restore the right to life of unborn children, it might impel the government to fund research that could remedy the health problems that affect this particular group of people.

Even if this were not possible, abortion can't be justified simply because pro-life advocates do not work to reduce natural miscarriages. Is it not appropriate to confront the man-made threats to human life before confronting the abundance of natural threats? Would we tell gun-control advocates who work to stop elementary-school shootings that they don't really care about elementary school students, because they don't work to reduce the much greater number of child deaths that result from cancer?

Another claim of alleged pro-life hypocrisy is that not all pro-life advocates mourn the loss of an embryo to miscarriage as they would mourn the loss of a born child. If the unborn are human, why don't we hold funerals for every miscarriage?

Even if this were true, it only reflects our lack of psychological attachment to the unborn, not any lack of humanity on their part. After all, countless human beings, young and old, die every day for whom we do not grieve, but our lack of grief or even our failure to give them a proper funeral (such as in impoverished or war-torn countries) doesn't prove they weren't human beings.

Since the miscarried unborn are not seen or touched, parents have not bonded as closely with those children, and so their emotional response would naturally be different than it would be to the death of a born child. However, I personally know many couples who do mourn their miscarried children just as they would mourn born children, so this argument simply would not apply to them.

The fire in the IVF clinic

One scenario fighters use to show that pro-life advocates don't believe the unborn are human is "the fire in the IVF clinic." According to this dilemma, you are in an in vitro fertilization clinic that is on fire and have a choice to save ten frozen embryos or one two-year old-child. Since most people would opt to save the two-year-old-child, pro-choice advocates claim this proves that pro-life advocates do not consider unborn children to be as valuable as born children. Of course, this entire scenario only proves that in a disaster we sometimes make a choice that involves more people dying.

Let's imagine the scenario involved five homeless people and the president of the United States. While all six have an equal right to life, the loss of the president may be more devastating to the country, and so I may choose to save him and let the five homeless men die as a result. However, my choice *not to save* the five homeless people wouldn't be the same as my choice in another circumstance to *directly kill* them and harvest their organs in order to save a terminally ill president.

Just because we might not save some humans in an emergency does not give us the right to kill those same humans for any reason we want. I once asked a critic who posed this objection whom he would save: one screaming nurse or five unconscious newborns? He begrudgingly—but honestly—admitted he'd save the nurse.

Most of us might choose to save the toddler over the embryos, because there are other relevant facts that are assumed, but not explicitly stated, about this case. For example, we may choose to save the two-year-old because we consider it worse for the toddler to painfully die in the fire than it would be for the five embryos to die painlessly. Or we might choose to save the toddler instead of the embryos because we know that frozen embryos have a poor chance of developing into adults. They might never be implanted, be killed in the de-thawing process, fail to implant, be naturally miscarried, or be reduced selectively later in the womb through abortion. It would be a waste to save the embryos that stand a high chance of dying before being born, and so saving the toddler would be a greater good.

Finally, our moral intuitions can also show that embryos in the IVF clinic are persons, regardless of whom we choose to save. With the increasing frequency of IVF births, there are many children and adults who now have the opportunity to look at a picture of an embryo in a petri dish and say, "That was *me* before they put me inside my mother."

I wonder what these grown children would think if we told them we thought it was okay to leave them to die in a laboratory fire? In fact, many infertile couples who use IVF see these embryos as their "children" and may, in the fire scenario, save their embryos over a born human being, especially if the alternative means they will never have children of their own.

However, some pro-life advocates have argued that embryo adoption is morally wrong, because it violates the way embryos and pregnancy should be treated. In their view, pregnancy should only come about as a result of the marital act, and any other way of causing pregnancy, including through IVF or embryo adoption, is intrinsically immoral.[270] If they are right, then even if the embryos in the IVF lab are human persons, the only moral option may be to let them perish and save the toddler, since the embryos are already "dying" in their unnatural cryogenic state, while the toddler is perfectly healthy.

The bottom line is that even if we are unsure about when or if we should save certain humans in certain scenarios, that doesn't change the central moral truth related to the issue of abortion: We should not directly kill innocent human beings simply because they are unwanted.

Feminists

Most feminists use arguments that range from the pragmatic (women need abortion to flourish in society) to the disqualifying (it's absurd to claim an embryo has the same value as an adult woman) to the autonomous (women are oppressed unless they have total control over their bodies).[271] The information in the previous chapters should be enough to address those arguments.

Apart from these arguments, feminists sometimes use rhetoric simply for the purpose of discrediting pro-life advocates. For example, they might accuse pro-life advocates who want to ban abortion of being "misogynistic," or being a person who hates women.

Pro-life advocates should counter this rhetoric by saying they firmly agree that men and women should be treated equally. It's especially helpful if you can identify areas where you agree feminists fight justly for women's rights (for instance, by encouraging the creation of laws that mandate their pay be equal to that of men). You can say that the pro-life movement fits in well with feminism, because pro-life advocates believe that all people, regardless of being male or female, should be treated equally.

Our position is not that "women shouldn't be allowed to have abortions." Instead it's that "neither men nor women should be allowed to harm unborn children." Men should not be allowed to abort children, and they should be charged with two criminal counts if they attack a pregnant woman. And neither should women be allowed to harm unborn children. What if a critic says you are trying to take away women's rights or you are "attacking women"? Redirect the conversation by saying that the issue of abortion affects both men and women and that you believe *all* individuals should have equal rights throughout their whole lives, including before birth. Always get back to the one question "What are the unborn?" as expediently as possible.

Feminists may respond by saying that banning abortion is an attack on women, because only women have abortions, and so this isn't about equal rights. But that's like saying a law against rape is an attack on men, because men commit the vast majority of rapes. Even though some feminists may want to deny it, men and women are biologically different, and that results in the law treating men and women not *unequally* but *differently*. Laws against abortion may prevent women from obtaining a certain surgery, but their primary purpose is to prevent both men and women from performing the work of an abortion provider, which has nothing to with what sex a person is.

Some pro-life advocates may find it useful to answer the charge of misogyny by claiming that feminists who support abortion are guilty of misopedia, or the hatred of children. How could someone not reach that conclusion, when feminists demand it be legal to kill unborn children? Feminists will probably respond that they don't hate children; they just deny the unborn are children (or persons). But isn't that still an attitude of hatred toward children? Wouldn't feminists say a man hated women precisely because he denied they were persons?

Indeed, how can feminists say they stand up for women's rights when many of them lobby against banning sex-selection abortions? Isn't support for killing fetuses in the womb because they are female misogyny at its worst?

I will caution the reader that such counter rhetoric must be used carefully. It may be a better tactic to use a softer approach. For example, Feminists for Life is an organization dedicated to articulating the principles of feminism in defense of unborn children. Its motto, "Women deserve better than abortion," is an excellent starting point for fruitful dialogue.

Regardless of the approach used, pro-life advocates must stay focused on the one question that matters most: "What are the unborn?" The pro-life movement is not about denying women any genuine rights. It is about securing equal rights for all human beings, and that includes all women, before and after they are born.

The post-abortive

At one of our JFA exhibits in Arizona a tall, muscular man was intimidating some of our volunteers. He spoke loudly and did his best to belittle them. I decided to step in.

"You know," I said, "I just think all humans should be treated equally, and even though abortion is really tough, it's not fair to treat the unborn in a way we would not treat two-year-olds. I just think we shouldn't kill people who are unwanted. That's all."

He became enraged. "That's the stupidest thing I've ever heard," he shouted. "You're an idiot."

As he yelled he kept walking toward me with clenched fists, and I backed away.

"Why are you walking backward?" he sneered. "You think I'm going to hit you?"

"I just don't like people in my personal space," I said.
One of our post-abortive volunteers was nearby, and I asked for her opinion. As the young man turned his attention to her testimony, I slipped away. I didn't feel like fighting someone whose arms were as thick as my midsection.

Our post-abortive volunteer told me later that after she spoke to him, the guy broke down and sobbed. Apparently, the day before, his girlfriend had told him she was going to abort their child, and that's why he had such an emotional reaction to my words.

If people are enraged or hysterical at your opposition to abortion, they are probably either post-abortive or they know someone who is. Their anger is a defense mechanism, because your opposition to abortion places them under judgment from either God or at least their own conscience. As a result, these people can't rationally discuss abortion, because their hurt feelings leave them raw and wounded.

If you sense that a past abortion experience is motivating an opponent, gently encourage her (or him) to speak with a qualified post-abortion counselor (and to seek the sacrament of reconciliation if she—or he—is Catholic). This person might be pro-choice in order to justify her past actions and mitigate any guilt she may still be feeling. Let her know that pro-life advocates believe all human beings have value and deserve to be treated with dignity. This includes not just unborn children but their mothers as well.

I'll explain more about how to help people find healing from abortion in Chapter 12 and in Appendix I. Remember that a pro-life ambassador doesn't yell or get upset at someone who uses him as an emotional punching bag. Of course, if you think someone is going to use you as a *literal* punching bag, by all means defend yourself (or flee, like I did!).

In conclusion, regardless of what kind of jab the fighter makes, the pro-life ambassador responds the same to each attack.

We can tolerate verbal abuse with grace, because we know that can help the unborn escape physical abuse. A pro-life ambassador is unfazed by the fighter's attempts at character assassination. We simply remind him that even if he is right and pro-lifers are massive hypocrites—even if I as a pro-lifer was secretly *an abortionist* because I wanted to make extra money—that hypocrisy would not change the fact that abortion takes the life of an innocent human being. Unless the fighter can show abortion does not unjustly kill a human being, he will be fighting a losing battle.

Engaging the fighter

The fighter's main concern: To sway the public against efforts to outlaw abortion by exposing how bad pro-life advocates are.

Your objective: Show that the personal character of pro-life advocates is irrelevant to the question of whether abortion should be legal.

★ ★ ★

Pro-choicer: How dare you judge women who have to make this terrible choice. You're just a bigoted, judgmental person.

Pro-lifer: I'm sorry if I've done something to anger you, but don't you think you're judging me?

PC: You deserve it. I mean, how many children have you adopted?

PL: Well, none. But how does that affect the question whether or not abortion kills a human being?

PC: Ha! See, you're using judgmental language again! All you want to do is enslave women and make them feel ashamed for controlling their bodies.

PL: That's not true. I care about women before and after birth. When do you think a woman's life begins? At birth?

PC: That doesn't matter. It's a religious question, and you're a religious fanatic who wants to enslave America under a Christo-fascist regime. Ignorant Christians like you shouldn't be allowed to roam free without a leash!

PL: Beat me up as much as you want; I can defend myself. But can we please talk about the unborn, who can't defend themselves at all? What about this issue has made you so upset? I really don't want to fight; I just want to understand where you're coming from, and I hope you can understand where I'm coming from.

PC: I'm upset because people like you judge me. I had an abortion.

PL: I'm sorry you've felt unfairly judged by pro-lifers. How have you been since the abortion? . . .

12

The Religious

Once during a pro-life outreach at the University of New Mexico, I was confronted by not only pro-choice students but also pro-choice adult activists, who came to campus to reinforce the student efforts to oppose us. These included representatives from Planned Parenthood, an Albuquerque atheist group, and a group called the Religious Coalition for Reproductive Choice (RCRC). I was talking to a young woman when one of the RCRC volunteers interrupted us.

"You shouldn't talk to him," she said to the young woman. "He's been trained by this group to lie to you."

I looked at her shirt with the RCRC logo emblazoned across the front. "Ma'am," I said, "have you been trained by your organization to do what you're accusing me of doing?"

She simply smiled, and as she walked away I noticed the motto of her organization on the back of her T-shirt: "Pro-faith, pro-family, pro-choice."

It might surprise you to learn that sides in the abortion debate are not neatly divided by religious demographics. There are atheists who oppose abortion and Christians who defend it.[272] In this chapter, we'll examine the arguments offered by pro-choice Christians who say that abortion is not only not a crime; it's not even a sin.

Is God pro-choice?

One general religious argument in defense of legal abortion claims that because God is "pro-choice" (i.e., he gave humans free will), he would want humans to be able to exercise that free will, so abortion should not be outlawed. On page 35 of

RCRC's booklet *Prayerfully Pro-Choice*, actress Whoopi Goldberg is quoted as saying, "I talk about God because God and I
are very close. God gives you choice. God gives you freedom
of choice. That's in the Bible."[273]

Goldberg is right that God gives human beings choices,
but he also expects us to live with the consequences of our
choices. In Deuteronomy 30:19, God tells the Israelites, "I
have set before you life and death, the blessing and the curse.
Choose life, then, that you and your descendants may live."
Jesus makes it clear that in the final judgment we will be
judged based on the choices we made in life. Those who failed
to love their brothers as they love themselves, Jesus says, "will
go off to eternal punishment, but the righteous to eternal
life" (Matt. 25:29).

Because God gave human beings free will does not mean
he condones everything we choose to do. Is God pro-choice
when it comes to humans who choose to murder, rape, drive
drunk, steal, or commit any other immoral act? Pro-choice
advocates would say no one should outlaw abortion even if
they think *God* wants them to outlaw it; so even pro-choice
advocates believe there is a limit to actions we may perform
with the free will God has given us.

It's true God gave us free will, and pro-life advocates believe
women should exercise that free will. Outlawing abortion does
nothing to inhibit free will, because people are free to break the
law. It is simply the right thing to do when unborn children
are being threatened by abortion.

Other pro-choice advocates claim that if embryos are human beings, the high number of miscarriages (some say as high
as 50 percent of all pregnancies) means that God is the greatest
abortionist in history. But that makes as much sense as saying
that the high number of born people who die makes God the
greatest serial killer of all time. God has the right to take human
life as well as to judge people in the afterlife. These are rights

human beings do not possess, and so human beings may not take innocent human life.

Some writers claim these embryos are not human beings precisely because God would never allow such a high mortality rate. According to professors Thomas Shannon and Allan Wolter, saying these embryos are fully human is almost "sacrilegious" due to the "bungling" it implies on the part of an all-wise Creator.[274] But would Shannon and Walter deny that infants are human beings even though there have been times in history when the infant mortality rate was as high as 50 percent?

It is not even certain that large numbers of *fully* human embryos are miscarried. What may have died in a miscarriage is human tissue that could never develop into a fully mature human being due to a genetic defect. Embryologists Keith Moore and T.V.N. Persaud write in their textbook, "The early loss of embryos appears to represent a disposal of abnormal conceptuses that could not have developed normally."[275]

My brother's keeper?

Another argument made by some religious pro-choice people is that they have no business telling women to not have abortions because that is "between her and God." But abortion is not a matter solely between a woman and God. It also involves the man who helped conceive the child, the woman's family, the abortion provider, and most important, the child.

Some of these critics think abortion is homicide, but they reason that in the afterlife God will punish those who commit abortion, so when it comes to persuading women not to have abortions, it is, in their words, "none of our business."

But would the religious critics say the same thing about rape, murder, or arson? If they saw someone about to burn down an orphanage, would they simply say, "Well, they'll burn in hell anyway, so what business is it of mine to try and stop them? It's between them and God." God calls us to root out injustice now and not to wait for him to do it later. Or, as Proverbs 24:11 exhorts us, "Rescue those who are being dragged to death."

Finally, some religious pro-choice advocates say that abortion is not wrong because aborted babies will go to heaven or be reincarnated and have another life.[276] Of course, this argument would justify killing *any* baby, or even an adult in the state of grace. If we wouldn't justify killing born children in a nursery in order to send them directly to heaven, then we cannot justify aborting unborn children.

The breath of life

There are three Scripture passages that Christian pro-choice advocates typically use to defend legal abortion. The first is Genesis 2:7, which says, "[T]hen the LORD God formed man of dust from the ground, and breathed into his nostrils the breath of life; and man became a living being." This means that until a baby breathes outside of the womb he or she is not a person and can be aborted.

There are numerous problems with this argument.[277] First, it proves too much, because many babies do not breathe immediately after birth and some can take up to a minute to breathe on their own. This argument would justify infanticide as well as abortion. Secondly, the unborn *do* breathe before birth, but through an umbilical cord rather than through their mouths. And, before they develop the umbilical cord, they absorb oxygen through the lining of their cells in a process called respiration. Not only that, some injured born humans must breathe through a tube in their throat. May we kill these humans because they don't breathe the "breath of life" through their nostrils like Adam did?

Finally, God had to infuse a human soul directly into Adam (or breathe the "breath of life" into him) because Adam was the first human being. Since all other human beings come into existence from other human beings, the requirement that God must "breathe" life into them the way he did for Adam is unsupported.

Abortion as God's plan

Another passage that is mentioned is Numbers 5:11–31, in which Mosaic Law requires a wife suspected of adultery by her husband to drink water mixed with dust from the tabernacle floor, which will allegedly cause a miscarriage if she has been unfaithful. One pro-choice author says this proves that "a planned abortion is part of God's law given to Moses."[278]

But, if anything, these verses would prove only that abortion is acceptable if God kills a child conceived in adultery. They would not justify legal abortion performed by a human being for any reason at any stage of pregnancy. Plus, God's killing of a child conceived in adultery would no more disprove that child's humanity than God's act of killing David or Pharaoh's firstborn sons would disprove those children's humanity. God is allowed to end human life; we are not. Finally, as Francis Beckwith notes, the passage does not seem to refer to the water causing a miscarriage but to causing the woman no longer to be fertile as a punishment for her adultery.[279]

An eye for an eye

The favorite passage of religious pro-choice advocates is Exodus 21:22–23, which describes what the punishment should be for accidentally harming an unborn child: "When men strive together, and hurt a woman with child, so that there is a miscarriage, and yet no harm follows, the one who hurt her shall be fined, according as the woman's husband shall lay upon him; and he shall pay as the judges determine. If any harm follows, then you shall give life for life." Critics use this passage to argue that if the unborn child were a full person, the punishment would not be a fine but the death penalty.

How does it follow that because someone is fined for *accidentally* killing an unborn child God would approve the *intentional* killing of an unborn child through abortion? After all, there is a punishment, so the child has some value and is not equivalent to disposable medical waste as he is in our legal system. In the preceding verses a man who accidentally kills his slave is not punished, but in the next verse the intentional killing of a slave is treated as grounds for serious punishment, possibly even the death penalty.[280]

There simply is no biblical directive about how to punish someone if he *intentionally* kills an unborn child, which is what happens in modern abortions. Therefore, it is inaccurate to say that the Bible allows intentional abortion because of the punishment prescribed for accidental miscarriage in these verses.

It is also not clear exactly what the word *injury* in these verses means. It could mean an injury that occurs to the pregnant woman, the unborn child, or both. One way to interpret the passage is that if the woman is caused to have an early delivery, then the penalty is a fine, but any further injury to the child is covered under the *lex talionis* law of "an eye for an eye."[281] Indeed, the text refers to a "child" coming forth, and this is a difficult fact for pro-choice commentators to evade.

As a final response, the pro-choice advocate may argue that abortion is permissible, because even if the Bible does affirm some kind of living presence within the womb, it never says explicitly that abortion is wrong. This is called an *argument from silence*, because the critic reasons that if abortion were wrong, the Bible would condemn it.

But consider this argument: "If an act were immoral, the Bible would condemn it. There are many acts (airplane hijacking, insurance fraud, election rigging) the Bible does not condemn. Therefore, those acts are not wrong." Clearly, just because an action is not condemned by name in the Bible does not mean that God would support it.

Pro-life Scripture verses

Although pro-choice advocates may twist Scripture to mean something it does not, it's important for pro-life advocates not to do the same thing. Two passages frequently cited by pro-life advocates lack conclusive pro-life evidence. The first is Jeremiah 1:5: "Before I formed you in the womb I knew you, and before you were born I consecrated you; I appointed you a prophet to the nations." Taken literally, this passage would mean God knew Jeremiah in some kind of preexisting state before he was conceived.[282] Clearly this passage is saying that before Jeremiah existed, God *foreknew* that he would be a prophet, not that he knew Jeremiah personally during that time.

Another common pro-life passage is Psalm 139:13: "For thou didst form my inward parts, thou didst knit me together in my mother's womb." But pro-choice critics are likely to reject passages from the Psalms as being poetic exaggerations. After all, the Psalms also say that God "shelters us under his wing" (Ps. 91:4), but we don't take that to mean God has feathers. Likewise, because the Bible talks about someone being "knit in their mothers womb" doesn't mean the person actually existed during gestation.

Nevertheless, some Scripture passages do seem to make a strong case that the unborn have a personal existence before birth. In Psalm 51:5, David laments, "Behold, I was brought forth in iniquity, and in sin did my mother conceive me." How could David be a sinner in the womb if he was not yet a person? In the New Testament, the Greek word for baby, *brephos*, is used for both born and unborn children. In Luke 1:44, a pregnant Elizabeth says to her cousin Mary, "at the moment the sound of your greeting reached my ears, the *brephos* in my womb leaped for joy." In Luke 2:12, the same Greek word is used to describe the newborn Jesus sleeping in the manger.

The argument from Scripture I prefer is a more modest one. I would simply argue that God forbids the killing of human beings (Exod. 20:13, Prov. 6:16–17), because human beings are made in his image (Gen. 1:26–27). Since we know from science and philosophy that the unborn are human beings, it follows that abortion is wrong. No special argument or appeal is needed to show that abortion is wrong, just as no argument or appeal to Scripture is needed to show that infanticide or rape is wrong.[283] Pope St. John Paul II wrote:

> The texts of Sacred Scripture never address the question of deliberate abortion and so do not directly and specifically condemn it. But they show such great respect for the human being in the mother's womb that they require as a logical consequence that God's commandment "You shall not kill" be extended to the unborn child as well.[284]

Pro-life tradition

Along with evidence from Scripture, evidence from Sacred Tradition holds that abortion is morally wrong. A first-century document called the *Didache* states, "You shall not procure abortion, nor destroy a newborn child" (2:1–2). By A.D. 314, the ecclesial Council of Ancyra thought it was being "lenient" in reducing a woman's penance for procuring an abortion to ten years of fasting (canon 21).

Some pro-choice advocates claim that the Church's teaching on abortion has changed, because some theologians such as Augustine speculated that human beings might receive their souls several months after conception. For one thing, those Church Fathers who believed ensoulment occurred after conception never endorsed the view that abortion was moral. For another, they operated under the mistaken view of human development espoused by Aristotle. He thought that unborn children progressed through vegetable and animal stages of life before their bodies were "animated" with a rational soul and they became human beings later in pregnancy.[285]

Other early Church writers like Tertullian made it clear that it does not matter "whether you take away a life that is born, or destroy one that is coming to birth. That *is* a man which is *going to be* one; you have the fruit already in its seed."[286] Tertullian believed "the soul also begins from conception; life taking its commencement at the same moment and place that the soul does."[287]

Early Christians did agree that it was a grave evil to kill the developing human life in the womb, regardless of whether or not God had "formed" it with a soul. This is powerfully articulated by St. Basil the Great, who wrote in the fourth century, "The woman who purposely destroys her unborn child is guilty of murder. With us there is no nice enquiry as to its being formed or unformed."[288]

Today we know that a biological human organism is not "formed" like a clay model but possesses a human genetic code that directs its intrinsic development. This makes it a human being whose life begins at conception and who deserves respect and protection under the law. The *Catechism of the Catholic Church* states, "Since the first century the Church has affirmed the moral evil of every procured abortion. This teaching has not changed and remains unchangeable. Direct abortion, that is to say, abortion willed either as an end or a means, is gravely contrary to the moral law."[289]

Arguing against tradition

Catholics for Choice, an organization started in 1973 by former nun Frances Kissling, is, according to its Web site, "the most effective counterpoint to the vocal, well-financed, and powerful Roman Catholic hierarchy." CFC's activities have included crowning its female president "Pope" at New York's St. Patrick's Cathedral and trying (unsuccessfully) to have Vatican City stripped of its position as a permanent observer at the United Nations.

CFC uses a variety of arguments to advance the idea that one can be a faithful Catholic and support legal abortion. For example, it claims that in the 1974 *Declaration on Procured Abortion,* the Vatican "acknowledged that it does not know when the fetus becomes a person." It highlighted this quote from the document: "There is not a unanimous tradition on this point [the exact moment of ensoulment] and authors are as yet in disagreement."[290]

This quote comes from a footnote in a section of the declaration that affirms the humanity of the unborn child from conception and condemns any discrimination against human beings, regardless of their level of development. The document says that the humanity of the unborn child from conception has been "confirmed by modern genetic science," and this fact is true apart from any discussion about when a human embryo receives an immortal soul.

It is true that there is disagreement among Christian theologians on exactly which moment an embryo receives a soul. But there is also no way to empirically prove a newborn infant, or anyone for that matter, has an immortal soul. Therefore, this argument from agnosticism proves too much, and it would justify killing humans at any stage of life. It would be more responsible to believe that biological human beings have a right to life, and that is why abortion, infanticide, and other forms of homicide are wrong.

Indeed, the footnote from the declaration goes on to say that a human life is still present in the womb, and this fact justifies prohibiting abortion. It also says that if we are unsure about the status of an embryo, then we should not risk killing a person whose existence in the womb is at least "probable" (just as we would not shoot a figure in the woods that was "probably" a hunter and not a deer).

Arguments from conscience and infallibility

Catholics for Choice promotes the idea that an individual's conscience is the sole and final authority in moral issues. It writes, "[T]he teaching on the primacy of conscience means that every individual must follow his or her own conscience—and respect the rights of others to do the same."[291] But the idea of a supreme and infallible individual conscience is illogical. For example, my conscience informs me that abortion is tantamount to murder, and it should be made illegal. Should I follow my conscience and work to outlaw abortion? If CFC says I should not do so because that interferes with other people's consciences, then CFC is wrong about conscience being the sole or final arbiter of truth.

Rather than being the final authority, conscience is like a compass that guides people in unfamiliar situations toward the true "moral" north. But just as a faulty compass will lead people astray, a faulty or ill-formed conscience will do the same. The *Catechism* states that while we "must always obey the certain judgment of [our] conscience," it's possible our conscience can make an "erroneous judgment" due to ignorance or even blindness caused by sin.[292]

CFC also asserts that because the immorality of abortion has not been infallibly defined by the pope, it is a teaching that Catholics are not bound to follow. Like many of CFC's arguments, this is a half-truth that camouflages a clear falsehood. It is true that no pope has infallibly declared abortion to be morally wrong; but Catholics are obligated to obey not just the special infallibility present in the pope's *ex cathedra* declarations, but also the teachings that are infallibly taught by the ordinary magisterium of the Church, or those doctrines that the bishops and the pope teach uniformly and definitively about the Faith.

In his encyclical *The Gospel of Life*, Pope St. John Paul II issued an authoritative statement that stops just short of extraordinary infallibility but relies on the ordinary sense of the term in order to underscore the binding nature of his teaching:

Therefore, by the authority which Christ conferred upon Peter and his Successors, in communion with the Bishops—who on various occasions have condemned abortion and who in the aforementioned consultation, albeit dispersed throughout the world, have shown unanimous agreement concerning this doctrine—*I declare that direct abortion, that is, abortion willed as an end or as a means, always constitutes a grave moral disorder,* since it is the deliberate killing of an innocent human being. This doctrine is based upon the natural law and upon the written Word of God, is transmitted by the Church's Tradition and taught by the ordinary and universal Magisterium.[293]

It's important to know that even if the pope were to infallibly declare abortion to be wrong, CFC would not accept this. In CFC's magazine *Conscience,* Rosemary Radford Ruether writes that if the pope were to infallibly define the Church's prohibition on contraception, it "would have the immediate effect of focusing Catholic dissent on the doctrine of infallibility itself. . . . A storm of dissent, and even ridicule, directed at infallibility itself would ensue from such a declaration."[294] So, rather than obey Church teaching, dissenters like CFC would simply reject whatever teaching they disagree with.

The fetus is not a person

A more sophisticated Catholic defense of abortion, which provides the academic muscle behind CFC's sound bites, is a book by Daniel Dombrowski and Robert Deltete: *A Brief, Liberal, Catholic Defense of Abortion.* The authors claim that it is the possession of a complex brain that can receive an immortal soul that makes something a person, as opposed to a mere animal, and fetuses lack this characteristic.

But if Dombrowski and Deltete are right, then why should we believe that newborn infants have souls? After all, a newborn's brain, like an early fetus's brain, is not complex enough to engage in rational thought. In fact, the newborn's brain is hardly more complex than a cow's brain. If that is the case, then why not treat infants like cattle?

Dombrowski and Deltete anticipate this objection and claim that infants do not have any biological traits that warrant granting them a right to life. However, they claim this fact should motivate us not toward the approval of infanticide but the "Franciscan protection of the lives of animals. [Born infants] are *actually* sentient and it is a fundamental moral axiom that no being that can experience pain or suffering ought to be forced to experience pain or suffering gratuitously."[295]

This leads Dombrowski and Deltete to a dilemma, because with anesthesia we can kill newborns *painlessly*. If it is not wrong to euthanize animals like cats, then it would not be wrong to euthanize infants who have brains as complex as a cat's. If it is wrong to euthanize infants, then veterinarians around the country should be rounded up and put on trial for euthanizing animals with brains that are similar to those of newborns.

Since I doubt Dombrowski and Deltete would accept either alternative, it seems that their argument defending abortion without conceding infanticide fails. The only logical explanation for why adults and infants equally possess a right to life is that both belong to a rational kind, or the human species. Of course, all unborn children belong to the human species, and this would justify granting them the right to life and prohibiting abortion.

Judge not

A common theme in religious pro-choice literature is that God will not condemn or judge women for having an abortion. The Religious Coalition for Reproductive Choice says, "God has given us the gift of free will and blesses decisions that are made thoughtfully, with knowledge and faith. Be assured that, no matter what you decide, you are a person who is loved and valued by God."[296] For women who feel guilty after abortions, RCRC gives instructions for a healing ritual. In one part of the ritual the minister consoles the grieving parents with the fact that at least they are still pro-choice. The minister says,

> However gently, the bud is broken.
> In pain and sorrow the Word is spoken:
> Not every essence shall come to be;
> It is in choosing that we are free.[297]

This is what the Lutheran theologian Dietrich Bonhoeffer called "cheap grace"—empty forgiveness without the need for genuine repentance.[298] It is true that no matter what we do, God loves us, and our sins cannot diminish his love for us. But when we sin it kills God's divine life within us. Fortunately, even as God respects our free will to reject him, his Son became a man and in a life of perfect obedience he undid the curses you and I bring upon ourselves through our constant disobedience.

God promises to give us new hearts and promises to cleanse us from our sins, provided we turn away from our sins and toward God. Abortion is no worse than any other serious sin that separates us from God. Christians should not cast out post-abortive women as some kind of "unforgivable other." Unlike other sins, however, abortion does require special kinds of healing because of the unique trauma that is involved.

To achieve that healing, I recommend women and men seek out post-abortive ministries such as Rachel's Vineyard, which was created by psychologist Theresa Burke. In her book *Forbidden Grief: The Unspoken Pain of Abortion,* Burke describes her experience counseling hundreds of women who suffered negative emotional side effects from their abortion decisions.

In order to begin this initial healing, women (and even men who've cooperated with abortions) are invited to a weekend retreat where they can share their stories with one another. Many of the participants have hidden their feelings for a long time, and the retreat gives them an opportunity to reflect on their experience and see where they need healing.

I attended one of these retreats with the permission of the participants so I could learn more about post-abortion healing. The most memorable moment was when we gathered around a bowl of water. Each participant placed a small floating candle representing their child who was aborted. After giving their children names, these women and men began to sing softly in unison, even as tears streamed down their faces, "Rock-a-bye, baby, on the treetop, when the wind blows, the cradle will rock . . ."

At the end of the retreat a priest was on hand to hear confessions and counsel women to understand that God forgives and loves them. He assured them they can trust their babies to God's care and have hope in the Savior who said, "Let the children come to me."[299] Jesus has specific words for post-abortive women and for anyone who has fallen into sin they are so ashamed of that they want to die. He says, "[T]here will be more joy in heaven over one sinner who repents than over ninety-nine righteous persons who need no repentance" (Luke 15:7).

Hiding or healing?

Some people might think that calling abortion "killing" and making arguments about the "deaths of unborn children" hurt women who have had abortions. While we should never intend to make someone feel guilt for a past sin, that should not deter our efforts to show our culture the reality of abortion.

After the Vietnam War, some veterans complained about being called "baby killers" in reference to events such as the

My Lai Massacre, where American troops were found guilty of killing innocent civilians, including women and infants, indiscriminately. While it was wrong to condemn all the veterans of that war for the immoral actions of a few, it was not wrong to call the My Lai Massacre what it was—baby killing. What post-abortive men and women need is not sheltering from the reality of abortion. They need an opportunity to heal and, if they feel called, to speak in defense of the unborn as well as the women who choose abortion. At the end of the Rachel's Vineyard retreat I attended, one woman said, "I just feel now that I want to do something. Like, I know what it's like, and I know what this does to babies, what it did to my baby. I feel like I can be a voice people have to listen to."

A person might be pro-choice in order to justify her past actions and mitigate any guilt she may still be feeling. Pope St. John Paul II recognized this and said a post-abortive woman's experience and ability to repent and trust in God can make her "among the most eloquent defenders of everyone's right to life."[300]

The pro-life movement should not shun or degrade post-abortive men and women but instead welcome them into the community. I remember one woman confiding in me that she would never go back to a pro-life meeting because one of the women there spoke with obvious revulsion about a friend who had three abortions. As you can guess, this woman I spoke with had had three abortions as well. In fact, half of all women who obtain abortions each year have had a previous abortion.

Instead of passing judgment, we are to be messengers of the gospel who pass along grace to all people we meet. Just as we aren't perfect in that goal and seek mercy and compassion when we fall, we should have mercy on others who fall and extend God's peace to them. St. Paul says, "Blessed be the God and Father of our Lord Jesus Christ, the Father of mercies and

God of all comfort, who comforts us in all our affliction, so that we may be able to comfort those who are in any affliction, with the comfort with which we ourselves are comforted by God" (2 Cor. 1:3–4).

Engaging the religious

The religious person's concern: There are religious reasons to believe that abortion is not wrong or should not concern outsiders.

Your objective: Show that there are no good religious reasons to justify abortion and redirect to the nonreligious reasons why abortion is a serious moral wrong.

★ ★ ★

Pro-choice: I don't see why Catholics get so hung up on abortion. It's not like Jesus ever said anything about it.

Pro-life: Are you saying that unless Jesus condemned something in Scripture there is nothing wrong with it? Jesus never said that child molestation was wrong, but would you agree that's not a good reason to make it legal?

PC: Well, yeah, sure.

PL: I'm glad we agree, but may I ask a question that might seem dumb? Why is child molestation wrong?

PC: Because it hurts innocent children.

PL: Okay, then, wouldn't someone like Jesus oppose abortion because it causes the death of very small children?

PC: I don't know. The Bible says that we are alive when we breathe, and fetuses have never taken the breath of life.

PL: Where in the Bible does it say that?

PC: Well, Adam wasn't alive until God breathed the breath of life into him.

PL: Right, but Adam was the first person God created. He was never alive in the womb like an unborn child is, right?

PC: I guess.

PL: So God would have to give Adam his soul directly. But there's no reason to think unborn children do not have immortal souls from the moment their bodies come into existence. Even if we aren't sure when the unborn receive their souls, can we agree they are living human beings?

PC: Sure.

PL: If we can agree on that, we can apply the principles in passages like Exodus 20:13 and Proverbs 6:16 that prohibit killing the innocent. Can you give me a reason to think those passages would not apply to unborn children?

PC: Look, I just think we shouldn't judge other people's situations. What they do is between them and God.

PL: Why do you think we shouldn't judge people's situations?

PC: Because Jesus says "Don't judge."

PL: Yes, but what Jesus said exactly in Matthew 7:1–2 is "Judge not, that you be not judged. For with the judgment you pronounce you will be judged, and the measure you give will be the measure you get." If I judge someone while being engaged in the same behavior I condemn, that makes me a hypocrite. But since I do not engage in killing innocent people, then why shouldn't I be able to say such an act is wrong?

PC: But aren't you being judgmental of women who
       have abortions when you say abortion is murder?

PL: You're right that human beings don't judge peo-
       ple's souls; only God can do that, since only God
       can see our hearts. But human beings can judge
       actions, and if an action hurts an innocent person,
       don't we have a duty to stop it? Loving our neigh-
       bor doesn't mean just being nice to him. It means
       helping him do good, avoid evil, and find healing
       if he does sin. This isn't done to hurt anyone but
       to help him come to know the God of love and
       to have a real relationship with him free from any
       sin that could pull him away from God.

Conclusion

I once asked a group of pro-life high school students, "How many of you would tell your parents if your sister was going to kill her two-year-old?" Immediately all their hands shot up. "Okay, how many of you would tell your parents if your sister was going to have an abortion?" Not a single hand went up. I asked them why, and some responded, "Well, it's so private," or "It's not my place to judge."

"But guys," I said, "what's the difference between killing a two-year-old outside the womb and a two-month-old in the womb?"

One of the students looked at the ultrasound image on his pro-life T-shirt and said, "I guess . . . there is no difference." These students called themselves pro-life, but they weren't ready to *act* like the killing of the unborn was wrong until someone prodded them into thinking hard about it.

Adults get caught in this mindset, too. Do you know anyone who is expecting a child or is about to become a mother? If you thought of a pregnant friend, you're wrong. That pregnant friend is not expecting a child and is not about to become a mother: She already has a child and she already is a mother.

While it is subtle, if we treat the unborn differently than we treat two-year-olds, then we have already bought into our culture's mentality that the unborn don't matter unless they are wanted, and even then they don't matter much.

The only remedy is to make a firm resolution to act like our belief that abortion ends the lives of human beings is really true. But this will not be easy. We will have to heed the call of Pope St. John Paul II to "be not afraid" and graciously make our opposition to abortion known in our schools and workplaces. The problem is, it's hard.

I'll admit: I'm scared to talk about abortion in public. My colleagues are often scared. And we are the trained advocates. Imagine people without training! They've got to be terrified. I can refute pro-choice arguments, but sometimes I just don't want to. At those times I don't want to refute an argument because I just want my hair cut. Or I just want my dinner. Or I just want my teeth cleaned. I don't want to answer the question, "What do you do for a living?"

See, most people don't ask you "What do you think about abortion?" because the topic is so unpleasant. But when I was a full-time pro-life advocate, I always looked for creative ways to answer the standard small-talk question, "What is your job?" My stock response was to say "I speak on bio-ethics" and then hope the conversation went somewhere else.

But in all those cases I was being selfish. I cared more about feeling comfortable than doing what was right. I'm not saying we should lecture everyone we meet about abortion. That would violate the pro-life apologist's cardinal rule of not being weird. There is a time and place for every conversation, but we should not be afraid to talk about abortion.

We must not be afraid. Too many lives, born and unborn, are counting on us to speak up for them. We can't be afraid to graciously but firmly insist that those who believe abortion should be legal defend their view that unborn human beings don't matter. After my wife and I endured the loss of our first child during pregnancy, she wrote an article that I found very moving. Here's an excerpt that underscores the need to, as my wife says, "make this personal":

> But as I miscarried, I also recalled the times when pro-choice advocates have defended their positions with rhetoric such as "It's not a baby," "It's not alive yet," or "It's not even a person." I immediately couldn't help but become really angry at these arguments that

belittle what I was feeling about my unborn child. If the pro-choice view is correct, women who miscarry are mourning nothing but the possibility of becoming pregnant, not an actual child she just lost. This is a lie, and it is insulting. Trent approached me, knowing something was wrong. "I think we need to start making this personal," I told him. He was confused, but I continued, "I mean, I think in the pro-life movement, we need to start using personal examples to be the voice of our children. We need to start saying statements such as 'So you're telling me when I miscarried, I have no right to think I actually had a baby I lost?'" A lot of people are advocates for legal abortion because they have intellectual arguments, but *more* people are defenders of legal abortion because they have emotional arguments. It's time we start being emotional right back, and showing them what the death of a child looks like.[301]

It's okay to get emotional, as long as we don't let our emotions override our reason or ability to be gracious. At times it will be frustrating when people seem like they won't listen or care. That is because people are complex and act not just with their heads but with their hearts. If people are emotionally attached to legal abortion, it will be difficult to persuade them that it should be illegal unless we can reach them on both an intellectual and an emotional level.

Imagine if a vegetarian had a powerful argument and some graphic images of a slaughterhouse and attempted to get you to give up eating meat (or some other favorite food). You may simply ignore rational arguments and evidence and cling to what you *want* to be true. I feel the same thing happens to pro-choice advocates who just *want* abortion to be legal. That is why we have to understand that persuasion is more than just good arguments; it is about reaching what St. Paul called "the inner man," or the place in our hearts where our most passionate desires reside.[302]

Once while I was on a campus in California I talked with a young woman for about an hour. We had covered almost all the arguments listed in the previous chapters, and both of us were becoming frustrated, because it seemed like the discussion was going around in circles. Suddenly, I noticed that she had a small, blue-and-white Israeli flag pin on her backpack. We talked a bit about Israel and our Jewish relatives, and I made the point that just as Jewish people throughout history have been dehumanized because they were unwanted in the eyes of others, I didn't want the unborn to be treated in the same way.

Within a few minutes the entire tone of the conversation changed. She told me, "This has really changed my mind on abortion. There's a lot I have to think about now." I was amazed that this simple example, hardly different from the other examples I used earlier in our conversation, had caused her to radically change her worldview. Jesus said, "For where your treasure is, there will your heart be also" (Matt. 6:21). This young woman now cared about the unborn because I was able to connect them to something she cared about. God could use my arguments to move not just her head but her heart as well.

It's important to remember that it is rarely just one conversation with a stranger that changes someone's mind. Rather, it is a long, gradual process of dialogue with a friend that is the most effective way to lead someone to truth.

My friend and fellow pro-life apologist Josh Brahm describes how a pro-choice friend of his became pro-life after months of conversation. He writes, "Two things were necessary conditions for her conversion: rigorous philosophical arguments and a loving friendship with someone on the other side." Why was a loving friendship so important? Josh says, "She found comfort in one thought: Even if every one of her pro-choice friends rejected her, she would have one pro-life friend on the other side welcoming her with loving arms."[303]

A pro-life advocate can spend a lifetime reading books, but if he never speaks to another person, then all of his study will be in vain. But if he speaks to other people with arrogance and not out of love, he will be, as Paul says, "a resounding gong" and have no worthwhile effect. It would be better for him to emulate the saintly octogenarian who prays, quietly and on her knees, with a smile on her face and a rosary in her hand, on a daily basis outside of an abortion facility.

But if he can "speak the truth in love," then he should allow God to use him in that way. Indeed, God has set before all of us divine appointments, or conversations with friends and even strangers where we can move their hearts toward caring for unborn human beings. Let's have faith and keep those appointments, appointments whose effects may be known only in the life to come.

Appendices

How to Talk to Pre- and Post-Abortive Women

As long as abortion is legal in this country, there will be only one way to truly stop it: persuade women not to choose it. This includes convincing friends and family not to choose abortion when they are faced with an unintended pregnancy as well as counseling strangers who enter abortion facilities. How should we talk to these women, as well as the men who may be encouraging them to choose abortion?

While the previous arguments in this book can be helpful to one degree or another, it's important to remember that they are designed for a general discussion of the issue, not for someone contemplating having an abortion. The latter case requires special approaches in order to overcome the stress involved in the situation. To make an analogy, there is a difference between making a philosophical argument against suicide and trying to talk someone down off a ledge. The latter case injects more emotion into the situation, and this may be even more important to confront than the logical arguments regarding the issue of abortion.

How should we confront those who are personally connected to abortion?[304] You will not succeed in saving the child of an abortion-minded woman unless she sees that you are trying to talk her out of an abortion for *her sake*, because you *genuinely care about her*.

Now, this doesn't mean that your concern for the child doesn't enter into the equation. However, if she sees you as a "fetus freak" who cares only about promoting an agenda or religious ideology, she will likely run into the arms of abortion providers, whose public image is that of a woman's advocate and helper. You must show her that because she is *now* a mother (even if she claims she is not ready to *become* one) your interest in saving her child coincides with your interest in her well-being. She needs to know that choosing abortion will be choosing to be the mother of a dead baby instead of a live one and that you don't want her to have to go through that experience.

Empathy

Before you engage this woman, pray for God's help to move her to love her child and to trust in God's care for her. Pray also for God to move *your* heart so you may know what precise words will resonate with this woman and her situation.

As you begin to speak with her, let this woman know that you feel sorry that she has to contemplate this choice and that she doesn't have to be alone when making her decision. Reassure her that she has a full range of options and that no situation is hopeless. Refrain from commenting on how she could have avoided her situation (birth control, abstinence, picking a better partner), because that won't change her immediate situation, where she feels like there is no way out except through having an abortion.

You have the power to open up possibilities to her she never knew existed, but they will be helpful only if you listen to her and understand her specific situation. For example, can she get help from parents, partner, or friends? What is her living situation? How does she feel about adoption? It is imperative that you be a "safe place" where this woman can confide and not someone who will berate her for making less than ideal choices in life.

It's possible that no matter how caring you are, she may be set on choosing abortion. Greg Cunningham of the Center for Bio-ethical Reform (CBR) puts it succinctly: "If a woman isn't more horrified of abortion than her pregnancy, then her child will die." CBR successfully uses graphic images of aborted children in order to show people the truth about abortion. I have seen graphic images cause women to walk out of abortion mills and other women to cancel appointments at these mills. However, these pictures should be used with the utmost care and respect for the person we are trying to help.

Get help

Once you have built a relationship of trust with this woman, and hopefully her partner as well, you will need to get some help. There are thousands of pro-life pregnancy resource centers across the country, and some of them offer discounted prenatal care, free ultrasounds, housing and job placement, STD testing, low-cost or free baby supplies, adoption referrals, and a myriad of other helpful services. They are staffed by people who are experienced in counseling women through unintended pregnancies, which can help take the pressure off you trying to do the counseling by yourself.

But unless you know about these centers and make it a commitment to take this woman to one (don't just give her a center's phone number), she may feel that these strangers could never help her through unexpected motherhood. At least not as well as someone she has some sort of trusting relationship with. Information about most of these PRCs is available on the Internet or in the phone book under "abortion alternatives."

Finally, to quote my friend Scott Klusendorf, "Never assume the baby is safe."[305] E-mail or call to make sure that she has not run into problems. In the early stages of pregnancy, when the only sign of the unborn child's existence is a little nausea, many women can be tempted by abortion in order to get their "normal life" back. Sometimes your intervention and promise of help are the only things that will make the difference.

Of course, it's possible that despite your best efforts this woman may still choose to abort her child. Or you may encounter a woman who chose abortion a long time ago. How should we talk with women, and men, who have had previous abortion experiences?

After abortion

Post-abortion grief is the result of a mother coming to grips with the realization that she has taken part in the killing of her child. Mothers who obtain abortions vary in their attitude toward the procedure, and this must be taken into account when talking to them. These attitudes include:

+ A denial of the humanity of the unborn child, such as thinking of it being "just cells" or "tissue" and abortion as "not being a big deal," but still being confused about the grief over her abortion.

+ An acceptance of abortion as the "lesser of two evils" when compared to motherhood. She may accept that the unborn is somewhat or totally human but see abortion as a terrible sacrifice she must make if she is going to "save her own life."

+ She may be religious and rationalize that she is "giving her baby back to God," and that "God will forgive her." She may also feel that God could never forgive her for what she's done and feel alienated from him.

+ She may have wanted the pregnancy but had the abortion for "health" reasons or was coerced into the procedure by a husband, boyfriend, doctor, or parents.

Although their circumstances may differ, each of these women will also be suffering from society's failure to provide an adequate grieving system for abortion. For example, a mother who miscarries is validated as having lost a child and allowed to grieve appropriately over that loss. A woman who has an abortion, however, is told that it was "the best decision she could have made," was "her choice or her right" or was "not a big deal, just a medical procedure."

After all, anyone can see the awkwardness of grieving over the death of a child when the death was planned and paid for by one or both of the child's parents. However, ignoring the problem is also a poor solution to the pain these women (and men) experience.

Conversation guidelines

Some women feel the grief of an abortion immediately following the procedure, while others don't feel the symptoms for many years. Times when emotional distress is most likely to occur include the anniversary date of the abortion or the anniversary of the expected due date of the baby. A post-abortive woman may also feel an onrush of negative feelings about her abortion in the presence of pregnant women, during discussions about abortion, or when she is in the presence of families with small children, especially children who would be the same age as her aborted child.

Listening is the most important skill to have when talking to a woman who has had an abortion. A common temptation (usually faced by men) is to try to say something that will make the woman feel better or solve her problem. However, just as abortion doesn't change the fact that a woman was pregnant, post-abortion counseling does not take away the fact that an abortion happened and that a child has died. Listen to how the woman is feeling, and ask questions to show you care and are interested in her well-being, questions like "How long have you had these feelings?" or "How are you handling everything since the abortion?" You can't take away her pain, but you can take away her loneliness.

Do not try to control the conversation or steer it in the direction you think it should go. If she wants to speak of a four-week-old embryo as a "baby," let her. If she needs to cry, yell, or not talk at all, let her. Above all else, keep her and her healing as the center of your focus. The grieving process is different for everyone, and this woman should be given whatever time she needs to work through it.

In addition, avoid your own personal commentary on abortion or statements that minimize her pain, such as noting the gestational age of her child, her life situation, or her reasons for having the abortion. Let her know that you feel sorry for her pain, but do not tell her that you "know how she feels," because if you haven't had an abortion, you don't know (and even if you have, you don't know that your experiences match).

Above all else, *never tell anyone about her abortion* unless you have been given permission to do so. The time may come when she is comfortable sharing her experience with others, and if she chooses to do so, she can be a huge help to other women in the same situation.

If you treat her grief as if she were grieving over the death of a born child, then you will probably act with the appropriate amount of compassion. This will prevent you from relying on clichés like "You can always have another child," "You were too young to be a mother," or worse, telling her "Suck it up and just get over it." Let her know it's okay to grieve, but also let her know there is hope and there are resources to help her through her grieving process so that she can experience the peace of Christ and the loving mercy of God offered through him.

Your best option to help her find this healing is to connect her with a local post-abortion counselor or a post-abortive retreat such as Rachel's Vineyard. A local Catholic priest can probably recommend suitable post-abortion counseling and be able to help this woman by administering the sacrament of reconciliation. I also recommend reading *Forbidden Grief: The Unspoken Pain of Abortion* by Dr. Theresa Burke, the founder of Rachel's Vineyard, to help understand abortion trauma and how to heal from it.[306]

Finally, be on the lookout for the woman becoming self-destructive or suicidal. If her grief becomes severe, you may need to seek professional help. If your friend seems to be contemplating suicide, call a suicide hotline immediately. It is far better to overreact than not to act before it's too late.

Answering Infanticide

Some philosophers agree with the pro-life claim that there is no moral difference between aborting a fetus and killing a newborn infant. However, rather than oppose both acts, as pro-life advocates do, they affirm the morality of both abortion and infanticide. Philosopher Peter Singer writes in his book *Practical Ethics*:

> At present parents can choose whether to keep or destroy their disabled offspring only if the disability happens to be detected during pregnancy. There is no logical basis for restricting parents' choice to these particular disabilities. If disabled newborn infants were not regarded as having a right to life until, say, a week or a month after birth it would allow parents, in consultation with their doctors, to choose on the basis of far greater knowledge of the infant's condition than is possible before birth.[307]

Singer does not sound crazy as he coolly explains his position in a soft-spoken Australian accent. Several years ago, during his presentation at Arizona State University on animal rights, many people nodded in agreement as Singer compared "speciesism," or the view that human beings deserve basic rights while animals do not, with racism and sexism. Fortunately, during the private question-and-answer session that followed, I had my chance to highlight the logical conclusion of Singer's beliefs before his adoring audience.

"Dr. Singer," I said, "my parents euthanized our pet dog because he was ill, and they no longer wanted to care for him. Were their actions wrong because my dog had interests that my parents were infringing upon?"

"If the dog was a significant burden, then, no," he replied. "So, considering that you said it is wrong to discriminate between species, would the situation be any different if my parents had euthanized my younger brother instead?"

Singer looked uncomfortable and said, "Well, it's different with infants, because there are emotions involved and—"

"But should a disabled newborn be treated any differently than a disabled dog?"

"No, the newborn and the dog would have the same value in either situation." Some attendees' eyes grew wide as they gasped at Singer's candid response, but many others nodded in agreement! Several people came up to me afterward and criticized my "narrow-minded" view that infants had a right to life.

Most pro-life advocates treat infanticide as something not to seriously argue against but simply to ridicule.[308] After all, even most pro-choice advocates agree that it is wrong to kill infants. But there is a growing trend in academia to legitimize infanticide, especially for sick or disabled infants. The danger comes when this trend receives legitimacy through academia before being passed onto the general public.

Rev. Richard John Neuhaus, founder of the journal *First Things*, said, "Thousands of ethicists and bioethicists, as they are called, professionally guide the unthinkable on its passage through the debatable on its way to becoming the justifiable, until it is finally established as the unexceptional."[309] This has motivated some pro-life advocates to put forward a rigorous critique of the case for infanticide, which includes some of the arguments presented here.[310]

Moral intuitions

There are several arguments the pro-life advocate can make against a defense of abortion that condones infanticide. First, we can ask, "What is wrong with trusting our moral intuitions when it comes to the wrongness of killing infants?" We think the external world actually exists and is not just a simulation, because we experience the external world and have no good reason to doubt our experiences or "intuitions" about it. In the same way, when we witness horrendous evils or injustices and we have a visceral intuition that those actions are just plain wrong, why not trust it?

What would we think of a firefighter who rescued ten cats from a burning building but left a one-month-old infant to die? Should we approve of eating handicapped humans who have the mental capacity of a cow? There would be nothing wrong with these acts if we considered newborns, adults with the intelligence of newborns, and animals to have the same value and the same rights.

Critics like Singer would probably say we should simply not eat infants or cows and that, all things being equal, it would be better to save ten cats than one baby (provided no human being who could experience more sadness than ten cats put together, such as the baby's mother, wanted the baby to live). He would say our intuition is warped in the same way a racist's intuition about the group he oppresses is warped.

Speaking of racism, Singer claims that we should not treat animals differently based on their species (or engage in what he calls speciesism) because species membership is as irrelevant to someone's value as race. But we legitimately use species distinctions all the time and do not consider pain or pleasure to be the deciding factors in our moral decisions. We use species distinctions to demonstrate, for example, whether a member of a species is "flourishing."[311] This is crucial, because the main concern that drives Singer's utilitarian ethical decisions is whether they will contribute to the happiness or "flourishing" of a being. Let's consider one case that helps us see that we do treat species differently.

If we had a drug that could give an animal the ability to read, should we use the drug on a cat or on a ten-year-old illiterate child? Both animals can't read, but we consider the human child disabled or hindered by illiteracy, while the cat is not hindered or disabled. Since we are justified in using species identity as a marker to judge whether a species is flourishing, it follows that species designation has some value in our moral judgments, and we should not be blind to the species involved in certain acts. We can then make a legitimate argument that when a newborn is deprived of life, it is a more serious act against an "individual's flourishing" than the killing of a cognitively similar animal like a chipmunk.

After-birth abortion

The philosophers Alberto Giubilini and Francesca Minerva have argued in a paper dubbed by the media as advocating "after-birth" abortion that a person must be any being who can value his own existence. They write:

> Both a fetus and a newborn certainly are human beings and potential persons, but neither is a "person" in the sense of "subject of a moral right to life." We take "person" to mean an individual who is capable of attributing to her own existence some (at least) basic value such that being deprived of this existence represents a loss to her. This means that many *non-human animals and mentally retarded human individuals are persons*, but that *all the individuals who are not in the condition of attributing any value to their own existence are not persons*. Merely being human is not in itself a reason for ascribing someone a right to life."[312]

One could object to this argument and say that asleep, drugged, or unconscious adult humans are not capable of valuing their own lives, but they are still persons. Giubilini and Minerva could respond that these persons do have the capacity to value their own lives and have valued them in the past.

That capacity is temporarily "blocked," and so they are simply *disabled* persons.

However, consider a forty-year-old male named Frank who was injured in a car accident. Frank is now only minimally conscious, on par with an infant in respect to cognitive abilities. Suppose that Frank's impairment is due to the fact that the accident caused part of his brain to be damaged and that this damage is the direct cause of his lack of function. Fortunately for Frank, it is the year 2065, and hospitals can restore damaged brain tissue in the same way that we can restore damaged pelvises (a process which would have mystified almost everyone in the nineteenth century, just as the process of brain restoration mystifies us now).

Now consider the claim that "a person is any human being who has the immediate biological capacity for rational thought." Under this definition, a thoughtful person would ask, "Is Frank a person?" Unlike the cases of being asleep or drugged, Frank is an injured adult who has to regrow his brain in order to be rational. It seems clear that Frank definitely does not have "the immediate biological capacity for rational thought" and this is not due to a mere "block" but to a substantial loss of brain matter that is needed for the capacity to have rational thought.

But if that means that Frank is not a person, then giving his brain restorative therapy would be akin to giving a cat hip-replacement surgery. It would be kind (albeit wasteful), but not wrong to withhold. But it seems that just as it would be wrong to deny a comatose patient a skin graft or other surgery that improved his health, it would be wrong to deny Frank the simple brain recovery surgery.

If the critic contends that Frank is a person by virtue of the fact that his brain has the capacity to regrow and develop to the point of having rational thought, then the critic must accept that the fetus is a person, because she too has the capacity to grow a brain that will under normal circumstances develop to the point of having rational thought. Why should we consider the fact that Frank can have his brain artificially developed through surgery morally relevant, while the fetus's ability to grow a brain naturally is not?

However, an objection may arise. Would that mean that a robot that has the capacity to develop a brain via artificial surgery is a person? I say no, because the robot's capacity to have a rational brain is extrinsic, and not intrinsic to the robot's nature. In that case, the robot didn't get a brain and become a person, but instead the person's brain got a robot body.

Unlike the robot, both injured Frank and any healthy infant both possess a *natural* capacity to grow brain tissue as a part of the kind of being they are. Robots must be built, while humans simply develop. If she is allowed to develop, a healthy infant will grow a brain large enough to have rational thought, because she is a rational being by nature (even if she can't function rationally). Likewise, Frank is a rational being by nature whose body's innate ability to grow a brain is simply aided by modern medicine.

If we are morally obligated to heal Frank by restoring his rational powers via external processes that encourage the natural growth of a brain (brain reconstruction surgery), then are we not morally obligated to instill rational powers in infants via external processes that encourage the natural growth of their brains (e.g., provide food and shelter)?

I answer that in both cases we are obligated, because rational beings, regardless of function, possess a right to life. While the brain restoration case may require extraordinary medical care (e.g., a $20 million surgery) and thus not be morally obligatory, the infant requires only ordinary care. If such ordinary care would allow Frank to heal his brain, then we should provide that same care to infants who have the natural ability to grow a brain that is capable of rational thought.

Metaphysical problems

Defenders of infanticide typically promote a psychological criteria of personhood that argues that a person is simply the sum total of his mental experiences. For them, a person is just a rational mind, and since infants do not have rational minds, they are not persons.

But there are deep problems with this view. For example, imagine I stepped into a machine that created an exact double of me. This machine causes me and the double it creates to lose consciousness briefly during the copying phase, after which the machine's technicians move us into separate rooms.

If a person is no more than a collection of mental states, since we both have identical memories, then both of us would be "Trent" (especially since neither of us would know if we were the original or the copy). But this leads to contradictions like "Trent is in two places at once" or "Trent is hungry and not hungry at the same time."[313]

While the "psychological view" of personhood leads to contradictions, the pro-life view of personhood—that a person is a substance or a being with a rational nature—does not. It would hold that the double was a new human organism that is *numerically* distinct from me while being *qualitatively* identical to me. The copy is merely someone who is a lot like me, but it would not be me, because I am a unique organism or rational substance.

Another condition that shows the problems with the psychological view is multiple personality disorder. If mental states make someone a human being, then our ability to cure someone of multiple personality disorder by erasing four of the alternate "personalities" from the patient's mind would be tantamount to murdering those four "people."[314] This should make us suspicious that a person is identical to a coherent set of mental states.

Finally, according to infanticide proponents, it is the loss of the conscious self that makes killing wrong, because we are essentially just self-conscious minds. Thus, if a being is killed prior to the development of its conscious self (such as in abortion), no harm occurs. Likewise, if the conscious self is lost at any point later in life (such as someone falling into an irreversible coma), then that person has died, even if his body is biologically alive.

However, imagine a case in which a four-year-old boy is dying from a rare disease. We have a drug that can save his life, but it will cause him to lose all of his memories and return him to the psychological state of an infant. Should we erase the boy's memories or let him die? I think most people would agree that we should save his life.

But under the infanticide proponent's view, the acts of letting the boy die and erasing his memories while saving his life are equivalent. Both acts destroy the conscious self, so there should be no difference, and hence no difficulty, in choosing the "correct" course of action. But since most people see death as being worse than the child losing his memories, I believe this provides evidence that a person is not just a mind but a union of body and mind. This implies that a person begins to exist prior to the development of a conscious mind after birth.[315]

Select Bibliography

Alcorn, Randy. *Pro-life Answers to Pro-choice Arguments.* Colorado Springs: Multnomah Books, 2000.

Arkes, Hadley. *Natural Rights and the Right to Choose.* New York: Cambridge University Press, 2004.

——. *First Things: An Inquiry into the First Principles of Morals and Justice.* Princeton, NJ: Princeton University Press, 1986.

Beckwith, Francis. *Defending Life: A Moral and Legal Case Against Abortion Choice.* New York: Cambridge University Press, 2007.

——. "Defending Abortion Philosophically: A Review of David Bonin's A Defense of Abortion. *Journal of Medicine & Philosophy*, 31 April 2006.

——. "A Critical Appraisal of Theological Arguments for Abortion Rights." *Bibliotheca Sacra* 148 no. 591 1991.

Berg, Thomas V., Marie T. Hilliard, and Mark F. Stegman. "Emergency Contraceptives & Catholic Healthcare: A New Look at the Science and the Moral Question." *Westchester Institute White Papers* 2, no. 1, June 2011.

Boonin, David. *A Defense of Abortion.* Cambridge: Cambridge University Press, 2003.

Brody, Baruch. *Abortion and the Sanctity of Human Life: A Philosophical View.* Cambridge, MA: MIT Press, 1975.

Burke, Theresa with David C. Reardon. *Forbidden Grief: The Unspoken Pain of Abortion.* Springfield, IL: Acorn Books, 2007.

Chikako, Takeshita. *The Global Biopolitics of the IUD: How Science Constructs Contraceptive Users and Women's Bodies.* USA: Massachusetts Institute of Technology, 2012.

Condic, Maureen L. "When Does Human Life Begin? A Scientific Perspective." *The Westchester Institute* 1 no. 1, October 2008.

Dawkins, Richard. *The God Delusion.* New York: Houghton Mifflin, 2006.

Dombrowski, Daniel A. and Robert Deltete. *A Brief, Liberal, Catholic Defense of Abortion.* Chicago: University of Illinois Press, 2000.

Garton, Jean Staker. *Who Broke the Baby?* Minneapolis: Bethany Fellowship, 1979.

George, Robert. "Infanticide and Moral Madness." *Journal of Medical Ethics* 39 no. 5, 2013.

George, Robert and Christopher Tollefsen. *Embryo: A Defense of Human Life.* New York: Doubleday, 2008.

Gilbert, Scott F. *Developmental Biology.* Sunderland, MA: Sinauer Associates, Inc.: June 30, 2013.

Giubilini, Alberto and Francesca Minerva. "After-birth Abortion: Why Should the Baby Live?" *Journal of Medical Ethics* 10.1136, 2011.

Halevy, Amir. "Beyond Brain Death?" *Journal of Medicine and Philosophy*, 26, no. 5, 2001.

Hern, Warren. *Abortion Practice.* Philadelphia: J.B. Lippincott Company, 1984.

Horan, Dennis J., Edward R. Grant, and Paige C. Cunningham. *Abortion and the Constitution: Reversing Roe v. Wade Through the Courts.* Washington, DC: Georgetown University Press, 1987.

Jaworski, Patricia. "Thinking About *The Silent Scream*: An Audio Documentary" in *Abortion Rights and Fetal 'Personhood.'* ed., Edd Doerr and James W. Prescott. Long Beach, CA: Americans for Religious Liberty, 1990.

Johnson, Abby. *Unplanned.* Carol Stream, IL: Tyndale House Publishers, 2010.

Kaczor, Christopher. *The Ethics of Abortion: Women's Rights, Human Life, and the Question of Justice.* New York: Routledge, 2011.

Klusendorf, Scott. *The Case for Life.* Wheaton, IL: Crossway Books, 2009.

————. *Pro-life 101: A Step-by-Step Guide to Making Your Case Persuasively.* San Pedro, CA: Stand to Reason Press, 2002.

Koukl, Greg. *Precious Unborn Human Persons.* San Pedro, CA: Stand to Reason Press, 1999.

————. *Tactics: A Game Plan for Discussing Your Christian Convictions.* Grand Rapids, MI: Zondervan, 2009.

Kreeft, Peter. *The Unaborted Socrates.* Downer's Grove, IL: InterVarsity Press, 1983.

Lee, Patrick and Germain Grisez. "Total Brain Death: A Reply to Alan Shewmon." *Bioethics* 26 no. 5, 2012.

————. *Abortion and Unborn Human Life.* Washington DC: Catholic University of America Press, 2010.

————. "The Pro-life Argument from Substantial Identity: A Defense." *Bioethics* Volume 18, Number 3, 2004.

Levitt, Steven and Stephen Dubner. *Freakonomics: A Rogue Economist Explores the Hidden Side of Everything.* New York: Harper Perennial, 2005.

Maguire, Daniel C. "A Catholic Theologian at an Abortion Clinic," in *The Ethics of Abortion* ed. Robert M. Baird and Stuart E. Rosenbaum. New York: Prometheus Books, 2001.

Markowitz, Sally. "A Feminist Defense of Abortion," in *The Abortion Controversy: 25 Years After Roe vs. Wade, A Reader* ed. Louis Pojman and Francis Beckwith. Canada: Wadsworth Publishing, 1998.

Marquis, Don. "Why Abortion Is Immoral," in *The Abortion Controversy: 25 Years After Roe vs. Wade: A Reader*, ed., Louis Pojman and Francis Beckwith. Canada: Wadsworth Publishing, 1998.

May, William. *Catholic Bioethics and the Gift of Human Life.* Huntington, IN: Our Sunday Visitor, 2000.

McCorvey, Norma. *Won by Love.* Nashville: Thomas Nelson Publishers, 1997.

McDonagh, Eileen. *Breaking the Abortion Deadlock: From Choice to Consent.* New York: Oxford University Press, 1996.

McMahan, Jeff. "Challenges to Human Equality." *The Journal of Ethics* 12 (2008).

Moore, Keith L. and T.V.N. Persaud. *The Developing Human: Clinically Oriented Embryology*, 9th edition. Philadelphia: Saunders, 2013.

Morowitz, Harold J. and James Trefil. *The Facts of Life: Science and the Abortion Controversy.* New York: Oxford University Press, 1992.

Nussbaum, Martha. *Frontiers of Justice: Disability, Nationality, Species Membership.* Cambridge, MA: Belknap Press, 2006.

O'Brien, George Dennis. *The Church and Abortion: A Catholic Dissent.* Maryland: Rowan and Littlefield Publishing, 2010.

O'Rahilly, Ronan and Fabiola Müller. *Human Embryology and Teratology*. New York: Wiley-Liss, 2001.

Pojman, Louis P. "Abortion: A Defense of the Personhood Argument" in *The Abortion Controversy: 25 Years After Roe v. Wade, A Reader*, ed., Louis Pojman and Francis Beckwith, Canada: Wadsworth Publishing, 1998.

Pope John Paul II. *Evangelium Vitae, 1995*.

Potter, E.L. and J.M. Craig. *Pathology of the Fetus and the Infant*. Chicago: Year Book Medical Publishers, 1975.

Rogers, Carl. *On Becoming a Person: A Therapist's View of Psychology*. New York: Houghton Mifflin Company, 1989.

Sadler T.W. *Langman's Medical Embryology*. Baltimore: Williams & Wilkins, 2010.

Sagan, Carl. *Billions & Billions: Thoughts on Life and Death at the Brink of the Millennium*. New York: Random House, 1997.

Schwartz, Stephen. *The Moral Question of Abortion*. Chicago: Loyola University Press, 1990.

Shannon, Thomas A. and Allan B. Wolter. "Reflections on the Moral Status of the Pre-Embryo." *Theological Studies*, December 1990.

Singer, Peter. *Practical Ethics*. Cambridge: Cambridge University Press, 2011.

Spitzer, Fr. Robert. *Ten Universal Principles: A Brief Philosophy of the Life Issues*. San Francisco: Ignatius Press, 2011.

Steinbock, Bonnie. *Life Before Birth: The Moral and Legal Status of Embryos and Fetuses*. New York: Oxford University Press, 1992.

Suarez, Antoine. "Hydatidiform Moles and Teratomas Confirm the Human Identity of the Preimplantation Embryo." *The Journal of Medicine and Philosophy* 15, no. 6, 1990.

Thomson, Judith Jarvis. "A Defense of Abortion" *Philosophy & Public Affairs* 1, no. 1, Fall 1971.

Tooley, Michael. *Abortion and Infanticide*. Oxford: Oxford University Press, 1983.

Tribe, Laurence H. *Abortion: The Clash of Absolutes*. New York: W.W. Norton & Company, 1990.

Wagner, Stephen. *Common Ground Without Compromise: 25 Questions to Create Dialogue on Abortion*. San Pedro, CA: Stand to Reason Press, 2008.

Warren, Mary Anne. "On the Moral and Legal Status of Abortion." *The Monist*, 57, no. 4, 1973.

Wennberg, Robert. *Life in the Balance: Exploring the Abortion Controversy*. Grand Rapids, MI: Eerdmans, 1985.

About the Author

Trent Horn is an apologist for Catholic Answers and previously served as the Respect Life coordinator for the Diocese of Phoenix. He holds an M.A. in theology and specializes in training Catholics to defend the pro-life worldview.

Endnotes

Introduction

1. Lydia Saad, "Pro-Choice Americans at Record-Low 41 percent," *Gallup Poltiics*, Gallup Inc., May 23, 2012, www.gallup.com/poll/154838/pro-choice-americans-record-low.aspx.

2. By general abortion bans I mean laws that would have prohibited almost all abortions both prior to and after fetal viability. Even laws that allow abortions for rape or the health of the mother but outlaw over 90 percent of all other abortions have not passed. For the "35 percent" figure see "June 2012 Poll for National Women's Law Center and Planned Parenthood Federation of America," Hart Research. Cited in Geoffrey Cowley, "More and more 'pro-life' Americans support abortion rights," *MSNBC*, September 13, 2013, www.msnbc.com/msnbc/more-and-more-pro-life-americans-support-ab.

3. To learn more about Justice for All visit its Web site, www.jfaweb.org.

4. They include *Defending Life: The Moral and Legal Case Against Abortion Choice* by Francis Beckwith (2007), *Abortion and Unborn Human Life* by Patrick Lee (2010), and *The Ethics of Abortion* by Christopher Kaczor (2012).

Chapter 1: What's at Stake?

5. This point is also made in Randy Alcorn, *Pro-life Answers to Pro-choice Arguments*, Multnomah Books, 2000, 38.

6. See also Stephen Wagner's description of the terms *pro-life, pro-choice*, and *advocate* that I have drawn from for this section. Stephen Wagner, *Common Ground Without Compromise: 25 Questions to Create Dialogue on Abortion*, Stand to Reason Press, 2008, 7.

7. At the time this abortionist was Dr. Warren Hern and his Web site was www.drhern.com.

8. Wanted fetuses are currently protected under the 2004 *Unborn Victims of Violence Act* (Public Law 108-212). Approximately thirty-five other states have similar laws but all exclude prosecuting an abortion provider for killing an unwanted fetus.

9. Rachel K. Jones and Jenna Jerman, "Abortion Incidence and Service Availability in the United States, 2011," *Perspectives on Sexual and Reproductive Health* 46, no. 1 (March 2014), 3, www.guttmacher.org/pubs/journals/psrh.46e0414.pdf.

10. Rachel K. Jones, Lawrence B. Finer and Susheela Singh, "Characteristics of U.S. Abortion Patients, 2008," Guttmacher Institute (May 2010), 8, www.guttmacher.org/pubs/US-Abortion-Patients.pdf.

11. Rachel K. Jones and M.L. Kavanaugh, "Changes in abortion rates between 2000 and 2008 and lifetime incidence of abortion," *Obstetrics & Gynecology* 117, no. 66 (June 2011),1358-1366, www.ncbi.nlm.nih.gov/pubmed/21606746.

12. Rachel K. Jones, Lawrence B. Finer and Susheela Singh, "Characteristics of U.S. Abortion Patients, 2008," 9.

13. Lawrence B. Finer, Lori F. Frohwirth, Lindsay A. Dauphinee, Susheela Singh, and Ann M. Moore, "Reasons U.S. Women Have Abortions: Quantitative and Qualitative Perspectives," *Perspectives on Sexual and Reproductive Health*, 37, no. 3 (2005), 114, www.guttmacher.org/pubs/psrh/full/3711005.pdf.

14. Abortions are either spontaneous (usually referred to as *miscarriages)* or they are caused intentionally *(induced abortions)*. Induced abortions are either "therapeutic," done in response to a health problem with the woman or child, or "elective," which means they are done for social or economic reasons.

15. The word *embryo* comes from a Greek word that means "growing in full," and the word *fetus* comes from a Latin word that means "offspring" or "young one." A human embryo becomes a human fetus at eight weeks, because that is when the major body parts and organs are now in place.

16. Some pro-life advocates prefer the term *pre-born child*, since it emphasizes the child is merely waiting to be born and does not undergo a radical transformation at birth, something the term *unborn* seems to imply. I have chosen to use the latter term, since it is still the more common term, and I don't think it is dehumanizing. However, I am open to changing my use of language on this subject.

17. Pope John Paul II, *Evangelium Vitae*, 99.

18. RU-486 is also known as mifeprex. Along with mifepristone and misoprostol, medical abortion procedures sometimes use methotrexate to facilitate the abortion process.

19. "Facts About Mifepristone (RU-486)," *Abortion Facts*, National Abortion Federation, www.prochoice.org/about_abortion/facts/facts_mifepristone.html.

20. Rachel K. Jones and Jenna Jerman, "Abortion Incidence and Service Availability in the United States, 2011," *Perspectives on Sexual and Reproductive Health* 46, no. 1 (March 2014), 3, www.guttmacher.org/pubs/journals/psrh.46e0414.pdf.

21. The drug Ella, which is claimed to be able to prevent pregnancy when taken as late as five days after intercourse, seems much more likely to kill a developing embryo. The FDA manufacturing label for Ella clearly states that, "Use of Ella is contraindicated during an existing or suspected pregnancy. Embryofetal loss was noted in all pregnant rats and in half of the pregnant rabbits following 12 and 13 days of dosing." Available online at www.accessdata.fda.gov/drugsatfda_docs/label/2010/022474s000lbl.pdf.

22. See Chapter 6's section "When the 'experts' disagree" for a more detailed reply to this issue.

23. "[I]n 1963, the U.S. Department of Health, Education, and Welfare defined abortion as 'all the measures which impair the ability of the zygote at any time between the instant of fertilization and the completion of labor.'" Chikako Takeshita, *The Global Biopolitics of the IUD: How Science Constructs Contraceptive Users and Women's Bodies*, Massachusetts Institute of Technology, 2012, 107.

24. In 1965 the American College of Obstetricians and Gynecologists declared, "Conception is the implantation of a fertilized ovum" (*Terms Used in Reference to the Fetus*. No. 1, Davis, September, 1965). This change seemed to be motivated by a desire to define pregnancy as beginning after implantation so that methods of birth control that destroyed an embryo could still be considered contraceptive.

25. Sheldon Segal et al., "Proceedings of the Second International Conference, Intra-Uterine Contraception, October 2-3, 1964," New York, *International Series*, Excerpta Medica Foundation, No. 86, 1965, 212.

26. While the manufacturer's label on Plan B says the drug might prevent an embryo from implanting in the uterus, some studies have shown that pregnancy rates among Plan B and non-Plan B users were the same when Plan B was taken after ovulation, indicating the drug did not prevent implantation (see N. Novikova, E. Weisberg, F. Z. Stanczyk, H. B. Croxatto, and I. S. Fraser. "Effectiveness of levonorgestrel emergency contraception given before or after ovulation: A pilot study," *Contraception* 75, 2007, 112-118. This issue is still disputed, so a cautious approach is recommended. For a defense of Plan B's "post-ovulatory" effects, see Thomas V. Berg, Marie T. Hilliard, and Mark F. Stegman, "Emergency Contraceptives & Catholic Healthcare: A New Look at the Science and the Moral Question," *Westchester Institute White Papers* 2, no. 1, June 2011, and Rebecca Peck and Juan R. Velez, "The Postovulatory Method of Action of Plan B," *National Catholic Bioethics Center*, December 2013. In regard to whether hormonal contraception can prevent an embryo from implanting in the womb, see Rich Poupard, "Does a Thin Uterine Lining Support the 'Pill as Baby Killer' Theory," *LTI Blog*, June 16, 2008, lti-blog.blogspot.com/2008/06/does-thin-uterine-lining-support-pill.html. Once again, the scientific conclusions in many of these arguments may be subject to further revision, so an attitude of caution against overstating or under-stating the dangers of these drugs is necessary.

27. "Facts About Mifepristone (RU-486)," *Abortion Facts*, National Abortion Federation, www.prochoice.org/about_abortion/facts/facts_mifepristone.html.

28. Pazol, "Abortion Surveillance—United States, 2008."

29. "Suction Curettage," *Informed Consent for Abortion*, Michigan Department of Community Health, www.michigan.gov/mdch/0,1607,7-132-2940_4909_6437_19077-46301--,00.html.

30. Pazol, "Abortion Surveillance—United States, 2008."

31. *Gonzales vs. Carhart*, 550 U.S. 124 (2007) Section I-A.

32. Warren Hern, *Abortion Practice*, J.B. Lippincott Company, 1984,142.

33. Elizabeth Gettleman writes, "[T]here is no such thing as a 'partial birth abortion.' This term was born of the clever marketing of the anti-choice movement (or "pro-life" as they like to be called) and has no medical foundation whatsoever," Elizabeth Gettleman, "Partial Birth Abortion Ban's Both Arbitrary and Dangerous" *Mother Jones*, April 18, 2007, www.motherjones.com/mojo/2007/04/partial-birth-abortion-bans-both-arbitrary-and-dangerous. But this argument is as silly as saying there is no such thing as a "heart attack" since doctors don't use that term and prefer the more technical term *myocardial infarction*.

34. American College of Obstetricians and Gynecologists Executive Board, Statement on Intact Dilation and Extraction, January 12, 1997, App. 599–560.

35. H.R. 1833, Partial-Birth Abortion Ban Act of 1995, "Factsheet." Available online at judiciary.house.gov/legacy/hr1833.htm. Haskell's comments can be found in the newsletter of the American Medical Association, *American Medical News*, July 5, 1993, 21.

36. In 1967, Colorado and California became the first states to repeal their abortion laws. Alaska and Hawaii soon followed, and in 1970 New York allowed abortion up to the twenty-fourth week, making it the sixteenth state to liberalize its abortion laws. Of those sixteen, twelve states had reformed their laws only to allow abortion for rape, fetal deformity, or to protect the life or health of the mother. Thirty-three other states between 1970 and 1973 debated the issue in their legislatures and all voted to maintain prohibitions against abortion, except when needed to save the life of a woman. See John and Barbara Willke, *Abortion: Questions and Answers*, Hayes Publishing Company, 2003, 33–34.

37. Norma McCorvey, *Won by Love*, Thomas Nelson Publishers, 1997, 29.

38. *Roe v. Wade*, 410 U.S. 113, Section VI. An excellent book on this subject is Dennis J. Horan, Edward R. Grant, and Paige C. Cunningham, *Abortion and the Constitution: Reversing Roe v. Wade Through the Courts*, Georgetown University Press, 1987. An 1871 report released by the American Medical Association also makes clear the reason abortion deserved to be outlawed. The "Report on Criminal Abortion" states that, "[M]en who cling to a noble profession only to dishonor it; men who seek not to save, but to destroy; men known not only to the profession, but to the public as abortionists. . . . These modern Herods, like their prototype, have a summary mode of dealing with their victims. They perform the triple office of Legislative, Judiciary, and Executive, and, to crown the tragedy, they become the executioners. . . . The abortionists are more destructive to human life than ten [foreign] armies." "Report on Criminal Abortion," *Transactions of the American Medical Association* 22, 1871, 240–257.

39. *Roe v. Wade*, 410 U.S. 113, Section VIII.

40. Ibid., Section IX.

41. Ibid., Section X.

42. Edward Lazarus, "The Lingering Problems with *Roe v. Wade*, and Why the Recent Senate Hearings on Michael McConnell's Nomination Only Underlined Them," *Findlaw.com,* October 3, 2002, writ.news. findlaw.com/lazarus/20021003.html.

43. The most dramatic change in abortion law since *Roe* was undoubtedly the 1992 *Planned Parenthood of Southeastern Pennsylvania v. Casey* U.S. Supreme Court decision, which essentially threw out Roe's trimester system and made viability the crucial dividing line. States could ban abortion after viability (as long as they left an incredibly large exception for a woman's "health"), but before viability states could restrict abortion only as long as it did not place an "undue burden" on the woman obtaining the abortion. The Court defined an undue burden as "the purpose or effect of placing a substantial obstacle in the path of a woman seeking an abortion of a nonviable fetus." The Court was now occupied with defining what exactly constituted such a

burden. For example, in Casey, the Court ruled that requiring a woman to have the consent of her husband in order to obtain an abortion was an undue burden while requiring a minor to have the consent of her parents was not.

44. "We agree with the District Court, 319 F.Supp. at 1058, that the medical judgment may be exercised in the light of all factors—physical, emotional, psychological, familial, and the woman's age—relevant to the well-being of the patient. All these factors may relate to health. This allows the attending physician the room he needs to make his best medical judgment." *Doe v. Bolton*, 410 U.S. 179, Section IV, Paragraph C.

45. Warren Hern, "Is Pregnancy Really Normal?" *Family Planning Perspectives* 3, No. 1, January 1971, www.drhern.com/pregnorml.htm.

46. In 2012, 12,765 people were murdered in the U.S., with 8,855 of the murders occurring with a firearm. "Expanded Homicide Data Table 8," *Crime in the United States 2012,* Federal Bureau of Investigation, www.fbi.gov/about-us/cjis/ucr/crime-in-the-u.s/2012/crime-in-the-u.s.-2012/offenses-known-to-law-enforcement/expanded-homicide/expanded_homicide_data_table_8_murder_victims_by_weapon_2008-2012.xls.

47. M. Antonia Biggs, Heather Gould, and Diana Greene Foster, "Understanding why women seek abortions in the U.S.," *BMC Women's Health* 13 no. 29, 2013, www.biomedcentral.com/1472-6874/13/29.

48. Cheryl Wetzstein, "Study ID's reasons for late-term abortions," *Washington Times,* December 10, 2013, www.washingtontimes.com/news/2013/dec/10/study-ids-reasons-for-late-term-abortions/?page=all.

49. Geoffrey Cowley, "More and more 'pro-life' Americans support abortion rights," *MSNBC*, September 13, 2013, www.msnbc.com/more-and-more-pro-life-americans-support-ab.

50. NBC News/Wall Street Journal Survey, Hart/M Study #13cInturff 018, January 12-15, 2013. Available online at msnbcmedia.msn.com/i/MSNBC/Sections/A_Politics/_Today_Stories_Teases/Supreme-court-question.pdf.

51. "Young Adults Least Likely Age Group to Know Roe v. Wade about Abortion," *Pew Research Center*, January 22, 2013, www.pewresearch. org/daily-number/young-adults-least-likely-age-group-to-know-roe-v-wade-about-abortion/.

Chapter 2: A Gracious Approach

52. JFA, like other pro-life exhibit outreaches, usually partners with local campus clubs that reserve space for the exhibit. If public universities allow any kind of exhibit to be set up, then they can't prohibit pro-life displays from being erected due simply to their shocking content. Such a prohibition would violate the First Amendment's guarantee of freedom of speech.

53. The ambassador model used by JFA was originally developed by the Christian apologetics organization Stand to Reason.

54. These skills are based on a previous set developed by the Justice for All team, which included "Asking Questions, Listening, and Finding Common Ground." Justice for All called these the "three essential skills" necessary for having productive conversations on any tough issue, especially abortion.

55. I prefer the term *abortion facility* to *abortion clinic*, because clinics are associated with healing people and saving lives, while abortion represents the opposite of those goals.

56. See Abby Johnson, *Unplanned*, Tyndale House Publishers, 2010, 33. The full quote reads, "My immediate thought was that if they cared about this woman, they wouldn't look so frightening with a Grim Reaper and a huge photo of an aborted fetus on display." Johnson also says, "We are there to love and befriend and pray for the clients who enter abortion clinics and the workers who staff them. Just as I was prayed for, loved, and befriended," Johnson, 253. For more information about *40 Days for Life*, visit www.40daysforlife.com.

57. "Bulletproof evidence" also means not giving women false information about the risks associated with abortion in order to stop them from having one. While it would be appropriate for pro-life advocates to warn women about *particular* abortion providers (such as the kind who have an

ambulance leaving their facility every week), it is not appropriate to claim that abortion is more dangerous for women than it actually is. In 2008, the CDC identified only twelve abortion-related deaths (Karen Pazol, et. al Abortion Surveillance—United States, 2009, *Morbidity and Mortality Weekly Report*, 61, no. 8, Centers for Disease Control and Prevention, (November 23, 2012, 1-44), while it claims that on average 650 women die from causes related to pregnancy each year (see "Pregnancy-Related Deaths," *Reproductive Health*, Centers for Disease Control, www.cdc.gov/reproductivehealth/MaternalInfantHealth/Pregnancy-relatedMortality. htm). I am extremely skeptical of the argument that abortion deaths are underreported and in reality abortion is more dangerous for women than childbirth, because that argument relies on evidence that is not known or available for criticism. If people think that pro-lifers lie or exaggerate in order to dissuade women from having abortions, then how can they trust us when we make a case that abortion is wrong? Why not just make the obvious case that abortion is more dangerous than childbirth for *the baby*?

58. A similar set of questions along with other helpful examples can be found in Scott Klusendorf, *The Case for Life*, Crossway Books, 2009, 149-156.

59. After citing the examples of the opinions held by Adolf Hitler and antebellum slaveholders, Fr. Robert Spitzer writes, "[E]ven though you want to respect the *person* who is asserting an opinion you must be careful about respecting the *content* of that opinion. The content of an opinion might be invalid and even unworthy of respect." Fr. Robert Spitzer, *Ten Universal Principles: A Brief Philosophy of the Life Issues*, Ignatius Press, 2011, 8.

60. This approach is called the *Socratic method* and is based on the dialectical style of one of the greatest philosophers of all time, Socrates.

61. You might be wondering, what if the young man had said pregnancy involves a woman having a "potential child" inside of her? I would then ask what the difference is between a "potential child" and a "real child," or what a "child" even is. After all, you can't be a potential X unless you are an actual Y. If the unborn is a potential child then it must be an actual something. I would ask what that something is and through

PERSUASIVE PRO-LIFE

what process it becomes a human being. I owe this to Peter Kreeft, *The Unaborted Socrates*, InterVarsity Press, 1983, 38.

62. Carl Rogers, *On Becoming a Person: A Therapist's View of Psychology*, Houghton Mifflin Company, 1989, 331-332.

63. Greg Koukl, *Tactics: A Game Plan for Discussing Your Christian Convictions*, Zondervan, 2009, 159-166.

64. John Paul II, *Redemptoris Missio*, 56.

65. Wagner, *Common Ground*, 6.

66. "I have noticed a growing interest among governments to sponsor programs intended to promote interreligious and intercultural dialogue. These are praiseworthy initiatives. At the same time, religious freedom, interreligious dialogue and faith-based education aim at something more than a consensus regarding ways to implement practical strategies for advancing peace. The broader purpose of dialogue is to discover the truth." Pope Benedict XVI, "Meeting With Representatives of Other Religions," *Apostolic Journey to the United States and Visit to the United Nations Headquarters*, The Holy See, April 17, 2008, www. vatican.va/holy_father/benedict_xvi/speeches/2008/april/documents/ hf_ben-xvi_spe_20080417_other-religions_en.html.

67. President Barack Obama, "Remarks by the President in Commencement Address at the University Of Notre Dame," *Speeches and Remarks*, The White House, May 17, 2009, www.whitehouse.gov/ the-press-office/remarks-president-notre-dame-commencement.

Chapter 3: The Pragmatists

68. Greg Koukl and Scott Klusendorf's "Making Abortion Unthinkable" curriculum helped me see the importance of focusing on this one question.

69. See Klusendorf, *The Case for Life*, 22-27. Mark Crutcher's *On Message: The Pro-life Handbook* also addresses pitfalls of answering the pragmatist on his own terms. He writes, "If your answer includes rhetoric about government welfare programs or charities raising money for the

poor, *you lose.*" Mark Crutcher, *On Message: The Pro-life Handbook*, Life Dynamics Inc., 2005, 10.

70. It does not work with so-called "body-rights" arguments, which concede that the unborn are as human as a two-year-old but say the unborn child's use of his mother's body justifies killing him, something that is not present with a toddler. This argument is examined in Chapter 8.

71. "Report: South Korean couple starved child while raising 'virtual baby,'" CNN, March 5, 2010, www.cnn.com/2010/WORLD/asiapcf/03/05/korea.baby.starved/index.html.

72. James Prescott, "Abortion or the Unwanted Child: A Choice for a Humanistic Society," *The Humanist*, March/April 1975, 13.

73. Meth is short for methamphetamine and is an illegal, highly addictive psychotropic drug with dangerous side effects.

74. Francis Beckwith, *Defending Life: A Moral and Legal Case Against Abortion Choice*, New York: Cambridge University Press, 2007, 50. Beckwith also correctly observes that many other arguments for abortion do not justify the pro-choice position of abortion being legal through all nine months of pregnancy for any or no reason at all. If abortion should be legal to ease overpopulation, then once population levels stabilize, shouldn't abortion be made illegal? Saying abortion is necessary for impoverished women would not justify abortion for wealthy women. Saying abortion must remain legal for women whose partners will abandon them won't justify keeping abortion legal for the women who have supportive partners.

75. *Roe v. Wade*, 410 U.S. 113, section eight (1973). "We, therefore, conclude that the right of personal privacy includes the abortion decision, but that this right is not unqualified, and must be considered against important state interests in regulation."

Chapter 4: The Tolerant

76. I recommend Greg Koukl and Francis Beckwith, *Relativism: Feet Firmly Planted in Mid-air*, Baker Books, 1998, as well as Peter Kreeft, *A*

Refutation of Moral Relativism: Interviews with an Absolutist, Ignatius Press, 1999.

77. Hadley Arkes shows in his book on abortion that it is self-contradictory for pro-choice advocates to argue that women have a "right to have an abortion" that is grounded in their human nature without affirming that all women, including unborn females, have a right to live that is also grounded in their human nature. See Hadley Arkes, *Natural Rights and the Right to Choose*, Cambridge University Press, 2004.

78. The legal principle that the Court's decision should respect its previous decisions is called *stare decisis*, which comes from the Latin phrase *Stare decisis et non quieta movere* or "to stand by decisions and not disturb the undisturbed." However, the longer a case remains "settled," the greater the chance it can be overturned, since this gives more time for a different political or social climate to arise that would cause the Court to look at a ruling in a new light.

79. *Lawrence v. Texas*, 539 U.S. 558 (2003).

80. *Citizens United v. Federal Election Commission*, 558 U.S. 310 (2010). Most critics of the case dispute the conclusion that donating money to political causes is a form of speech and so corporations, and legal persons, have a right to free speech and can donate as much money as they want toward independent political expenditures. Although this case reinforced legal personhood for corporations, it did not create it. This idea was first affirmed by the Court in cases like *Dartmouth College v. Woodward* (1819) and *Santa Clara County v. Southern Pacific Railroad* (1886). Critics who argue against corporate personhood include UC Berkeley professor of public policy Robert Reich, who said, "I'll believe corporations are people when Texas executes one." Robert Reich, "Why BP Isn't a Criminal," *robertreich.org*, November 16, 2012, robertreich.org/post/35848994755. Mr. Reich seems unaware that the state of Texas routinely executes corporations by declaring them bankrupt.

81. Interview in the Dubuque, Iowa, *Telegraph Herald*, July 2004.

82. Pope John Paul II, *Evangelium Vitae*, 90.

83. Laurence H. Tribe, *Abortion: The Clash of Absolutes,* W.W. Norton & Company, 1990, 116.

84. While most of these proposals seem disingenuous, the closest I've seen to being a genuine compromise is William Saletan, "Abortion: Safe, Legal, and Never," *Slate Magazine,* January 26, 2005, www.slate.com/articles/health_and_science/human_nature/2005/01/safe_legal_and_never.html. He writes, "Not safe, legal, and rare. Safe, legal, and never. Once you embrace that truth—that the ideal number of abortions is zero—voters open their ears."

85. In addition, why should pro-life advocates be expected to compromise and promote contraception when pro-choice advocates probably won't compromise and promote showing graphic images of abortion to the public?

86. *Planned Parenthood of Southeastern Pennsylvania v. Casey,* 505 U.S. 833 (1992), Section I-e.

87. Pope John Paul II, *Evangelium Vitae,* 13.

88. Naomi Wolf, "Our Bodies, Our Souls," *New Republic,* October 16, 1995.

89. Mary Elizabeth Williams, "So What If Abortion Ends Life?" *Salon.com,* January 23, 2013, www.salon.com/2013/01/23/so_what_if_abortion_ends_life/.

90. Evan Esar, *The Treasury of Humorous Quotations,* 1951, 103.

91. Wolf, *Our Bodies,* 1995.

92. For accurate, high-definition, and documented photographs of aborted humans, I recommend the Center for Bio-Ethical Reform (CBR), whose Web site is www.abortionno.org. Information on the authenticity of CBR's abortion images can be found at www.abortionno.org/abortion-photos/verifying-photograph-authenticity/.

Chapter 5: The Distractors

93. Greg Koukl, *Precious Unborn Human Persons,* Stand to Reason Press, 1999, 7. By "abortion" Koukl means "elective abortion," and in other

writings he has affirmed that abortion can be moral when it is done to save a woman's life.

94. Some critics will argue that this argument assumes a deontological view of ethics, or that the concepts of "right" and "wrong" involve violating rights or moral principles. If one assumes instead a consequentialist view of ethics, like utilitarianism, or that an act is moral if it produces the most favorable consequences, then killing an innocent person through abortion can be moral. For a critique of this argument, see Lee, *Abortion and Unborn Human Life*, 140-164.

95. In his critique of the pro-life position, Richard Dawkins spends several pages criticizing the "Beethoven Argument," Richard Dawkins, *The God Delusion*, Houghton Mifflin, 2006, 337-339. What is of course disappointing is that, like his treatment of the arguments for the existence of God, Dawkins has refuted only the weakest arguments for the pro-life position.

96. Some critics ask me, "Would it have been wrong for Hitler's mother to have aborted him?" The answer is yes, because when he was a fetus Adolf Hitler was an innocent human being who had a right to life. He had done nothing up to that point to justify being killed.

97. For a recent review of the evidence that casts doubt on fetal pain before the third trimester, see S.J. Lee, H. Ralston, E.A. Drey, J. Partridge, and M.A. Rosen, "Fetal Pain: A Systematic Multidisciplinary Review of the Evidence," *Journal of the American Medical Association*, 294 no. 8, 2005, 947-954. I understand the concern that some who argue against fetal pain may have a bias toward keeping abortion legal, so it is important to critically examine all the evidence surrounding this issue.

98. Roy Bowen Ward, "Is the Fetus a Person?," *Mission Journal*, January, 1986. Cited in Klusendorf, *Case for Life*, 135.

99. A. Chandra, G.M. Martinez, W.D. Mosher, J.C. Abma, and J. Jones, "Fertility, family planning, and reproductive health of U.S. women: Data from the 2002 National Survey of Family Growth," National Center for Health Statistics, *Vital Health Stat* 23 no. 25, 2005, table 82.

100. I obtained this information from personal conversations with pregnancy center directors, though national statistics showed that between

1989 and 1995 less than 2 percent of children born to never-married women were placed for adoption. This is a dramatic decline from pre-Roe rates, when almost one in every five children born to white women was placed for adoption. Among African American women, the number was close to zero and was extremely low even before 1973. A. Chandra, J. Abma, P. Maza, and C. Bachrach, "Adoption, adoption seeking, and relinquishment for adoption in the United States," Vital and Health Statistics of the Centers for Disease Control and Prevention, *Advance Data* No. 306, 1999, www.cdc.gov/nchs/data/ad/ad306.pdf.

101. Steven Levitt and Stephen Dubner, *Freakonomics: A Rogue Economist Explores the Hidden Side of Everything*, Harper Perennial, 2005, 115-146. Other writers have criticized Levitt's and Dubner's hypothesis and proposed other explanations for crime decrease in the 1990s, including the end of the "crack wars" of the 1980s and even changes in childhood exposure to lead. While interesting, the relationship of abortion to crime rates is irrelevant to the moral or legal status of abortion.

102. Advocates of this approach, such as Paul Swope of the Caring Foundation, say the pro-life movement "must show that abortion is actually not in a woman's own self-interest, and that the choice of life offers hope and a positive, expanded sense of self." Paul Swope, "Abortion: A Failure to Communicate," *First Things*, April 1998, www.firstthings. com/article/2008/11/004-abortion-a-failure-to-communicate-49. For an excellent rebuttal to Swope's approach see Scott Klusendorf, "The Vanishing Pro-life Apologist: Putting the 'Life' Back into the Abortion Debate," *Christian Research Journal*, 22 no.1, 1999, www.equip.org/articles/the-vanishing-pro-life-apologist-putting-the-life-back-into-the-abortion-debate/.

103. The question of whether or not abortion causes negative health consequences for women is fiercely debated. Most major medical organizations deny this claim, but they also support legal abortion and could be biased. Pro-life advocates generally support the claim but bias could seep into their findings as well. Since the issue of abortion's relationship to pathologies such as breast cancer or clinical depression does not play a key feature in my argument against abortion in this book, I have chosen not to engage the issue or present my take on the matter.

104. This is evidenced on the Web site www.thanksabortion.com

105. See E.M. Dadlez and W.L. Andrews, "Post-abortion syndrome: creating an affliction," *Bioethics* 24, no. 9, November 2010, 445-452.

106. It's important to remember that "unwantedness" is not a property that a child possesses in the same way a child is blue-eyed. Saying a child is unwanted reflects an attitude of the child's parents. The child would no doubt be "wanted" by many couples who are waiting to adopt children.

Chapter 6: The Skeptics

107. *Roe v. Wade*, 410 U.S. 113 (1973), section 9-b.

108. Carl Sagan, *Billions & Billions: Thoughts on Life and Death at the Brink of the Millennium*, Random House Publishing, 1997, 201.

109. The original version can be found in Wagner, *Common Ground*, 69.

110. A critic might object that Darwinian evolution could cause a human to give birth to a non-human. This is implausible as the process of evolution gives rise to slight changes in entire populations, not radical changes in isolated individuals. Furthermore, if we encountered species that have different DNA but still possess the capacity for rational thought, then they would be persons, because they would be individuals who belong to a rational kind.

111. Some critics say, "A blueprint is not a house, and an embryo with human DNA is not a human being." The problem with this analogy is that pro-life advocates don't say a strand of human DNA is a human being (or "a blueprint is a house"), but that an embryo with DNA is a human being. A human embryo is more like a set of instructions within a complex computer that can acquire new parts and build itself while remaining a computer through its entire process of growth.

112. Not all humans have 46 chromosomes. Some humans have more than that, such as people with Trisomy 21 or Klinefelter's syndrome, who have 47 chromosomes. Some humans have less, such as people with Turner's syndrome, who have only one X chromosome and therefore have a total of 45 chromosomes.

113. The same is true for the word *zygote*, which refers to a human being at the one-celled stage of life.

114. Technically, a woman is not pregnant until her offspring implants within the womb.

115. See "Definition of *organism* in English," Oxford Dictionaries, ox-forddictionaries.com/us/definition/american_english/organism.

116. A critic could object that human tissue can develop into a human being through cloning. However, cloning simply replaces the substantial change that occurs at conception (23 chromosomes + 23 chromosomes = a new human being) with another substantial change (46 chromosomes + 0 chromosomes in an empty ovum = a new human being). Cloning reveals that body cells have an extrinsic capacity to develop into a new human being, just as sperm and egg have this extrinsic capacity. This is different than the intrinsic capacity of an embryo or fetus that develops on its own and requires no further genetic information or substantial changes in its being in order to grow into a mature member of our species.

117. E.L. Potter, and J.M. Craig, *Pathology of the Fetus and the Infant*, 3rd edition, Year Book Medical Publishers, 1975, page vii. Robert George and Christopher Tollefsen also summarize this point well: "Here, then, is the bottom line: A human embryo is not something different in kind from a human being, like a rock, or a potato, or a rhinoceros. A human embryo is a whole living member of the species *Homo sapiens* in the earliest stage of his or her natural development. Unless severely damaged or denied or deprived of a suitable environment, an embryonic human being will, by directing it own integral organic functioning, develop himself or herself to the next more mature developmental stage, i.e., the fetal stage. The embryonic, fetal, child, and adolescent stages are stages in the development of a determinate and enduring entity—a human being—who comes into existence as a single-celled organism (a zygote) and develops, if all goes well, into adulthood many years later." Robert George and Christopher Tollefsen, *Embryo: A Defense of Human Life,* New York: Doubleday, 2008, 50-51.

118. These tumors are called *teratomas*, which comes, not surprisingly, from the Greek word for "monster." See also Antoine Suarez, "Hydatidiform Moles and Teratomas Confirm the Human Identity of the Preimplantation Embryo," *The Journal of Medicine and Philosophy*, 15, no. 6, 1990, 630.

119. Peter Singer, *Practical Ethics*, 3rd edition, Cambridge University Press, 2011, 73.

120. For a critique of the view that the pretwinning embryo is just a collection of potential human beings, and not a single unified organism, see George and Tollefsen, *Embryo*, 149-158.

121. Patrick Lee, *Abortion and Unborn Human Life*, Catholic University of America Press, 2010, 96. For a comprehensive treatment of this subject, see 93-101.

122. Some critics argue that because the mother's messenger RNA (or mRNA), as opposed the embryo's DNA, guides the growth of the early embryo up to the eight-cell stage, it is not an individual organism until that point. Instead, these critics claim that the cells of the early embryo are an "aggregated entity" within the zona pellucida that the mRNA directs. Instead of being a unified whole, the cells are a mere "collection of parts" in the same way a collection of bottles in a bag are not a unified entity but merely an aggregate of individual entities within a protective barrier. Robert George and Christopher Tollefsen in their book *Embryo* object to this view. They argue that even though the mRNA guides cell development, there are other forms of communication present between the dividing cells at this stage (i.e., they are not truly independent like the bottles in the bag). In particular, there is evidence of interaction between blastomeres at the four-cell and even two-cell stage as they prepare to specialize and form the embryo's trophoblast and inner cell mass. They claim this represents an inner unity within the embryo that, while aided by the mRNA molecules in development, is still a unified being on a path of self-directed development. The embryo may cooperate with the mRNA but is not completely "constructed" by it. See George and Tollefsen, *Embryo*, 157-158.

123. See Thomas L. Johnson, "Why the Embryo or Fetus Is Not a Parasite," Libertarians for Life, 1974, www.l4l.org/library/notparas.html.

124. See the 1943 Nazi pamphlet *Der Jude als Weltparasit* or *The Jew as World Parasite*, German Propaganda Archive, www.calvin.edu/academic/cas/gpa/weltparasit.htm.

125. "Planned Parenthood Minnesota, North Dakota, South Dakota; Carol E. Ball, M.D. v. Mike Rounds, Governor, in his official capacity; Larry Long, Attorney General, in his official capacity," United States Court of Appeals for the Eighth Circuit No. 05-3093, section I, filed June 27, 2008.

126. Ronan O'Rahilly and Fabiola Müller, *Human Embryology and Teratology*, 3rd edition, Wiley-Liss, 2001, 8. The full quote reads, "Although human life is a continuous process, fertilization (which, incidentally, is not a 'moment') is a critical landmark because, under ordinary circumstances, a new, genetically distinct human organism is formed when the chromosomes of the male and female pronuclei blend in the oocyte."

127. Keith L. Moore and T.V.N. Persaud, *The Developing Human: Clinically Oriented Embryology*, 9th edition, Saunders, 2013, 2. The full quote reads, "Human development begins at fertilization, approximately 14 days after the onset of the last normal menstrual period." T.W. Sadler, *Langman's Medical Embryology*, 11th edition, Williams & Wilkins, 2010, 13. The full quote reads, "Development begins with fertilization, the process by which the male gamete, the sperm, and the female gamete, the oocyte, unite to give rise to a zygote."

128. Scott F. Gilbert. *Developmental Biology*, 10th edition, Sinauer Associates, Inc., June 30, 2013.

129. David Boonin, *A Defense of Abortion*, Cambridge University Press, Cambridge, 2003, 20.

130. Peter Singer, *Practical Ethics*, 2nd edition, Cambridge University Press, 1993, 73.

131. The closest I've found is an essay by biologist Scott Gilbert that was published as part of an online supplement to the ninth edition of his textbook *Developmental Biology*, titled, "When does human life begin?" The essay claims that there are numerous points at which human

life begins and that ultimately the question is a moral one that science cannot answer (the essay was removed from the textbook Web site but can still be found online). Gilbert clearly seems to mean the debate over when a "human person" or "valuable human" begins to exist is a moral one, and he's right. But as I wrote earlier, the tenth edition of his own textbook seems to affirm that the scientific question is resolved, as the fourth chapter is bluntly titled "Fertilization: Beginning a New Organism."

132. *The Sean Hannity Show*, May 14, 2014.

133. Philip Bump, "Marco Rubio demanded people look at the science on abortion. So we did," *Washington Post,* May 15, 2014, www.washingtonpost.com/blogs/the-fix/wp/2014/05/15/marco-rubio-demanded-people-look-at-the-science-on-abortion-so-we-did/.

134. David Boonin, *A Defense of Abortion*, Cambridge University Press, 2003, 93.

135. Report, Subcommittee on Separation of Powers to Senate Judiciary Committee S-158, 97th Congress, 1st Session, 1981, 7.

136. Richard Stith, "Arguing with Pro-Choicers," *First Things,* November 4, 2006, www.firstthings.com/onthesquare/2006/11/stith-arguing-with-pro-choicer.

137. Indeed, the English word *develop* comes from the Old French word *desveloper*, which means "to unroll that which is wrapped up." When an unborn child develops he "unrolls" the humanity already wrapped up within his genetic code.

138. When skeptics say we don't know the exact moment sperm and egg become a zygote or we don't know exactly when variations in the human genome become a new species (such as the extinct *homo sapiens idaltu*) and therefore we can't know if an embryo is alive or if a certain organism is human, they may be committing the fallacy of the beard. This fallacy occurs when someone says, "Well, since we can't know when stubble ends and a beard begins without drawing an arbitrary line or imposing our own 'conventional labeling system,' then we can never know when anyone has a beard." But that's silly. I

can tell bearded faces from clean-shaven ones even though I cannot directly pinpoint when stubble becomes a beard. Much the same way, in most cases I know when one organism is human and another is not, even though there are examples where I'm not sure (such as an extinct hominid species). Likewise, even though the process of fertilization is not instantaneous and it is difficult to point out exactly when it ends, this does not prove that a zygote, or the end product of fertilization, is not a human being. Francis Beckwith argues that this agnosticism (which he agrees commits the beard fallacy) cuts both ways. Pro-choice advocates usually pick the acquisition of certain traits as being that which makes an entity human (e.g., sentience or rationality). But it is just as difficult, if not more so, to identify when those traits emerge than it is to identify when the process of fertilization is complete. See Francis Beckwith, "Defending Abortion Philosophically: A Review of David Bonin's A Defense of Abortion," *Journal of Medicine & Philosophy*, 31, April 2006, 177-203.

Chapter 7: The Disqualifiers

139. "It is hardly necessary to express the further thought that readers will surely have already had—namely, that it would be dangerously invidious to give public expression to a view that accords a higher degree of moral inviolability to people with higher psychological capacities or a worthier moral nature. Even if such a view were true, it is virtually certain that if it were widely espoused and recognized as true, it would then be distorted or otherwise abused in efforts to justify the unjustifiable.

"All this leaves me profoundly uncomfortable. It seems virtually unthinkable to abandon our egalitarian commitments, or even to accept that they might be justified only in some indirect way—for example, because it is for the best, all things considered, to treat all people as equals and to inculcate the belief that all are indeed one another's moral equals, even though in reality they are not. Yet the challenges to the equal wrongness thesis, which is a central element of liberal egalitarian morality, support Mulgan's skepticism about the compatibility our all-or-nothing egalitarian beliefs with the fact that the properties on which our moral status appears to supervene are all matters of degree. It is hard to avoid the sense that our egalitarian commitments rest on distressingly insecure foundations." Jeff McMahan, "Challenges to Human Equality," *The Journal of Ethics,* 12, 2008, 81–104.

140. I owe this argument to Steve Wagner, who tells me that the philosopher J.P. Moreland heavily influenced his version of the argument.

141. Boethius used the phrase "*Naturæ rationalis individua substantia*" to describe what a "person" was in his *"De persona et duabus naturis,"* This is also called "the substance view" of the human person. A substance is something that maintains its identity and value through change. Imagine your family had a car, but in the past twenty years your father changed 90 percent of the car's parts. Is the car you're looking at now the *same* car your Dad bought twenty years ago? No, because the car is an object that becomes a different thing when you change the majority of its parts. The car has no inner essence that maintains its identity (or its value!) over time. But now look in the mirror. You have 90 percent new body parts since you were a baby, but you can look at a photo of yourself as a baby and say, "That was me!" Even through all those changes, you have the same identity and value you had as a baby, despite the fact that most of your "parts" are different. This is because you are a *substance*, or a thing that maintains its value and identity through change. The word *substance* comes from a Latin word that means "to stand under." Even though your body has undergone an incredible number of changes in your life, something "stands under" those changes to connect them. In fact, all living creatures exist as different kinds of substances. According to the substance view, while the accidental properties a human being possesses (such as the ability to think or feel) may change over time, there is something that makes humans valuable that does not change over time but remains constant. This essential or unchanging property of being a person is what makes it true that *you* were once a child, *you* were once an infant, *you* were once a fetus, and *you* were even once a tiny one-celled embryo (or what's called a zygote). Through all of those changes in size and ability, you had the essential property of intrinsic value and personal identity. You had, still have, and will continue to have, a right to life. See also Patrick Lee, "The Pro-life Argument from Substantial Identity: A Defense," *Bioethics,* vol. 18, no. 3, 2004, Beckwith, *Defending Life,* 132-134, and a similar view called "The Constitutive Property Argument" in

Christopher Kaczor, *The Ethics of Abortion: Women's Rights, Human Life, and the Question of Justice*, Routledge, 2011, 105-120.

142. This view of personhood helps answer a common pro-choice question: "Why does having human DNA make it wrong to abort a fetus?" The answer is that the human fetus not only has human DNA but is also a human organism or a human being. Unlike other animals, the members of our species can develop into beings capable of pursuing transcendent goods like justice or beauty, which makes us unique and deserving of rights, including the right to life. Now, this doesn't mean persons can abuse or torture non-persons such as pets. It instead means that along with having moral duties toward the helpless, human beings have moral rights that compel us to treat one other in "the right way." Indeed, we are the only known species who even understands what "rights" are! Now, some critics mistake this argument for a simpler one based on potentiality. They falsely characterize it as saying, "The unborn will potentially be persons, which means they are now persons." But that is as illogical as saying that a candidate will potentially be the President so he is now the President. However, the argument I'm proposing says that what you essentially are does not change over time. If you were a person at any point in your existence, you always were a person (even if you could not function like a person), and you always will be a person until you cease to exist. The potential to act in personal ways is a sign that someone is a member of a rational kind, not the reason they are a person. For example, one of the essential features of a rational animal is that it can reproduce and think rationally, but most humans only have the *potential* to think rationally for the first two years of life and only the *potential* to reproduce for the first twelve to thirteen years of life. But humans under the age of thirteen are still rational animals, even if they can't function in these ways by virtue of the kind of being they are. The same simply applies to their status as persons. See Kaczor, *Ethics of Abortion*, 98.

143. Stephen Schwartz, *The Moral Question of Abortion*, Loyola University Press, 1990, 15-19. An earlier version of this argument, though without the acronym SLED, can be found in Jean Staker Garton, *Who Broke the Baby?*, Bethany Fellowship, 1979, 38-39. Kreeft originally listed the differences as size, development, dependence, and mobility in his 1983 book on abortion, *Unaborted Socrates*, 56.

144. Dawkins, *The God Delusion*, 333.

145. Daniel C. Maguire, "A Catholic Theologian at an Abortion Clinic" in *The Ethics of Abortion* ed. Robert M. Baird and Stuart E. Rosenbaum, New York, 2001, 205.

146. Dawkins, *The God Delusion*, 336.

147. The example of a comatose person can be used effectively if the pro-life advocate makes it clear he is talking about a *reversible* coma such as one that lasts for, say, nine months.

148. Some critics argue that the pro-life view of personhood is undermined by those who are permanently unconscious, whom critics don't believe are persons but seem to be persons under the pro-life view. I suspect what is driving most people's intuitions that the permanently unconscious do not have a right to life is the counterintuitive claim that it would be murder to take such a being off artificial life support. A permanently unconscious person may have a right to life, but the level of medical treatment needed to sustain him may not be warranted due to a hopeless prognosis. Even defenders of the substance view, like Francis Beckwith, admit that the removal of life support for such a being is a "legitimate, though disputed, question." (See Beckwith, *Defending Life*, 137.) However, if the comatose do not require extraordinary care (such as a heart-lung machine), then I believe it is wrong to kill them, either directly or indirectly, by depriving them of ordinary care all humans deserve, such as being given food and water. Amir Halevy argues that the intuition most of us probably have against burying or cremating a breathing human body counterbalances the intuition that the permanently unconscious do not have a right to life. See Amir Halevy, "Beyond Brain Death?," *Journal of Medicine and Philosophy*, 26, no. 5, 2001, 498.

149. Judith Jarvis Thomson, "A Defense of Abortion," *Philosophy & Public Affairs* 1, no. 1, Fall 1971.

150. Peter Singer and Helen Kuhse, "On Letting Handicapped Infants Die," in *The Right Thing to Do: Basic Readings in Moral Philosophy*, ed., James Rachels, Random House, 1989, 146. Of course, Singer and Kuhse go on to adopt a solution that is diametrically opposed to the pro-life

position: "The solution, however, is not to accept the pro-life view that the fetus is a human being with the same moral status as yours or mine. The solution is the very opposite: to abandon the idea that all human life is of equal worth."

151. Maria A. Morgan, Robert L. Goldenberg, and Jay Schulkin, "Obstetrician-gynecologists' practices regarding preterm birth at the limit of viability," *Journal of Maternal-Fetal and Neonatal Medicine*, vol. 21, no. 2, 2008, 115-121.

152. Kaczor goes on to say, "There is no reason to think that individually unsound arguments against personhood somehow when taken as a group demonstrate that not all human beings should be respected as persons, whether those human beings are living in Ireland or living in utero," Kaczor, *Ethics of Abortion*, 86.

153. The philosopher Wayne Sumner is a defender of this position. For a critique, see Lee, *Abortion and Unborn Human Life*, 47-56.

154. Susan Brink, *The Fourth Trimester: Understanding, Protecting, and Nurturing an Infant through the First Three Months*, University of California Press, 2013. Description available online at www.ucpress.edu/book. php?isbn=9780520267121#.

155. "No one would suggest that a fetus could have a claim to fill the Chair of Logic at one of our universities; and we would not wish quite yet to seeks its advice on anything important; and we should probably not regard him as eligible to vote in any state other than Massachusetts. All of these rights and privileges would be inappropriate to the condition or attributes of the fetus. But nothing that renders him unqualified for these special rights would diminish in any way the most elementary right that could be claimed for any human being, or even for an animal: the right not to be killed without the rendering of reasons that satisfy the strict standards of 'justification.'" Hadley Arkes, *First Things: An Inquiry into the First Principles of Morals and Justice*, Princeton University Press, 1986, 366. Quoted in Klusendorf, *Case for Life*, 62-63.

156. Of course, some humans may have more *instrumental* value, or value in what they can do, because they are of a certain age or level of

development. For example, a healthy adult has more instrumental value, or can do more and be of more worth, than a newborn infant. But both adults and newborns have the same intrinsic value, or value in what they are. This makes it equally wrong to kill either.

157. Granted, one can be halfway through the *process* of pregnancy just as one can be halfway through a human lifespan, but one either is or is not pregnant just as one either is or is not human.

158. "The blood is circulating and the heart begins to beat on the 21st or the 22nd day." Keith L. Moore and T.V.N. Persaud, *The Developing Human: Clinically Oriented Embryology*, 9th edition, Saunders, 2011, 64.

159. See Phillips Verner Bradford and Harvey Blume, *Ota Benga: The Pygmy in the Zoo*, St. Martin's Press, 1993.

160. Some pro-choice advocates argue that a fetus becomes a person at quickening because at this moment it has "interacted" with other human beings and this is a necessary condition for personhood. But why should someone's rights or value depend on whether they have "interacted" with other human beings? Do I cease to be a person if I become a hermit? Do dogs and cats become persons when humans adopt them and begin to have a social relationship with them? In addition, why can't we say the fetus has been "interacting" with the mother since implantation if not conception itself? This criterion seems to be designed to exclude the unborn from being considered persons instead of giving us an objective definition of what a person is.

161. Patricia Jaworski, "Thinking About *The Silent Scream*: An Audio Documentary" in *Abortion Rights and Fetal 'Personhood'*, ed. Edd Doerr and James W. Prescott, Americans for Religious Liberty, 1990, 57. Another interview in the same documentary makes the claim that specifically having a cerebral cortex, or the more developed upper brain, is necessary for personhood, because this is the organ that is necessary for "human-like behavior," ibid., 59. Many pro-choice authors have defended the "cortex criterion," but for different reasons. Harold J. Morowitz and James Trefil in their book *The Facts of Life: Science and the Abortion Controversy* claim the cortex is the biological structure that makes human beings

different from all other animals and thus what gives human beings their "humanness" or special value. Harold J. Morowitz and James Trefil, *The Facts of Life: Science and the Abortion Controversy*, Oxford University Press, 1992, 62. However, Boonin points out that possession of a cortex may be a necessary condition for personhood in this argument, but it is not a sufficient condition, because there are humans who possess a cortex but cannot act in distinctly human ways (such as infants). He argues, as I do in this book, that any defense of the cortical criterion grounded in the physical nature of the brain will either include fetuses or exclude infants, Boonin, *Defense of Abortion*, 121-122. Boonin himself believes the cortex is associated with personhood, but only because it produces "ideal, dispositional desires" that are necessary for his own theory of personhood to succeed.

162. Baruch Brody, *Abortion and the Sanctity of Human Life: A Philosophical View*, MIT Press, 1975. Some pro-life advocates are fond of saying that "brain waves" occur when an embryo is forty days old. Although I am convinced by an article from pro-choice advocate Margaret Sykes that this statement is inaccurate and that embryos do not have brain waves at this stage of development similar to what born humans possess. See Margaret Sykes, "'Brain Waves' When???" at www.svss-uspda.ch/pdf/brain_waves.pdf. However, my argument for the personhood of the unborn does not depend on them having a brain that functions at a certain level, but on their being a member of rational kind who are ordered toward growing brains capable of engaging in rational thought.

163. There is controversy over whether brain death leads to the death of a human organism in light of Alan Shewmon's research on the subject. For a more in-depth discussion of this issue, I refer the reader to Patrick Lee and Germain Grisez, "Total Brain Death: A Reply to Alan Shewmon," *Bioethics* 26 no. 5, 2012, 275-284.

164. See also Maureen L. Condic, "When Does Human Life Begin? A Scientific Perspective," *The Westchester Institute* 1 no. 1, October 2008, www.westchesterinstitute.net/images/wi_whitepaper_life_print.pdf.

165. Schwartz, *The Moral Question of Abortion*, 52.

166. Conor Liston and Jerome Kagan, "Brain Development: Memory Enhancement in Early Childhood," *Nature* 419, 2002, 896, www.nature. com/nature/journal/v419/n6910/abs/419896a.html. Cited in Scott Klusendorf, "Abortion Debate: A Short Defense of the Pro-Life Position," *Life Training Institute*, www.prolifetraining.com/Articles/abortion-debate.pdf.

167. The classic study on this is Beulah Amsterdam, "Mirror self-image reactions before age two," *Developmental Psychobiology* 5, no. 4, 1972, 297–305, onlinelibrary.wiley.com/doi/10.1002/dev.420050403/abstract. In Amsterdam's study, only 65 percent of children by age two were able to recognize themselves in a mirror. The "mirror test" is a typical assessment of self-awareness, which would be a necessary though not sufficient condition for rational ability. There is no evidence of self-awareness or rationality in newborns.

168. Of course, not everyone rejects infanticide, as is evidenced in the writings of Michael Tooley, Peter Singer, and, more recently, the ethicists Alberto Giubilini and Francesca Minerva. See Appendix II for how to discuss abortion with those who have no objection to infanticide.

169. This example comes from philosopher Robert Wennberg, who writes, "If I were cheated out of an inheritance that I didn't know I had, I would be harmed regardless of whether I knew about the chicanery. Deprivation of a good (be it an inheritance or self-conscious existence) constitutes harm even if one is ignorant of that deprivation." Robert Wennberg, *Life in the Balance: Exploring the Abortion Controversy*, Eerdmans, 1985, 98. Quoted in Beckwith, *Defending Life*, 145.

170. The idea that abortion is wrong because it deprives someone of his future life experiences is the foundation for another argument against abortion I have not explored in this book, though I am a fan of what is called the "future-like-ours" (FLO) argument. It was created by Don Marquis at the University of Kansas. Marquis writes, "Therefore, when I die, I am deprived of all the value of my future. Inflicting this loss on me is ultimately what makes killing wrong. This being the case, it would seem that what makes killing any adult human being prima facie

seriously wrong is the loss of his future." According to the FLO account, adult humans, infants, suicidal people, and the unborn would also have a FLO, thus making it wrong to kill them, even if they do not currently desire to live (which is the case with the suicidal or the unborn). It's important to note that Marquis argues only that the FLO is a *sufficient* condition for the wrongness of killing, not a *necessary* condition. Marquis admits that some people, like the terminally ill, may not have a FLO, but that for other reasons it may still be wrong to kill them. See Don Marquis, "Why Abortion Is Immoral," in *The Abortion Controversy: 25 Years After Roe vs. Wade: A Reader*, ed., Louis Pojman and Francis Beckwith, Wadsworth Publishing, 1998, 345, 349.

171. Perhaps the most significant defense of a "desires-based" account of personhood is Boonin, *Defense of Abortion*, 122-129. Boonin argues that a being is a person if it has any ideal, dispositional desires for a future-like-ours. An ideal desire is a desire a being would have it were properly informed about the world and a dispositional desire is one a being has without consciously thinking about it. Boonin is adamant, however, that a being cannot have an ideal desire to live without having at least one actual desire. The fatal objection to Boonin's view is that fetuses engineered not to have any desires or children who are injured and lose their memories and revert to the psychological state of a fetus would also not possess a right to life. A more in-depth critique can be found in Beckwith, *Defending Abortion Philosophically*, 177-203.

172. See Beckwith, *Defending Life*, 148, and Lee, *Abortion and Unborn Human Life*, 21-22. Even more shocking would be the cloning of a celebrity using discarded genetic material and then altering the clone during her embryonic stage of life so that she never attains consciousness and can instead be developed into the world's most realistic "sex doll." One pro-choice medical professor I spoke with admitted that the brainless clone could not be harmed and the only thing wrong with creating the sex doll would be if it harmed the celebrity's reputation! The pro-life advocate is able to condemn this disgusting act because he believes that all human beings have a right to grow and develop at a normal rate throughout their lives. This process of growth and development should not be interrupted through harmful techniques such as lobotomies or abortion, which violate a human being's basic rights.

173. Ethicist Bonnie Steinbock attempts to justify the right to life of a similar unconscious newborn girl while still allowing for the abortion of unconscious fetuses. She writes, "[A]lthough strictly speaking she does not have interests of her own [like fetuses we are allowed to abort], we treat her as if she did, because she is so close to having them." Bonnie Steinbock, *Life Before Birth: The Moral and Legal Status of Embryos and Fetuses*, Oxford University Press, 1992, 61-62. This reply is unsatisfactory, because one could easily argue that embryos and fetuses are "close" to having interests as well. In fact, if the born child were in a coma for several years that would make all fetuses "closer" to being persons than this disabled newborn that Steinbock claims is prima facie wrong to kill. Kaczor also shares my assessment of Steinbock's argument (Kaczor, *Ethics of Abortion*, 77).

174. Not all people share this conclusion. Radical animal-rights activists believe that either all sentient animals are persons whose rights must be respected or that no being has "rights," and morality is solely determined by the amount of pain or pleasure an action causes among sentient beings. The eighteenth- and nineteenth-century philosopher Jeremy Bentham summarized this attitude in the phrase, "The question is not, 'Can they reason?' nor, 'Can they talk?' but 'Can they suffer?'" The phrase is derived from his 1823 work, *An Introduction to the Principles of Morals and Legislation*.

175. Some pro-choice advocates respond that a person is any *human being* who is sentient, but this is obviously a case of special pleading. What makes sentient humans worthy of protection but not any other sentient animals? If it is because humans have a capacity to be rational persons, then why not respect the unborn child, who also shares that same basic capacity?

176. The critic could escape my rebuttal by saying that a person is any *biological human being* who can survive outside of the womb. But this is once again a case of special pleading in the same way that saying only sentient *biological human beings* are persons. Why not say a person is any biological *male* human being who can survive outside of the womb? Such a definition of personhood is just as arbitrary.

177. *In Re A (Children) (Conjoined Twins: Surgical Separation) [2001] Fam 147*, Court of Appeal, Ward, Brooke And Robert Walker LJJ,

182, www.mentalhealthlaw.co.uk/images/Re_A_%28Conjoined_
Twins%29_%282001%29_Fam_147_report.pdf.

178. A critic could object that fertilization is a process that takes even
longer than birth and so it is just as absurd a criterion for personhood.
The difference is that in fertilization two body parts are transforming into
one body and so it is natural that we might not know exactly when in
this process a human being comes into existence. Birth does not involve
transformation but motion and so the process of birth becomes absurd
as a marker for personhood because nothing is changing about the fetus
as the different parts of its body emerge from the uterus.

179. I know some pro-life advocates who celebrate their approximate
conception days, and in Asian cultures it is common for someone to be
labeled one year of age at birth. Catholics celebrate the day Jesus was
conceived (the Annunciation) and the day Mary was conceived (the
Immaculate Conception).

180. Another argument claims that the United Nations defines the
moment we have rights as being at birth, not conception. According
to the first article of the 1948 Universal Declaration of Human Rights,
"All human beings are born free and equal in dignity and rights." First,
this article may not imply that birth is what divides humans who have
rights from those who don't, since legal abortion was very uncommon
in 1948. Second, even if it did mean this, it could simply be mistaken.
Pro-choice advocates probably reject article 16, which says that "Men
and women of full age . . . have the right to marry and to found a family."
In the rest of the document rights are given to "everyone," but in this
article alone they are given to "men and women," which implies that
only men and women can be joined together in marriage, and so this
declaration precludes the legal right to so-called same-sex "marriage."
If pro-choice advocates can believe that the declaration erred in regard
to what marriage is, pro-life advocates should be free to believe the
declaration "erred" (if this was even the case) on which humans have
rights and dignity.

181. This comes from personally observing Stephanie in dialogue with
pro-choice advocates.

Chapter 8: The Autonomists

182. *McFall v. Shimp*, 10 Pa. D. & C. 3d 90 (1978).

183. Colin Gleeson, "Chomsky criticises restrictive abortion laws," *The Irish Times*, April 3, 2013, www.irishtimes.com/news/social-affairs/chomsky-criticises-restrictive-abortion-laws-1.1346993.

184. Kreeft, *Unaborted Socrates*, 45-47.

185. Amanda Marcotte, "Really Sex Really?" *RH Reality Check Blog*, www.rhrealitycheck.org/blog/2009/06/28/really-sex-really. This is not to say that this excerpt represents Marcotte's entire defense of abortion. In the past, Marcotte has also argued that because a fetus typically lacks sentience it is not a person and would not have a right to life. However, the right to bodily autonomy is a major, perhaps crucial, part of Marcotte's case.

186. Sally Markowitz, "A Feminist Defense of Abortion" in *The Abortion Controversy: 25 Years After Roe vs. Wade: A Reader*, ed., Louis Pojman and Francis Beckwith, Wadsworth Publishing, 1998, 390-391.

187. Louis P. Pojman, "Abortion: A Defense of the Personhood Argument," in *The Abortion Controversy: 25 Years After Roe vs. Wade: A Reader* ed., Louis Pojman and Francis Beckwith, Wadsworth Publishing, 1998, 278.

188. Warren, "On the Moral and Legal Status of Abortion."

189. As examples of this refusal, Blackmun lists *Jacobson v. Massachusetts*, 197 U.S. 11 (1905) (vaccination) and *Buck v. Bell*, 274 U.S. 200 (1927) (sterilization). *Roe v. Wade* 410 U.S. 113, section VIII.

190. The thalidomide example is from Rich Poupard of the Life Training Institute. See Rich Poupard, *"Suffer the Violinist: Why the Pro-Abortion Argument from Bodily Autonomy Fails,"* *Christian Research Journal* 30, no. 4, 2007.

191. Samantha Broussard-Wilson, "Reaction to Shvarts: Outrage, shock, disgust," *Yale Daily News*, April 18, 2008, www.yaledailynews.com/news/university-news/2008/04/18/reaction-to-shvarts-outrage-shock-disgust/.

192. In a newspaper editorial describing the first sit-ins protesting segregated lunch counters in Greensboro, North Carolina, the editorial writer claimed that racial segregation was about conflicting "moral principles." He writes, "Involved are moral, legal and economic questions, and they impinge on one another. Negro students have a sound moral position when they protest a policy which caters to their business at nine counters and slaps them in the face at the 10th. Stores have a sound legal position when they say the law allows them to choose their clientele and serve or reject whomever they see fit." "Common Sense and the Public Safety," *Greensboro Daily News*, Saturday, February 20, 1960, www.sitins.com/clipping_022060b.shtml.

193. See *State of North Carolina v. Jesse Black* 60 N.C. 266 (June 1864). "A husband is responsible for the acts of his wife and he is required to govern his household, and for that purpose the law permits him to use towards his wife such a degree of force as is necessary to control an unruly temper and make her behave herself; and unless some permanent injury be inflicted, or there be an excess of violence, or such a degree of cruelty as shows that it is inflicted to gratify his own bad passions, the law will not invade the domestic forum, or go behind the curtain," sobek.colorado.edu/~mciverj/2481_60NC266.html.

194. It is important to remember that Thomson is not offering an argument by analogy "in defense of abortion" so much as she is offering a counterexample to the pro-life argument against abortion. Though I disagree with Watkin's ultimate assessment, I think this part of his assessment needs to be mentioned. Michael Watkins, "Re-Reading Thomson: Thomson's Unanswered Challenge," *Journal of Libertarian Studies*, vol. 20, no. 4, Fall 2006, 41–59.

195. Judith Jarvis Thomson, "A Defense of Abortion," *Philosophy and Public Affairs*, vol. 1, no. 1, 1971, 47-66.

196. William Parent, "Editor's introduction" in Judith Jarvis Thomson, *Rights, Restitution, and Risk*, Cambridge, MA: Harvard University Press, 1986, vii-x.

197. The names of these objections come from Boonin, *Defense of Abortion*. I am aware that there are other objections to Thomson's argument

made by pro-life advocates. However, for the sake of space and clarity, I have only included what I believe to be the most powerful objections to the argument.

198. Tony George, "Good Samaritan on Life Support," *Justice for All*, 2009, www.jfaweb.org/Training/George_Anthony_GSonLife-Support.pdf.

199. Thomson, *"A Defense of Abortion."*

200. Now, some people will certainly deny that sex is ordered toward pregnancy. Here I can only agree with Beckwith that such a rewriting of human nature is a "Herculean task" that may be impossible to achieve (Beckwith, *Defending Life*, 193). Certainly sexual intercourse has more than one purpose. For example, it bonds couples emotionally, which itself is good for any babies who are created. However, just as we can come to the conclusion that eating is for the acquiring of nutrition even if one only cares about the taste of food, by examining the design of the digestive system, we can come to the conclusion that sex is for procreation, even if some people care only for the pleasure of sex, by examining the design of the reproductive system. See Edward Feser, *The Last Superstition: A Refutation of the New Atheism*, St. Augustine's Press, 2008, 141-153.

201. This objection is made by F.M. Kamm in *Creation and Abortion: A Study in Moral and Legal Philosophy*, Oxford University Press, 1992. For a critique, see Lee, *Abortion and Unborn Human Life,* 135-136.

202. Klusendorf, *Case for Life*, 195.

203. Michael Tooley, *Abortion and Infanticide*, Oxford University Press, 1983, 45.

204. It's important to phrase the counterexamples in these ways instead of just asking if a woman may neglect her born children or choose not to breastfeed them. Autonomists will object that men and women have responsibilities toward infants once they take them home from the hospital, because such an act "tacitly consents" to caring for the child, as they have removed the child from a situation where he is cared for and assumed "guardianship" over him.

205. Beckwith, *Defending Life*, 195. See also *S.F. v. Alabama ex rel. T.M.*, 695 So. 2d 1186 (Ala. Civ. App. 1996) for a real-life example of a man being compelled to provide child support payments to a woman who sexually assaulted him. Even men who cannot consent to sex, because they are too young or unconscious at the time of the act, can still be held liable to pay child support.

206. Some people may object that there is no difference in this case between giving birth to a child in the woods and finding a child who has been abandoned and is unrelated to you. I cannot go into the issues in great depth; I believe that most people will see that a woman has greater responsibility to her own child than she does to an unrelated one. For example, I doubt that anyone would consider parents morally blameworthy if, in saving their own child's life, they refrain from an action that could have saved many more children. I believe this intuition shows that parents really do have obligations to their own children that surpass the obligations they have to strangers. Although some of my pro-life colleagues have explored this issue and have put forward an interesting case for the view that anyone, stranger or not, who needs the ordinary use of my body to live, provided that I am the only one who can provide such assistance, has a right to use my body in order to sustain themselves. See Stephen Wagner, et al., "De Facto Guardian and Abortion: A Response to the Strongest Violinist," www.jfaweb.org/Training/DeFactoGuardian-v03.pdf.

207. Kaczor, *Ethics of Abortion*, 184-185.

208. If those parents were unable to fulfill their duties, the duty to care for these children would radiate out to next of kin and finally to the state or even the international community. Although the level of duty that would be required would reduce as the field grew wider, so that if there are children whose own nations abandoned them, the moral duty imposed on the international community would be very low for each member of the international community.

209. This is similar to an objection raised by Boonin, *A Defense of Abortion*, 172-173, involving a doctor who gives the dying violinist a drug that saves his life but will damage his kidneys, thus requiring the use of the doctor's kidneys several years later. Boonin's primary argument

against the responsibility objection is that, as in the kidney case this student presented me, a pregnant woman is responsible only for the unborn child's existence and not his neediness (or the reason he cannot survive on his own), and so she is not obligated to sustain the child's life, even though she is responsible for the fact that the child exists. But this reply neglects the case of being responsible for the existence of a being who is "needy by nature" and thus being responsible for why someone can't survive on his own. It also relies on analogies that claim there is no morally relevant distinction to graciously extending someone's life and creating someone in a needy condition. For a more in-depth reply, see Beckwith, *"Defending Abortion Philosophically,"* Lee, *Abortion and Unborn Human Life*, 121-130, and Kaczor, *Ethics of Abortion*, 163-165.

210. See also Stephanie Gray, "A Kidney versus the Uterus," *Ethics & Medics* vol. 34 no. 10, October 2009.

211. This is also known as the "killing vs. letting die" objection, which I have subsumed into the "organ use objection." Under my view, denying someone the extraordinary use of an organ in order to keep them from dying from an unrelated ailment is a moral case of "letting die," while denying someone the ordinary use of an organ they need to survive is a case of immoral killing.

212. Eileen McDonagh, *Breaking the Abortion Deadlock: From Choice to Consent*, Oxford University Press, 1996, 12.

213. Klusendorf, *Case for Life*, 191-193.

214. This argument comes from Beckwith's reply to McDonagh, available online at bearspace.baylor.edu/Francis_Beckwith/www/Sites/ BeckwithReplyToMcDonagh.pdf. One objection to this argument is that if we abort this pregnancy, we deny this woman the right to have this particular child, which could cause great harm. However, if we stop this man from having sex with the woman, she could always choose to have sex with him later, but she can't choose to have this particular pregnancy again. But we could modify the example and say the man is a handsome drifter whom we may not be able to find again, and perhaps this woman has a penchant for "handsome drifter" fantasies. Or it could be a man with superior genes who will disappear like the drifter, and the

woman wouldn't want to miss this opportunity to bear superior children. It also won't work to say that we would allow the pregnancy to continue if we knew that if the woman were conscious she would have wanted the pregnancy to continue. After all, we wouldn't allow a man to have sex with an unconscious woman, even if we thought the woman would have sex with this particular man (maybe it is her husband visiting her in the hospital). This shows that while sexual intercourse requires explicit consent, pregnancy is a prima facie good, or good in and of itself, that we would allow to continue even without knowledge that a woman still wants to be pregnant.

215. Beckwith, *Defending Life*, 175-176.

Chapter 9: The Concerned

216. The woman in the picture was Gerri Santoro, who in 1964 became pregnant as the result of an extramarital affair with a married man named Clyde Dixon. Santoro fled with her children from her abusive husband, but when her husband planned to visit the girls, she checked into a motel with Dixon on June 8, 1964, and he attempted to abort her pregnancy. Santoro began to bleed profusely, and Dixon fled the scene, leaving her to die. A grisly photograph of her corpse has become a rallying cry among pro-choice advocates. See Janet Maslin, "Film Festival Review: The Woman Behind a Grisly Photo," *New York Times*, March 31, 1995, www.nytimes.com/1995/03/31/movies/film-festival-review-the-woman-behind-a-grisly-photo.html.) What makes this case ironic is that Santoro was six and a half months pregnant, which places Santoro's abortion in the third trimester. Since the abortion was not needed to preserve Santoro's life or health (the only threat to her life came from outside her body), in most states Santoro's abortion would *still* have been illegal.

217. For more information, see the World Health Organization's fact sheet, "Female genital mutilation," available online at www.who.int/mediacentre/factsheets/fs241/en/.

218. Mary Anne Warren, "On the Moral and Legal Status of Abortion," *The Monist*, vol. 57, no. 4, 1973. Some pro-choice advocates offer a sophisticated back-alley abortion objection and admit for the sake of

the argument that the unborn are human beings but then create a false dilemma for the pro-life advocate. He may say, "Isn't it better to keep abortion legal so only the fetus dies, as opposed to making abortion illegal and creating the situation where both the mother and child die in an illegal abortion? Isn't it better to save one life than lose two?" But this argument assumes that women can never choose the third option of giving birth and placing the child for adoption. In fact, it demeans women and assumes that we must keep abortion legal because apparently women will have no regard for their own well-being and will hurt themselves instead of waiting to safely give birth and then either place their child for adoption or raise the child themselves.

219. Christopher Tietze and Stanley K Henshaw, *Induced Abortion: A World Review*, The Guttmacher Institute, 1986. Cited in "History of abortion," *The National Abortion Federation,* at www.prochoice.org/about_abortion/history_abortion.html.

220. Barbara J. Syska, Thomas W. Hilgers, M.D., and Dennis O'Hare, "An Objective Model for Estimating Criminal Abortions and Its Implications for Public Policy" in *New Perspectives on Human Abortion*, ed., Thomas Hilgers, M.D., Dennis J. Horan, and David Mall, University Publications of America, 1981, 171.

221. This claim seems to go back to Frederick Taussig's 1936 study, *Abortion Spontaneous and Induced Medical and Social Aspects.* The study is horribly flawed, because it wildly extrapolates numbers found only in New York City and has no relevance today, especially since the safety of surgery in general has dramatically improved due to the advent of modern surgical techniques and the introduction of antibiotics such as penicillin.

222. Laurie D. Elam-Evans and Lilo T. Strauss, et al., "Abortion Surveillance, United States—2000," *Morbidity and Mortality Weekly Report (MMWR).* Centers for Disease Control and Prevention, November 28, 2003, table 19, www.cdc.gov/mmwr/preview/mmwrhtml/ss5212a1.htm#tab19.

223. Mary Steichen Calderone, "Illegal Abortion as a Public Health Problem," *American Journal of Public Health Nations Health*, vol. 50 no. 7, July 1960, 949.

224. Even when the studies compensate for this, they often botch the statistics. For example, Koch et al (2012) found that even though Mexico's Federal District legalized abortion in 2007, maternal mortality rates were declining steadily before that, and estimations by pro-choice advocates of abortion and maternal mortality rates were greatly exaggerated. See E. Koch., P. Aracena, S. Gatica M. Bravo, A. Huerta-Zepeda, B.C. Calhoun, "Fundamental discrepancies in abortion estimates and abortion-related mortality: A reevaluation of recent studies in Mexico with special reference to the International Classification of Diseases," *International Journal of Women's Health,* no. 4, December 2012, 613-623.

225. "Maternal Mortality Rates," *The World Fact Book,* Central Intelligence Agency, 2010, www.cia.gov/library/publications/the-world-factbook/rankorder/2223rank.html.

226. For example, see Ushma D. Upadhyay, et al., "Denial of Abortion Because of Provider Gestational Age Limits in the United States," *American Journal of Public Health,* August 15, 2013. The study concluded, "Adolescents and women who did not recognize their pregnancies early were most likely to delay seeking care. The most common reason for D.G. Kilpatrick, and C.L. Best, K. Sundberg, A. Tabor, Danish Fetal Medicine Research Group, delay was having to raise money for travel and procedure costs. We estimated that each year more than 4,000 U.S. women are denied an abortion because of facility gestational limits and must carry unwanted pregnancies to term."

227. Those who do break the law usually try to buy medication that causes abortions without having a prescription for that medication. See, for example, Susan Donaldson James, "Nursing Home Worker Charged with Illegal Abortion of Teen; Ordered Drugs Online," *ABC News,* March 7, 2014, abcnews.go.com/Health/pa-woman-charged-illegal-abortion-teen/story?id=22802782.

228. Available online at: http://www.youtube.com/watch?v= Uk6t_tdOkwo.

229. This argument is rejected by George Dennis O'Brien in his book *The Church and Abortion: A Catholic Dissent,* Rowan and Littlefield Publishing, 2010, 26-27. He says that "to will the ends is to will the means,"

and since Catholic bishops are not vocal about inflicting criminal penalties upon women who choose abortion, they should give up publicly trying to outlaw abortion. O'Brien's argument is less than convincing. What would he make of states that in an effort to get teen girls out of prostitution and not throw them in jail criminalize buying sex but not selling it? After all, to will the end of prostitution is to will the means of arresting these teen girls, right? I don't see any conflict in passing imperfect laws in order to achieve some level of justice instead of passing no laws and failing to achieve any just ends.

230. Other pro-life advocates say that women would always be given legal immunity so that abortion providers could be convicted from their testimony, but this would not explain what to do with women who self-abort. In addition, couldn't we find other evidence to indict the abortion provider besides the woman's testimony?

231. Angela Hatcher, "Campbell County mother can't be charged in baby's death," NBC 12 News, December 16, 2009, www.nbc12.com/Global/story.asp?S=11690000.

232. In Great Britain, infanticide is recognized as a separate crime as a result of the 1938 Infanticide Act. In jurisdictions like the United States, there is no separate charge for infanticide, but the distinction is present in the severity of the sentence.

233. This includes Amy Grossberg and Brian Peterson, who were sentenced to three years' imprisonment, and Melissa Drexler, who killed her infant after giving birth at her prom and was released on parole after three years. But this should not be construed to mean all infant killers are given light sentences. A woman who maliciously and repeatedly killed infants would be an example of someone who is fully culpable for her crimes (provided she was not insane) and would be subject to much harsher penalties. One example would be Genene Jones, who may have killed up to fifty infants as a nurse and was sentenced in 1985 to ninety-nine years in prison.

234. Subsequent bills amended this language to reflect the fact that human beings also begin to exist at twinning after fertilization has taken place.

235. Ruth Padawer, "The Two-Minus-One Pregnancy," *New York Times*, August 10, 2011, www.nytimes.com/2011/08/14/magazine/the-two-minus-one-pregnancy.html?pagewanted=all&_r=0.

Chapter 10: The Conflicted

236. I owe this phrase to Steve Wagner.

237. Gallup Polling, "Abortion," June 9-12, 2011, www.gallup.com/poll/1576/abortion.aspx.

238. In medical literature, this condition is known as *Fibrodysplasia ossificans progressive*.

239. Beckwith, *Defending Life*, 103-104, describes a similar illustration used by Germain Grisez and Stephen Krayson.

240. Some critics may actually bite the bullet and say that they would kill a born child who had a terrible disease, and therefore they can consistently affirm the morality of abortion. With these critics you'll have to discuss the ethics of euthanasia and whether it is better for doctors to kill pain or to kill patients. For a Catholic perspective, I recommend William May's *Catholic Bioethics and the Gift of Life*, 2000. For a secular perspective, I recommend Wesley Smith's book *Forced Exit*, 2006, as a good introduction to why euthanasia is bad public policy.

241. R.L. Kramer, R.K. Jarve, Y. Yaron, M.P. Johnson, J. Lampinen, S.B. Kasperski, and M.I. Evans, "Determinants of parental decisions after the prenatal diagnosis of Down syndrome," *American Journal of Medical Genetics*, vol. 79, no. 3, 1998, 172-174. This study placed the percent of women who terminate after receiving the diagnosis at 86.9 percent. Other localized studies have reached similar conclusions, but it is not wise to derive a national average from these studies, since some communities may be more open and accepting of children with Down syndrome and thus have lower abortion rates.

242. C.K. Ekelund, F.S. Jorgensen, O.B. Petersen, K. Sundberg, A. Tabor, and Danish Fetal Medicine Research Group, "Impact of a new national screening policy for Down's syndrome in Denmark: population based cohort study," *British Medical Journal* 337, 2008.

243. John Eligon and Michael Schwirtz, "Senate Candidate Provokes Ire with 'Legitimate Rape' Comment," *New York Times,* August 19, 2012, www.nytimes.com/2012/08/20/us/politics/todd-akin-provokes-ire-with-legitimate-rape-comment.html.

244. See Melisa M. Holmes, Heidi S. Resnick, D.G. Kilpatrick, and C.L. Best, "Rape-related pregnancy: Estimates and descriptive characteristics from a national sample of women," *American Journal of Obstetrics & Gynecology* 175, no. 2, August 1996, 320-325. The study concluded that women had a five percent chance of becoming pregnant after rape. Among women in the study who became pregnant resulting from rape, "32.2 percent opted to keep the infant whereas 50 percent underwent abortion and 5.9 percent placed the infant for adoption; an additional 11.8 percent had spontaneous abortion." The authors conclude that rape-related pregnancy "occurs with significant frequency."

245. Jonathan Weisman, "Rape Remark Jolts a Senate Race, and the Presidential One, Too," *New York Times,* October 25, 2012, www.nytimes.com/2012/10/25/us/politics/using-mourdocks-rape-comment-against-romney.html.

246. Michael A. Memoli, "Obama objects to Mourdock's rape comment, skewers Trump," *Los Angeles Times,* October 24, 2012, articles.latimes.com/2012/oct/24/nation/la-na-obama-skewers-donald-trump-richard-mourdock-on-tonight-show-20121024.

247. See *Kennedy v. Louisiana,* 554 U.S. 407 (2008).

248. One white paper that describes this issue says, "The absence of consent in a sexual assault morally renders the prevention of fertilization, after the assault, an act of self-defense rather than a contraceptive act." Thomas V. Berg, Marie T. Hilliard, and Mark F. Stegman, "Emergency Contraceptives & Catholic Healthcare: A New Look at the Science and the Moral Question," *Westchester Institute White Papers* 2, no. 1, June 2011, 14. This paper also describes in detail other Catholic theologians who support the use of contraception in defense against the sex cells emitted by a rapist and explains why such an act does not contradict the Church's stance on the immorality of contraception in general.

249. United States Conference of Catholic Bishops, "Ethical and Religious Directives for Catholic Health Care Services, 5th edition, USCCB, November 17, 2009, paragraph 36. This paragraph goes on to say, "It is not permissible, however, to initiate or to recommend treatments that have as their purpose or direct effect the removal, destruction, or interference with the implantation of a fertilized ovum." While it is acceptable to destroy a rapist's sperm in self-defense, it is not acceptable to directly destroy one's own child in order to no longer be pregnant.

250. Note that everything I've said about rape also applies to pregnancies that result from incest, such as when a father rapes his own daughter. Saying that the child who is created is a genetic monster who shouldn't be allowed to live is incredibly offensive to people who were conceived in incest and have the same external appearance as anyone else.

251. F. Gary Cunningham et al., *Williams Obstetrics*, 20th edition, Appleton & Lange, 1996, 151.

252. Technically, there is a "fourth stage." Some women claim that the strain of pregnancy is so great that they will kill themselves unless they can have an abortion. In this case, it is argued, the pregnancy is a "threat to the mother's life." But in this case it is not the pregnancy that is threatening the woman but her mental instability. Just as we would not kill a toddler because his mother was threatening suicide if the child is allowed to live, we should not kill an unborn child for the same reason.

253. Hern, *Abortion Practice*, 106.

254. United States Conference of Catholic Bishops, "Ethical and Religious Directives for Catholic Health Care Services," 5th edition, *USCCB*, November 17, 2009, paragraph 47.

255. While it is accepted among ethicists that salpingectomy, or the removal of the fallopian tube, is a morally licit means to resolve ectopic pregnancy, there is a dispute among Catholic medical ethicists over the whether salpingostomy (removing the embryo without removing the tube) or administering methotrexate (which slows the embryo's growth and results in the embryo dying and detaching on its own) are licit. At the time of this publishing, in the absence of official Church teaching on the subject, Catholics may accept or reject all three options in accordance

with their conscience. One critique of the alternative methods of resolving ectopic pregnancies states, "The Congregation for the Doctrine of the Faith, in conjunction with the Pontifical Academy for Life, should study the issue of tubal pregnancies and offer sound guidelines for what Catholics may or may not do to resolve them." Marie Anderson, Robert L. Fastiggi, David E. Hargroder, Rev. Joseph C. Howard, Jr., and C. Ward Kischer, "Ectopic Pregnancy and Catholic Morality A Response to Recent Arguments in Favor of Salpingostomy and Methotrexate," *National Catholic Bioethics Quarterly,* vol. 11, no. 1, Spring 2011.

256. "In 46 states legal abortion is permitted to preserve the life of the mother; three states allow, in addition, preservation of the health of the mother." Mary Steichen Calderone, "Illegal Abortion as a Public Health Problem," *American Journal of Public Health Nations Health,* vol. 50, no. 7, July 1960, 948. Calderone was referencing a 1958 Planned Parenthood conference that took place before Alaska and Hawaii were states. She says in other places a woman's threat of suicide would justify abortion, and she never mentions a state where abortion is prohibited even if a woman's life is in danger. Calderone also admits that, even in her day, "it is hardly ever necessary today to consider the life of a mother as threatened by a pregnancy" (948-949).

257. Catholic opposition to such abortions is described in paragraph 45 of the Ethical and Religious Directives for Catholic Health Care Services.

258. Thomas Murphy Goodwin, "Medicalizing Abortion Decisions," *First Things,* March 1996, www.firstthings.com/article/2007/10/003-medicalizing-abortion-decisions-15.

259. Klusendorf, *Case for Life,* 175.

260. See also Kaczor, *Ethics of Abortion,* 193-210.

Chapter 11: The Fighter

261. A critic could respond that the child is not like an enemy soldier and is more like an innocent hallucinating person who *might* hurt us. Therefore, we can use deadly force to remove the child from the uterus in order to protect the mother. The critic might say, "After all, no one

knows which pregnancies will become fatal, so all abortions should be legal. With this approach a woman has the maximum ability to protect her own life in case her pregnancy should go awry." But this argument proves too much. Six hundred fifty women die every year in the U.S. from pregnancy complications, but more than 1,500 women in 2007 alone were murdered by their intimate partners. (See Shannan Catalano et al., "Female Victims of Violence," *Bureau of Justice Statistics Selected Findings,* September 2009, 2.) In fact, a 2011 article in the journal *Obstetrics and Gynecology* has led several media outlets to issue statements like, "Expectant mothers are more likely to die from murder or suicide than several of the most common pregnancy-related medical problems" (Kerry Grens, "Murder, Suicide top medical deaths in pregnancy," Reuters, October 26, 2011, www.reuters.com/article/2011/10/26/us-deaths-pregnancy-idUSTRE79P7OK20111026.) In light of these statistics, should women have the right to kill their husbands and boyfriends? A critic might say, "After all, no one knows which intimate partners will become fatal, so all partner killings should be legal. With this approach a woman has the maximum ability to protect her life in case her relationship should go awry." Clearly this argument fails, because the woman's intimate partner is an innocent human being with a right to life. If a woman may not kill her husband or boyfriend because he *might* murder her in the future, then surely a woman may not kill her unborn child because he *might* be part of a sequence of events in which her pregnancy becomes dangerous. In both cases the threat is too remote to justify using lethal force.

262. The U.S. Supreme Court declared a moratorium on capital punishment in *Furman v. Georgia* (1972) before reinstating it in *Gregg v. Georgia* (1976). For statistics comparing deaths from abortion and capital punishment, see www.deathpenaltyinfo.org/number-executions-state-and-region-1976, which counts approximately 1,200 executions as taking place since 1976.

263. Sanger's eugenic streak is easily seen in her magazine *Birth Control Review.* The November 1921 issue is a prime example. Sanger boldly announces at the top of the first page, "Birth Control: To create a race of thoroughbreds."

264. Beckwith, *Defending Life* (126), makes a similar argument.

265. Helen Alvaré, Greg Pfundstein, Matthew Schmitz, and Ryan T. Anderson, "The Lazy Slander of the Pro-Life Cause," *The Witherspoon Institute,* January 17, 2011, www.thepublicdiscourse.com/2011/01/2380/.

266. Joseph Cardinal Bernardin, "A Consistent Ethic of Life: An American-Catholic Dialogue," Gannon Lecture, Fordham University, December 6, 1983, www.hnp.org/publications/hnpfocus/BConsistentEthic1983.pdf.

267. Thomas L. Friedman, "Why I Am Pro-life," *New York Times,* October 27, 2012, www.nytimes.com/2012/10/28/opinion/sunday/friedman-why-i-am-pro-life.html?_r=0.

268. For the death penalty, see paragraph 2267, and for just war, see paragraph 2309 in the *Catechism of the Catholic Church.*

269. Joseph Cardinal Bernardin, "A Consistent Ethic of Life: Continuing the Dialogue," The William Wade Lecture Series, St. Louis University, March 11, 1984.

270. See Fr. Tadeusz Pacholczyk, "What Should We Do with the Frozen Embryos?", *Catholic Education Resource Center,* 2009, www.catholiceducation.org/articles/medical_ethics/me0137.htm.

271. Feminists may also say that women need abortion so that they can socially compete with men and be equal to them (Tribe, *Clash of Absolutes,* 105). Apparently, since men can easily walk away from unwanted parenthood and women cannot, women need abortion in order to be equal with men. But instead of saying women have to lower themselves to the level of men in order to be "equal to them," why not force men to rise to the dignity of women and compel them to be responsible fathers? This would just as effectively remove the alleged inequality between men and women without relying on legal abortion. One could also argue that if women need abortion to overcome nature's "sexist" design that allows only men to have sex and not become pregnant, then wouldn't men "need" artificial wombs and have a right to said wombs in order to overcome nature's "sexist" design that only women can have sex and

become pregnant? Valuing sex that is isolated from pregnancy or treating pregnancy like a disease seems to reinforce a male view of sex that would be the antithesis of what authentic feminists should be promoting.

Chapter 12: The Religious

272. For more information about atheists who oppose abortion, visit www.secularprolife.org.

273. Goldberg's quote originally came from her entry in Angela Bonavoglia, *The Choices We Made: Twenty Five Men and Women Speak Out About Abortion*, Four Walls Eight Windows, 2001, 121.

274. Thomas A. Shannon and Allan B. Wolter, "Reflections on the Moral Status of the Pre-Embryo," *Theological Studies*, December 1990, 619. For a thorough critique of Shannon and Wolter's arguments, see Lee, *Abortion and Unborn Human Life*, 83-107.

275. Keith Moore and T.V.N. Persaud, *The Developing Human: Clinically Oriented Embryology*, 9th edition, W.B. Saunders, 2013, 36.

276. A reader might ask what *does* happen to unbaptized babies that have been aborted. The honest answer is, we don't know. While theologians once speculated that these babies went to a pleasant state in the afterlife called "limbo," this was never taught as Catholic doctrine. In 2007, the Vatican's International Theological Commission released a document titled *The Hope of Salvation for Infants Who Die Without Being Baptized* that stated that, based on God's desire to save all men and his request to "let the children come to me," there are "reasons for prayerful hope, rather than grounds for sure knowledge" that unbaptized babies will go to heaven; but this should not be understood to mean that baptism is not generally necessary for entrance into heaven.

277. Similar points are raised by Klusendorf, *The Case for Life,* 143-144.

278. Francis Beckwith, "A Critical Appraisal of Theological Arguments for Abortion Rights," *Bibliotheca Sacra*, vol. 148 no. 591, 1991, 337-355.

279. Ibid. Beckwith also notes that some religious critics use Ecclesiastes 11:5 to argue that it is presumptuous to claim that we know the unborn are human beings. I have seen this in O'Brien, *The Church and Abortion,*

73. It says, "Just as you know not how the breath of life fashions the human frame in the mother's womb, so you know not the work of God which he is accomplishing in the universe." If this argument were true, it would also make it presumptuous to say the unborn are not human beings. As a result, we should not kill the unborn, since we are ignorant of their true moral status. However, this verse has nothing to do with when a child receives a soul. The writer is saying only that just as the people of his time do not understand how God works in creating a child in the womb, we do not know how God works in the universe as a whole. The verse never says we do not know if a child exists in the womb, it says only we do not know how God interacts with that child's development.

280. Exodus 21:20-21.

281. For a more in-depth treatment of this passage, see Greg Koukl, "What Exodus 21:22 Says About Abortion," *Stand to Reason*, February 4, 2013, www.str.org/articles/what-exodus-21-22-says-about-abortion#. U4DfGi_gLjB. I disagree with Koukl's assessment of Catholicism, which is present in a few articles on his Web site, but his work on pro-life apologetics is good.

282. Mormons actually do take the passage this literally and believe that human souls preexisted eternally before conception. The problem with this interpretation is that it confuses real existence with ideal existence, or existence in God's mind. Prior to Jeremiah's creation, God knew him as an idea of a prophet in his mind, not as an existing being with him. Another example of ideal existence is Romans 4:17, where Paul describes how Abraham was called a father of many nations before he had any children because God had knowledge of Abraham's future in mind. We can reject the concept of real preexistence for human beings prior to conception, because Scripture never describes someone like Jeremiah knowing God before conception, even though God knew him in an ideal way. Paragraph 366 of the *Catechism of the Catholic Church* says, "The Church teaches that every spiritual soul is created immediately by God—it is not 'produced' by the parents—and also that it is immortal," which implies that souls are not eternal but are created by God at conception.

283. See also Klusendorf, *The Case for Life*, 135-137.

284. Pope John Paul II, *Evangelium Vitae*, 61.

285. Moral theologian William May says that Aquinas, whose writings were heavily influenced by Aristotle, "mistakenly thought, because he relied on the inadequate biological knowledge of his day, that in human generation the male seed was alone the active element, he concluded that the body first formed by maternal blood by this seed was only vegetative in nature. . . . But note that for St. Thomas the *bodies* generated were *not* human in nature. . . . St. Thomas, were he alive today and cognizant of the biological evidence known today, would not hesitate in conclud-ing that the *body* that comes to be when fertilization is completed is indubitably a *human* body and hence that its organizing and vivifying principle can only be a *human soul*, an intellectual or spiritual soul." William May, *Catholic Bioethics and the Gift of Human Life*, Our Sunday Visitor, 2000, 164-165.

286. *Apology* 9:8.

287. *The Soul*, 27.

288. *First Canonical Letter*, canon II.

289. CCC 2271. In regards to canon law on abortion, certain questions are liable to spring up in the minds of many people. Can a Catholic be excommunicated for having an abortion? Can a pro-choice politician be excommunicated for his commitment to legal abortion? In order to answer these questions, we have to understand excommunication. It is not a decree that a person is no longer Catholic. It is instead, in the words of Pope John Paul II, a way to "make an individual fully aware of the gravity of a certain sin and then to foster genuine conversion and repentance" (*Evangelium Vitae, 62*). A person who is excommunicated is barred from receiving the sacraments until he repents of his sins and seeks reconciliation. The section of canon law that covers abortion is canon 1398, which states, "A person who procures a completed abor-tion incurs a *latae sententiae* excommunication." This means that a person who obtains a successful abortion, or one that results in the child's death, is excommunicated without a formal decree by an ecclesial body, or the punishment is "automatic"—assuming certain conditions are met. According to canon 1329, this punishment also applies to accomplices

who made the abortion possible (such as the doctor who performed the abortion or the boyfriend who paid for it). However, a person cannot be excommunicated if she did not know abortion was an excommunicable offense, she was a minor less than sixteen years old, or she was affected by a mitigating circumstance such as grave fear (see canons 1323-1324). The act of abortion itself would still be objectively and gravely sinful. Canon 1398 does not apply to people who use the political process to make abortion legal, so these people do not incur automatic excommunication. However, canon 915 states that people who are "obstinately persevering in manifest grave sin are not to be admitted to Holy Communion," which many have argued should be applied to Catholic politicians who support legal abortion. The U.S. Conference of Catholic Bishops' 2004 document "Catholics in Political Life" states, "[S]uch decisions rest with the individual bishop in accord with the established canonical and pastoral principles."

290. "The Truth About Catholics and Abortion," *Catholics for Choice* (2011), www.catholicsforchoice.org/documents/TruthaboutCatholicsandAbortion.pdf.

291. Ibid.

292. CCC 1790-1791.

293. Pope John Paul II, *Evangelium Vitae*, 62.

294. Rosemary Radford Ruether, "Catholics and Abortion: Authority vs. Dissent," *Conscience*, March–April 1989.

295. Daniel A. Dombrowski and Robert Deltete, *A Brief, Liberal, Catholic Defense of Abortion*, University of Illinois Press, 2000, 73. For a critique of a similar "delayed hominzation theory," see Lee, *Abortion and Unborn Human Life*, 83-93.

296. "Considering abortion?" *Religious Coalition for Reproductive Choice*, www.rcrc.org/issues/consideringabortion.cfm.

297. "Prayerfully Pro-choice: Resources for Worship," *Religious Coalition for Reproductive Choice*, March 2004, 92, www.rcrc.org/pdf/Prayerfully.pdf.

298. "Cheap grace is the grace we bestow on ourselves. Cheap grace is the preaching of forgiveness without requiring repentance, baptism without church discipline, Communion without confession, absolution without personal confession. Cheap grace is grace without discipleship, grace without the cross, grace without Jesus Christ, living and incarnate." Dietrich Bonhoeffer, *The Cost of Discipleship*, Touchstone, 1959, 44-45. See also Romans 6:1-2: "What then shall we say? Shall we persist in sin that grace may abound? Of course not! How can we who died to sin yet live in it?"

299. Luke 18:15-17, Matthew 19:13-15, Mark 10:13-16.

300. Pope John Paul II, *Evangelium Vitae*, 99.

301. "From My Wife," *trenthorn.com,* trenthorn.com/2014/01/27/from-my-wife/.

302. See 2 Corinthians 4:16.

303. Josh Brahm, "My formerly pro-choice friend now self-identifies as pro-life!", *Joshbrahm.com*, May 19, 2014, joshbrahm.com/relational-apologetics-formerly-pro-choice-friend-deanna-now-pro-life/.

Appendix I: How to Talk to Pre- and Post-Abortive Women

304. The information in this section comes from the author's personal experience and through the work of post-abortion support groups like Silent No More and Rachel's Vineyard. See www.silentnomoreawareness.org and www.rachelsvineyard.org for more information.

305. Scott Klusendorf, *Pro-life 101: A Step-by-Step Guide to Making Your Case Persuasively*, Stand to Reason Press, 2002, 45. The tips in this section are adapted from Klusendorf, *Pro-life 101*, 44-47 and Karen Black's "Manual for Sidewalk Counseling."

Appendix II: Answering Infanticide

306. Theresa Burke with David C. Reardon. *Forbidden Grief: The Unspoken Pain of Abortion*, Acorn Books, 2007.

307. Singer, *Practical Ethics*, 166.

308. Even Robert George, known for his thoughtful replies to pro-choice advocates, writes in reply to Guiblini and Minerva's recent defense of infanticide, "Whatever errors of fact and judgment are made possible by the complexities of human development or a prenatal child's hiddenness in the womb—though in the age of the sonogram, the child is hidden only from those who wish to avert their gaze—it should be plain to see that killing an infant because he or she is unwanted is evil. The advocacy of that, or of its moral permissibility, is what should take one aback, not a declaration by me or anyone else that such advocacy should be denounced as moral madness." In his response, George seems to argue that the wrongness of infanticide should be obvious to any rational observer and not require a sophisticated argument to denounce it. See Robert George, "Infanticide and Moral Madness," *Journal of Medical Ethics, vol.* 39, no. 5, 2013, 299-301.

309. Richard John Neuhaus, "The Return of Eugenics," *Commentary*, April 1988, 19.

310. See Lee, *Abortion and Unborn Human Life*, 8-46, and Kaczor, *Ethics of Abortion*, 13-37, 105-120.

311. Martha Nussbaum, *Frontiers of Justice: Disability, Nationality, Species Membership*, Belknap Press, 2006. Cited in Kaczor, *Ethics of Abortion*, 25.

312. Alberto Giubilini and Francesca Minerva, "After-Birth Abortion: Why Should the Baby Live?", *Journal of Medical Ethics*, 10.1136, 2011.

313. A similar example, which helped me finalize this thought experiment, is found in Eric T. Olson, *The Stanford Encyclopedia of Philosophy*, Fall 2004 edition, Edward N. Zalta, ed., plato.stanford.edu/entries/identity-personal/. I will add that the common solution given to this thought experiment—that a person survives death provided no copy has been made of him (also called the no-branching requirement)—seems ad hoc and unjustifiable.

314. Kazcor, *The Ethics of Abortion*, 115.

315. Don Marquis used this thought experiment with Michael Tooley in an online discussion at www.philostv.com/

don-marquis-and-michael-tooley. I also believe this intuition would apply to adults who would rather be given "a second life" than see the demise of their own bodies. Although such adults may also worry about what will happen to their bodies when the mind of an infant inhabits them, so this may sway their intuitions on this case, I don't think it would show they see themselves only as being a mind, since they would worry about the state of "their" body after death. Just as we don't worry about how our cars are used after we sell them (because we are not our cars), why would we worry about how our bodies are used unless we are indeed are bodies?